Entrepreneur®
MAGAZINE'S

W9-BDJ-771

startup

Start Your Own

MAIL ORDER BUSINESS

Your Step-by-Step Guide to Success

Terry and Rob Adams

EP
Entrepreneur
Press

Editorial Director: Jere L. Calmes
Managing Editor: Marla Markman
Cover Design: Beth Hansen-Winter
Production: Eliot House Productions
Composition: Ed Stevens

This publication is designed to provide accurate and authoritative information in regard to the subject matter covered. It is sold with the understanding that the publisher is not engaged in rendering legal, accounting, or other professional services. If legal advice or other expert assistance is required, the services of a competent professional person should be sought.

Library of Congress Cataloging-in-Publication Data

Adams, Terry, 1952–
  Start your own mail order business/by Terry Adams, Rob Adams.
     p.   cm.   —(Entrepreneur magazine's start up) (Entrepreneur magazines's business start-up series; #1015)
   ISBN 1-891984-79-9
    1. Mail-order business—Management. 2. New business enterprises—Management. I. Adams, Rob, 1950– II. Title. III. Series. IV. Entrepreneur business start-up guide; no. 1015.

HF5466.A2173 2003
658.8'.72—dc21   2002192795

Printed in Canada

10 09 08 07 06 05 04   10 9 8 7 6 5 4 3 2

Contents

Chapter 4

Packaging Your Business: Choosing a Name and a Structure

Chapter 5

Into the Money Bag: Figuring Your Finances

▲

Chapter 11
Pushing the Envelope, Part 2:
Print, Radio, TV, and Internet Advertising 189

Chapter 12
The Check's in the Mail: Money Management 209

Preface

You're holding this book, either in your hands, on your lap, or on your desk—probably dangerously near a spillable cup of coffee—because you're one of those people who likes to live on the edge. You're contemplating starting your own business.

This is one of the most exhilarating things you can do for yourself and your family. It's also one of the scariest. Owning your own business means you're the boss, the big wheel, the head cheese. You make the rules. You lay down the law. It also means you can't call in sick (especially when you're also the only employee), you can't let somebody else worry about making enough to cover payroll and expenses, and you can't defer that cranky client or intimidating IRS letter to a higher authority. You're it.

We're assuming you've picked up this particular book on starting and running a mail order business for one or more of the following reasons:

- You have a background in the mail order field.
- You're an avid fan of The Home Shopping Network, your mailbox is stuffed with every catalog ever printed, and you think mail order would be a fun and exciting business.
- You have a background in sales or distribution and feel that sales is sales, no matter what kind.
- You have no background or fascination with any of the above but believe mail order is a hot opportunity and are willing to take a chance.

Which did you choose? (Didn't know it was a test, did you?)

Well, you can relax because there is no wrong answer. Any of these responses is entirely correct so long as you realize that *they all involve a lot of learning and a lot of hard work*. They can also involve a heck of a lot of fun, as well as a tremendous amount of personal and professional satisfaction.

Our goal here is to tell you everything you need to know to:

- decide whether a mail order business is the right business for you,
- get your business started successfully,
- keep your business running successfully, and
- make friends and influence people. (That's actually part of Chapters 10 and 11, which are about advertising and public relations.)

We've interviewed lots of people out there on the front lines of the industry—all around the country—to find out how the mail order business really works and what makes it tick. And we've set aside lots of places for them to tell their own stories and give their own hard-won advice and suggestions, a sort of virtual round-table discussion group, with you placed right in the thick of things. (For a listing of these successful business owners, see our Appendix.) We've broken our chapters into manageable sections on every aspect of start-up and operations. And we've left some space for your creativity to soar.

We've packed our pages with helpful hints so that you can get up and running on your new venture as quickly as possible. And we've provided a resource section crammed with contacts and sources.

So sit back—don't spill that coffee!—start reading and get ready to become a mail order pro.

Mail Order
Mania

Mail order is one of the hottest industries right now. It's not new—in fact, it can be traced back more than a century. But it's in demand, by consumers and entrepreneurs alike. Why? Reasons abound, both personal and commercial.

This chapter explores the flourishing business of mail order—a sort of in-your-lap TV news magazine report without the commercials. We'll delve into the steadily rising economic success of the field and dip into the secrets of America's mail order industry.

Wish Fulfillment

Everybody loves to get something in the mail—except, of course, those pesky bills. A letter—or especially a package—delivered to your door is like a birthday gift any time of the year. It's wish fulfillment. Even if the contents are something as mundane as kitchen towels or a car mat, that package makes you feel like you've received something special and exciting. And the anticipation of waiting for the mail carrier or UPS delivery person to arrive with your parcel is half the fun. So it's no wonder that mail order is in demand.

The venerable Sears Roebuck catalog, a pioneer mail order piece, was dubbed "The Wish Book" because it gave you the power to choose whatever you wanted and have that wish granted simply by sending off your order form and payment. Sears, however, was not the first mail order company.

Mail Order's Dad

The title of Father of Mail Order goes to Aaron Montgomery Ward, a savvy traveling salesman who in 1872 decided direct mail was a terrific way to get quality merchandise to rural Americans who frequently suffered at the mercy of substandard goods. The 28-year-old entrepreneur founded his company—and America's shop-by-mail industry—with a single sheet of paper listing 163 products, the cornerstone of what would become the Montgomery Ward catalog.

Sears, Roebuck and Co., founded by former railway station agent Richard W. Sears and watchmaker Alvah C. Roebuck, came into being about 20 years later. By 1895, the Sears catalog weighed in at a hefty 532 pages, crammed with everything a shopper could want, from shoes and buggies to fishing tackle and furniture. A few years later, you could even buy a house from the Sears catalog.

Today, mail order is still an exciting, high-demand source of merchandise. The Direct Marketing Association (also known as the DMA) estimates that each year more than 131 million Americans order a product or service by phone or mail.

Why are we including phone sales in our mail order figures? Because mail order is actually an inaccurate moniker for *direct marketing*, which includes any form of shop-at-home-or-office order placement, from mail to

Stat Fact

According to a recent report by the National Mail Order Association, annual U.S. mail order sales have reached $318.5 billion.

telephone, fax, and e-mail. Because most people use the term *mail order* to cover these broad bases, we'll continue to do so within these pages.

What makes mail order so hot today? As we have said, reasons abound. One is the same as when Aaron Ward had his brainstorm—the convenience of shopping from home. Ward, however, based his marketing strategy on the fact that his customers were rural and didn't have access to the higher-quality goods available in urban areas.

Off-Duty Shopping

In today's marketplace, most customers can easily access any number of retail stores but don't have the time. More and more Americans are part of a two-income household, a team stretched taut between work and child raising, with scant time for leisure—much less shopping. These people want to spend their off-duty hours in more rewarding pursuits than traipsing through the mall. Single parents, stretched even further to be in several places at once, have reached the same anti-shopping conclusion. And Americans as a whole have shed the more-is-better consumerism of the 1980s in favor of meeting their profound desire for simple quality time at home with family.

So mail order, again, fulfills wishes. It grants consumers the ability to shop in peace and quiet from, as the old saw goes, the privacy of their own homes. There's no need to power up the old automobile, no need to rush out of the house to reach the mall before it closes, no need to jockey for a parking space, and no need to schlep that tired and cranky child or significant other along at your heels when you may be tired and cranky yourself.

Instead, you can pore through the pages of mail order catalogs that offer just about everything you can imagine—with your feet up, a cup of coffee at hand, and the kids and spouse either "shopping" with you in similar comfort or somewhere else in the house happily going about their own affairs.

If you have questions, you pick up the phone, key in a number (usually toll-free), and talk to a knowledgeable customer assistant. No more frustration trying to track down elusive store clerks who often don't have the answers anyway. When you're ready to buy, you order by phone, mail or e-mail in minutes. No more standing in line! And that's not all. Mail order shoppers aren't restricted by store hours. With a catalog, you can shop at 3 A.M. if the mood strikes you. Instead of fighting for the department store's ghoulishly lit dressing rooms, you can try on mail ordered garments in front of your own bedroom mirror. And, of course, there's no worry about pickpockets or purse snatchers. No wonder mail order is the modern shopper's paradise!

The Flip Side

What's the flip side to mail order's advantages? Although we'd be lying if we said there wasn't one, mail order's negative points are few. One is that consumers can't handle the merchandise until after they've paid for it. As a buyer, you have to rely on pictures and text to give you the full flavor of the goods. You can never be entirely sure of the size, color, or quality until it's been delivered. Of course, if you don't like what you get, you can almost always return it, but this takes a certain amount of effort and eliminates most of the fun, especially if you need (or want) the product right away.

Another mail order minus is the time element. You have to wait for delivery, whereas if you ran out to the mall, you could have the merchandise in your home the same day. Most mail order companies will ship your goodies overnight by FedEx if you're willing to pay extra for the service, but if you're not, you face a certain lag time between order and delivery. And if those goodies happen to be the wrong fit or the wrong color, there's an even greater delay while you send them back and wait—again—for the replacements to arrive.

The last mail order negative is a sort of stigma bearing the word "scam." Although many mail order companies, from L.L. Bean to Lands' End to Lillian Vernon (a lot of Ls!), have sterling reputations, the idea persists in some minds that mail order is a hotbed of phony merchandise hawkers. Because there were (and still are) send money wolves devouring customer lambs, the Federal Trade Commission created the *Mail Order Merchandise Rule* (now called the *Mail or Telephone Order Merchandise Rule*) in 1975 to regulate direct-marketing businesses. We'll explore this in depth in Chapter 2, but for now let's just say that Big Brother is watching out for mail order customers.

Brain Cell Application

So far, we've examined mail order from the consumer's perspective. Now let's take a look at the industry from the businessperson's point of view. What do we see? An industry that is potentially lucrative for the savvy, hardworking entrepreneur and that has the advantage of requiring relatively little in the way of start-up expenses, specialized skills, or intensive apprenticeship—as opposed to, say, professions like brain surgery, high rise construction, or even restaurant management.

Bear in mind, however, that this doesn't mean you can make a fortune without lifting a finger or applying a brain cell. In order to be successful in mail order, you'll need a generous measure of hard work, a concerted and constant study of the industry as a whole as well as your particular niche, and the ability to roll with the punches. You'll also need to be prepared to have a lot of fun!

That said, let's take a look at the reasons entrepreneurs love mail order. One is that it's as convenient for the direct marketer as it is for the consumer. Since your customers' visits are all virtual, you can work from home—basing your operations in a spare bedroom, at the kitchen table, or even in a corner of the garage, if necessary, until your efforts bear enough fruit to furnish a "real" office.

Mail Order Moonlighting

Mail order offers the option of starting your business part-time. In fact, many direct marketers insist that moonlighting is the wisest way to go. John Schulte, chairman of the National Mail Order Association (NMOA), believes traditional and Internet-based mail order are the last frontiers for the little guy. "You can find ways to make things happen part-time from your kitchen table," says Schulte.

Competition in the mail order biz is tough. But if you start out part-time, you can allow yourself on-the-job training without on-the-job financial anxieties. And if you don't want to sever the ties with your full-time employer until you know you can make it on your own, mail order is an ideal business for you.

What else makes mail order shine for the start-up entrepreneur? You don't need a lot of inventory. You can sell merchandise through a drop-ship arrangement. No, we aren't suggesting that you parachute goods to customers like in the Berlin Airlift. Drop-shipping is an arrangement in which a third party such as a manufacturer or wholesaler sells you the merchandise but keeps it in his warehouse and delivers it to your customer for you after you've made the sale. Or you can start out with one product or service, rather than go the L.L. Bean 16,000-products route, and keep your inventory manageable as you grow.

Keep in mind that mail order lends itself to services as well as merchandise. You can offer everything from antique appraisal to desktop publishing to genealogical research—and for most services, your inventory list will be minimal.

Yet another mail order plus: You don't need to ship the product until your customer's check or credit card clears the bank. Unlike your store-bound retail colleagues, you've got no bounced-check worries, mate!

The Top Contender

What are mail order's minuses from the business owner's viewpoint? Again, there are few, with the top contender being the tough competition from all the other direct marketers out there. As a mail order maven, you'll have to be clever, creative, and persistent—and this book will help.

The other major minus from the direct marketer's side of the fence is the old "scam"

Fun Fact

In 1931, the cost of a brand-new Coldspot electric refrigerator—Sears' own make, now called Kenmore—was $137.50. In 1957, you could purchase a fridge from the *Sears* catalog in your choice of green, pink, yellow, or white.

▲

stigma we mentioned earlier. Customers who wouldn't hesitate to hand over their money in a retail store can balk at sending it through the mail, over the phone, or over the Internet via credit card.

Counting Your Coconuts

What can you expect to make as a mail order entrepreneur? The amount is entirely up to you, depending only on how serious you are and how willing you are to work for the rewards. One of the entrepreneurs we interviewed for this book brings in annual gross revenues of $150,000; another brings in more than $1 million. Schulte of the NMOA says annual incomes for the industry range from $40,000 to more than $100,000, depending on how long the business has been in operation and how much has been invested in building the business.

By a mail order company's fourth or fifth birthday, Schulte says, about 60 percent will find themselves in the $0 to $40,000 bracket, about 25 percent will fall into the $40,000 to $100,000 category, and a final 15 percent will land in the $100,000-plus range.

The Minneapolis-based direct-mail expert estimates that it takes two to four years to break even with a mail order operation. "Profitability," he advises, "comes at about the same time, in three to five years. You want to start breaking even right away, but the real profits come when you have a solid customer base that buys from you with some frequency. It takes a few years to build up this base."

Wind Beneath Your Wings

Here's the big secret to keeping the wind in your sails and beneath your wings as a mail order moonlighter: Offer a product or service that appeals to a well-defined market segment—for example, horse lovers or off-road vehicle buffs. Targeting a specific audience rather than the general public keeps you from getting mowed under by the major mail order players who have bigger, splashier catalogs and far larger mailing lists than you'll be working with.

A specific market isn't necessarily a small one. Lands' End began in 1963 as a purveyor of marine hardware and sails—products with a decidedly limited market. Somewhere along the time line (1974 to be exact), the company began adding clothing for the yachtsperson to its merchandise list. Today, Lands' End is renowned for classy casual wear, rather than jibs and mainsails, and boasts annual earnings of more than $990 million.

And while success doesn't come overnight to most, it doesn't come at all to some. "Only about 20 percent make it," cautions Schulte. This isn't a reason to quit before you start, but it's a darn good reason to get everything you can going for you before you start. That's why you bought this book! And its pages will guide you through every stage of starting your mail order company. Researching the points that pertain to the specific type of mail order business you want to start—and then following through—will be up to you.

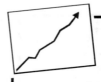

Stat Fact

Just how much are people spending on mail order products? According to the National Mail Order Association, recent annual consumer mail order sales weighed in at $630 per person.

Crank-Up Costs

One of the Catch-22s of being in business for yourself is that you need money to make money—in other words, you need start-up funds. With mail order, you can start off with a much more manageable investment than your peers in retail or manufacturing. Because you can begin as a one-person show in your own home, you automatically eliminate expenses like rent and employees. As an added bonus, equipment costs are relatively low: Your major outlays will be for a computer, software, two to three phone lines, a phone with multiline capability, a fax machine, and Internet access. This whittles your other initial expenses down to inventory and advertising—which, if you plan to go the catalog route, can be considerable.

But don't get too carried away with the idea of starting on the proverbial shoestring. There's a downside, which is that starting small can limit your company's potential growth.

"You really have to have backup in terms of finances," advises Greer T., a cataloger in Canton, Ohio. "It always costs more than you think it's going to. A lot of businesses fail because they don't have the financial backup."

Maxwell Sroge, president of the mail order consulting firm Maxwell Sroge Company Inc., agrees. Undercapitalization, he says, is one of the main reasons mail order entrepreneurs fail. You can start with a limited investment, but you'll have to be especially creative, and you'll have to really focus your energies on what many experts see as the lifeblood of the successful mail order business: the repeat customer. (We'll

Fun Fact

L.L. Bean Inc., a premier mail order retailer, was born in 1912 when Leon Leonwood Bean, a 40-year-old Maine outdoorsman, decided he'd had just about enough of having cold, wet feet while tramping around in the woods. The resourceful Mr. Bean created the Maine Hunting Shoe, which he not only wore but also sold exclusively by mail, and which became the "sole" of today's 16,000-product mail order operation.

Beware!

You may come across ads from companies purporting to set you up in the mail order business—distributors who will supply you with all the catalogs, advertising copy, equipment, and inventory necessary to get up and running. These are not a good bet. To be successful in mail order, you need your own special niche—not a boilerplate program tailored to nobody.

explore the secrets to winning repeat customers throughout this book.)

For now, let's say you can expect your start-up costs to range from about $5,000 to somewhere over the $250,000 mark, depending on what sort of operation you start with. If you plan to start small, with a brochure-sized catalog or a print ad, your start-up figure will be relatively low. If you decide to start out with a 48-page catalog to rival those of Lands' End and J. Crew and mail it to 100,000 people, you're looking at a lot more money. "It's very easy to eat up $250,000 to $500,000 in starting a catalog today," Sroge says.

"Can people do it cheaper than that?" Sroge asks. "Sure." You can do a catalog from your kitchen table, design it yourself on a computer, and go with a much smaller mailing. You're not going to go from nothing to Lands' End, with its annual nine-figure revenues, overnight—but then, do you need to?

In this book, we're going to show you how to do things from a variety of perspectives, but the emphasis will be on doing them as reasonably as possible so that you can keep your costs to a minimum. Then, as we've said, the rest will be up to you!

Rock of Gibraltar

Besides start-up costs and profits, two other important factors to consider are risk and stability. You want a business that, like the Rock of Gibraltar, is here to stay. Mail order definitely qualifies as a "keeper" business, but choosing a business with a proven track record isn't the key to overnight success.

Even with its relatively long history, mail order's stability rates a "moderate" on the business start-up scale. Once you get to the point where you've got a good customer base—which can take a few years—your company should be on a firm foundation.

While everyone's heard tales of somebody who made it rich in mail order overnight, that somebody was either the exception to the rule or an urban legend like the stories of alligators in the New York sewer system—entertaining to hear about, but not necessarily true. As we mentioned earlier, industry experts agree that most direct-marketing businesses don't become profitable until three to five years after the initial investment. Mail order can be lucrative, and you can have a heck of a lot of fun getting there, but you have to be willing to put in lots of time, effort, and start-up capital—and you have to be willing to take risks.

The risk factor in starting a mail order business is also considered moderate—less than opening a tofu taco restaurant but more than selling 10-cent cups of coffee to caffeine-deprived commuters. The reason, as we've said, is that the competition is tough. Unless you've got the right combination of factors— an understanding of your potential customers' wants and needs matched with top-notch marketing skills—you'll have a hard time making it. Not to worry, though. There's a method to the magic of finding that perfect combination, and we'll show it to you in Chapter 3.

Fun Fact

Omaha Steaks first began sending its beefy products by mail in 1952. Since then, the company's steaks have been sent to Presidents Eisenhower and Kennedy and to the governors of all 50 states, and they've been given as gifts to heads of state in Denmark, Norway, and Sweden.

The Right Stuff

OK, you've decided that running a mail order business is potentially profitable. You're willing to invest not only the money but the time to learn the ropes and become established as a pro. What else should you consider? Your personality.

Total Strangers

That hallmark of the upscale mail order industry, the Spiegel catalog, got its start in Chicago in 1865 when Civil War veteran Joseph Spiegel—fresh out of a Confederate prison—launched a home furnishings store. Business flourished and survived the Great Fire of 1871 because Spiegel, whose warehouse was demolished, managed to salvage and store the furniture stock in his backyard.

But although this prudent move allowed the store to bounce back from disaster, it wasn't the company's greatest innovation. First came a retailing concept that was revolutionary in 1892: offering credit via installment plans. Then, in 1905, Spiegel's son, Arthur, got even more radical, suggesting catalog sales backed up by installment credit through the mail. Spiegel Senior initially balked at the idea, claiming it was ridiculous to offer credit to total strangers; but he eventually gave in.

A test catalog sent to Chicagoans met with instant success and, thus the Spiegel mail order business was born, giving rise, in turn, to a number of new ideas, including the first Christmas catalog and the use of photography instead of line drawings to show products.

▲

Traits of the Trade

Hey kids! Take this fun quiz, and find out if you've got what it takes to become a mail order maven.

1. My idea of a fun evening is:
   a) watching *The Postman Always Rings Twice* on video.
   b) snuggling up with a hot toddy and a rough draft of my catalog advertising copy.
   c) cruising around town singing "Please, Mr. Postman."

2. Here's how I usually send Christmas gifts to relatives who live out of state:
   a) I wait until December 24, stuff the gifts into old grocery bags with the addresses scribbled in crayon, then rush down to the post office and stand in a huge, snaky line with all the other procrastinators, hoping my gifts arrive in time and intact.
   b) I wrap my gifts carefully in specially selected packaging no later than December 10, call my predesignated FedEx or UPS courier (I've already checked to see which is cheaper and faster), and then follow up to make sure the gifts have arrived on time and intact.
   c) I usually just hope no one notices I forgot to send gifts.

3. Here's how I manage my library books:
   a) I return them as soon as I receive the first overdue notice!
   b) I carefully note the due date and return them on or before that time.
   c) I try to get them out from under the sofa when I get the collection letter from the city attorney's office.

4. When I want to sell my car, I:
   a) write "For Sale" on the windshield in shaving cream and hope the next rain doesn't wash it off.
   b) write a snappy advertisement, call my local newspapers to get the best ad rates, place the ad with the top few, and then determine which ones net the best results before renewing the ad.
   c) hope a tree falls on the car in the night so I can collect the insurance money.

5. I would best describe my self-motivational abilities as follows:
   a) I manage to get things done sooner or later.
   b) I love setting goals and accomplishing tasks!
   c) My self-starter frequently sticks.

Traits of the Trade, continued

6. If asked to sell Girl Scout cookies, I would:

   a) buy ten boxes myself so I wouldn't have to decide how to market them.

   b) sell one variety on one street and a second variety on another, keep accurate records of sales, compare which variety sold the most, and then request more boxes of that one to sell.

   c) politely decline.

   Answers: *If you chose "B" for each answer, you passed with flying colors! You've got what it takes to become a mail order maven. You're creative, organized, an efficient time manager, and self-motivated, and you possess a good accounting bent.*

Not everyone is cut out to be a mail order maven. This is not, for example, a career for the creativity-challenged. If you're one of those folks who'd rather undergo a root canal than come up with peppy advertising copy, then you don't want to be in mail order. It's also not a career for the math-phobic. Believe it or not, there's a lot of number-crunching involved in the mail order business. It's fun because it tells you how well your creative ideas are doing, but if you're a person who draws the line at working with figures, then you don't want to be in mail order, either.

This is also not a career for the time-management deficient. If you're a star procrastinator who can't seem to send anything out in the mail until it's already overdue, then you should definitely look elsewhere for entrepreneurial satisfaction.

If, on the other hand, you delight in dreaming up advertising ideas, you enjoy calculating how well your plans are paying off, and you're an efficient time manager, then a mail order company is probably a good business for you to start.

Mix It Up

This doesn't mean that only ad agency executives or accountants need apply. Mail order entrepreneurs come from all avenues of life. The ones we interviewed for this book represented a variety of careers: food writer and cooking teacher, mom, computer information specialist, bookkeeper, and romance writer.

The tip here is that all of these entrepreneurs figured out how to make their backgrounds and interests work for them in their new careers. They've taken the skills and enthusiasm they've already acquired and applied them to the mail order business—which is crucial to being a successful direct marketer.

"It's very good for people who have a special knowledge, skill, or interest that they want to share," John Schulte of the NMOA advises, "and who can find a way to contact others who share the same passion." And that's exactly what the entrepreneurs we interviewed have done.

Beth H., a food writer and cooking teacher, got into mail order through her knowledge of foods for people on a gluten-free diet. "I started in January of '93," the Connecticut resident recalls. "My son and I are both [allergic to glutens], so I started making mixes that I could use for myself. Then I converted them into formulas that I could mix up in large batches and started offering them to people in various support groups around the country. By July, I was so overwhelmed with requests that I couldn't keep up. I had to go to somebody to help me make them. It's really grown from there."

And Beth's business has definitely grown. From five products and a small flier sent to support groups, she's expanded to a line of products that fills a 28-page catalog and mail order sales around the world.

Ah, Romance

Mary M. also has a background as a writer—in her case, screenwriting and historical romances. When an auto accident rear-ended her writing career, Mary and her writing partner, her daughter-in-law, Michelle, who's also a graphic artist, brainstormed what else they could do that would allow them to continue their artistic expression while bringing in an income.

"It was an effort of combining everything we love," the St. Louis entrepreneur explains. "Michelle could contribute her graphic arts abilities, and I could do the writing. We both love decorating, and, of course, romance was the primary theme. So we decided to offer romantic gifts and home décor that conveys the spirit and style of romance. It's reflected in everything we offer."

Mary and Michelle spent a year just planning the business. "We knew nothing," Mary says candidly. "I had been in wholesaling years before, but it was totally different from what we're doing now. I did some interior design, which I always loved, but I really had no idea how to work with purchasing wholesale goods from vendors."

Three years later the partners are pros at dealing with mail order vendors and suppliers and are busy converting their paper catalog operation into a Web-based one.

Getting the Message Out

Greer T., a mail order entrepreneur based in Canton, Ohio, knew exactly what kind of merchandise she wanted to sell. "It was always in me that I wanted to have a children's boutique," she says, "and there was a children's boutique here in town that I loved. But I saw it taken over by three different owners in ten years, and I realized that small boutiques have a really hard time doing business. But if you can do a catalog and get your message out there, you can increase your business."

And that's exactly what the mother of four preteens did. She opened her boutique

Stat Fact

Mail order isn't just for home consumers. The National Mail Order Association says business-to-business sales tally in at $85.3 billion, or 27 percent of all direct-marketing sales.

on two fronts—a retail store in Canton and a mail order catalog with customers across the country. Greer had no experience in mail order when she started out. But she armed herself with a copy of Entrepreneur's business start-up *Start Your Own Mail Order Business*.

"I'm still learning the cost avenues of mail order," Greer says. "Your printing costs are high, along with your costs to do the photography, the scans, and the typesetting. I write my own copy, so I don't need a copywriter. But I have to pay a typesetter and a photographer. Purchasing a mailing list is expensive; so is mailing your product. You learn [all this] through experience."

After one year in business, the Ohio entrepreneur says, "We're doing well. It's steady, but it's difficult. You have to keep going at it. You put so much into it that nobody could have explained to you."

Hey, Sports Fans

Kate W., whose mail order company caters to a very different market, echoes this view. "I think that in your first couple of years, your learning curve is tremendous," the Overland Park, Kansas, resident says. Kate began her business two and a half years ago and bases her product line on her alma mater's football team.

"My husband is a huge, huge fan, and he wears [the team's logo on] everything," the Midwestern entrepreneur explains. "He wears the watch, shirts galore, everything. We're both graduates of the university, so we're big fans."

And as Kate discovered, she and her husband weren't the only "expatriate" fans. Graduates from their university had moved all around the country, and they all were eager for team logo products. "We found that any time we went anywhere, wherever we lived," Kate says, "people would say, 'That's cool; where did you get it?'"

Kate decided she'd like to start selling team merchandise, but her husband nixed the idea of a retail store because of the costs involved. The former bookkeeper wasn't deterred. She kept thinking about the concept and arrived at a goal: to engage people like herself and her husband, alumni who had moved away from the city where

Fun Fact

Lillian Vernon, the doyenne of mail order merchandise, began her empire at her kitchen table in 1951 as a 21-year-old pregnant housewife. Lillian's first marketing effort was a line of monogrammed belts and handbags sold through ads in *Seventeen* magazine.

the university is located but still had plenty of team spirit.

Finally, Kate hit on mail order as the perfect vehicle. "We decided on it because we could keep down the costs of everything associated with a retail outlet, like rent and employees. It could be done on a smaller basis, with just me starting the business. We could do nationwide distribution, which was ultimately what I wanted to do."

Filling a Need

Caryn O. began her company based on a lifelong knowledge of her products and, like Kate, as a way to fill the needs of people she knew were potential customers. "I didn't have a background in mail order, but I've always been around people in the fabric business," Caryn says. "My grandparents and great-grandparents had all been in the garment and fabric industry. So I was familiar with textiles—the industry, the people in it, and which companies were reputable."

And she knew what people needed within the industry. "I saw a need [among] small manufacturers who are constantly struggling to stay in business and constantly going out of business because they're forced to buy more than they need to get good pricing," the Roswell, Georgia, entrepreneur explains. "I saw a need for people who do crafts to be able to make extra money for their families. They needed to be able to get fabric at a good price. I also saw a [way to help] home sewers who might have children in the home and find it difficult to get out when they need something or find their selections limited to their local stores.

"So, for all those reasons, I tried to create a business that could help these different people fill their needs and help other businesses stay in business and make money."

And Caryn has fulfilled her vision. Today, her company is in its 16th year of operation, employs ten people, and has customers all over the world.

Midnight Brainstorm

Liz L. started her mail order company with a brainstorm in the middle of the night. "I had a toddler at the time," the upstate New Yorker says, "and I must have been thinking 'What can I do? I have two kids at home.' So I came up with the idea to do my shirts."

Liz's shirts are kid-geared tees in four educational designs—with a twist. The designs are printed upside down so the child can see them and learn. Liz started her company 12 years ago, screen-printing her shirts herself. As other businesses discovered her screen-printing abilities, they began to request her services to the degree that she found herself operating a full-time screen-printed promotional products company. Today, Liz has scaled back on this aspect of the business to devote herself to her tees, which are in great demand for kids from the preschool set right up to teens.

Be Your Own Boss

Mike M. is at the start of his mail order adventure. "I've always had a desire to be my own boss, like a lot of people have," the Byron, California, resident says. So while on vacation in Hawaii, he (like Greer T.) read Entrepreneur's *Start Your Own Mail Order Business*. "My wife and I decided we would dabble in this," Mike explains, "which we did."

They formed a corporation and chose a marketable product at a gift show. "We started much smaller than I would have liked, but it's kind of fun," he says. Then something happened to change Mike's view of the business. The company he'd worked at for five years was purchased by a larger corporation, and Mike was notified that his job was about to end. "I'm on my own, come the first of the year," the fledgling entrepreneur says, "so we're going to dive into [the mail order business] full-time."

And he's excited about it. He and his wife, both longtime boaters, are researching and designing a special product for boaters which they plan to have out soon. "[Mail order fulfills] a lot of start-up entrepreneurial desires," Mike says. "You don't have a lot of 8-to-5, and you don't have to be as regulated."

Mail Order Passion

And while "doing your own thing" is a definite plus in the mail order business, it's not the only thing to consider. The most important factor in mail order success, the one stressed again and again by entrepreneurs and industry experts alike, is passion—for the mail order industry as a whole and for your product line in particular. After all, you're going to be working with this merchandise for a long time, so make sure it's something you love and believe in.

"Passion brings success," advises Schulte of the NMOA. "If you're in the business just to make money but have no passion, your success—if at all—will be short-lived. Your competition will beat you every time." And, he adds, "Nothing sells like sincerity."

Fun Fact

That quintessential mail order haven for bibliophiles, the Book-of-the-Month Club (BOMC), sent out its first books in 1926. Less than a century later, the BOMC reported shipping more than 570 million books—enough to supply every American household with five volumes.

Future Forecast

If you're still reading, we assume you've decided to take the plunge and forge ahead with your new career. There is, however, one more thing to take into consideration: the industry prognosis.

Fortunately, the prognosis is good. As we saw at the start of the chapter, there's a great big, beautiful tomorrow for the direct-marketing industry. Unless aliens from the planet Zarcon land on the White House lawn and enslave us all, the industry outlook is healthy. On the other hand, if aliens from the planet Zarcon landed on the White House lawn, they would probably bring with them greater opportunities for mail order—of the intergalactic kind.

It's always possible, of course, that economic disaster will befall the country, making it difficult for customers to afford retail merchandise of any kind. But history so far has shown mail order to be an industry that has not only survived but thrived through every downturn and depression over the past century. Barring a cataclysmic disaster, the future of mail order is bright.

So fasten your seat belt, bring your tray table to the upright position and let's start your learning curve. Next chapter: Mail Order 101!

Mail
Order 101

You've decided to take on mail order as your business. Good! The world is your mailbag, with opportunities around every bend. But as with any business, you can't really be successful until you know what you're doing. So step on into the hallowed halls of Mail Order 101, and let's get learning.

▲

Trade Secrets

You can start your mail order company from one of three basic tangents:

- Offering one or a few products
- Offering one or a few services
- Offering a variety of products

No one of these is necessarily better than another. It all depends on what products or services you decide to sell and how you decide to sell them. This is one of the really great things about mail order: You can design and structure your company just about any way that suits you—so long as it suits your potential customers as well. The more focused your company is on a specific customer base, the more successful you're likely to be.

One-Hit Wonder

One of the biggest secrets to mail order success is the repeat customer. If you plan on a long and star-studded career in the industry, you will need to keep your customers coming back for more. You don't want to be the equivalent of the music industry's "one-hit wonder," debuting with one great product, after which you sink into mail order oblivion. Instead, you want to constantly consider what you can offer your customers after they've purchased your initial product or service.

For example, if you plan to start with a no-spill coffee mug for car cafe latte aficionados, then you'll want to follow up with a no-splootch jelly doughnut (especially for police officers—it could be the seed of a police officers' specialty catalog!). Or how about a fast-food lap tray? Whatever you choose, you'll want a new item that will entice the same customers who bought your first product.

The rule here is actually the same as it is in retail—keep your products in the same "family." A golf pro shop isn't going to do well selling dog food because customers who walk in wanting to buy tees and clubs aren't likely to buy kibble. And the mail order customer who sends in for your first product, a hummingbird feeder, probably won't buy your next offering if it's something unrelated, say, glow-in-the-dark paper clips. But if your next product is a home for unwed sparrows or a bat house, then you'll have that customer hooked. Which is good, because repeat customers are the ones who make your

> **Tip...**
>
> **Smart Tip**
>
> It's not just offering the right products that keeps people coming back for more. Quality and customer service are essential to customer loyalty, so set these attributes as cornerstones of your business and keep them there.

business a success. So much so, in fact, that experts insist you don't make any money at all off your first sale—that it's the return customer who secures your profits.

As you'll soon see, a lot of time, effort, and money goes into finding those initial customers. To lose them after a single marketing campaign is bad management, not to mention just plain silly.

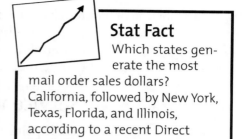

Stat Fact
Which states generate the most mail order sales dollars? California, followed by New York, Texas, Florida, and Illinois, according to a recent Direct Marketing Association report.

Target Practice

Another major key to mail order success is target marketing, the art of specializing within a specific market: nature lovers who are bird enthusiasts, for example. Mail order consultant Maxwell Sroge of Maxwell Sroge Company Inc., concurs. "If it wasn't for the improved techniques in target marketing," he says, "the increases in paper and postage costs would have destroyed the industry a long time ago."

These paper and postage cost increases—which have made printing and mailing catalogs more and more expensive as the years roll by—were responsible, at least in part, for the downfall of two of mail order's most time-honored icons, the Sears and the Montgomery Ward catalogs.

But while the pioneering twosome went the way of the Roman Empire, other mail order marketers prospered. Why? They developed target markets, offering select groups of products to select clientele. Instead of spending vast sums of money on the

Who Fits the Profile?

If you could draw a portrait of the quintessential mail order shopper, this is what she (yes, she's a female) would look like:

○ Female (This gender does 58 percent of all mail order shopping.)
○ Age 35 to 44
○ Earns upwards of $40,000 per year
○ College-educated
○ Professional/managerial career
○ Homeowner

mass distribution of booster-chair-size catalogs, they pared down printing and postage costs by sending out small catalogs with carefully selected merchandise to those most likely to buy those particular products. The result? They made more profit per dollar spent than the bigger guys. And they're still around!

Service with a Stamp

In this book, we're generally going to discuss mail order products in terms of merchandise, but keep in mind that what you sell can just as easily be a service instead of a product. According to the Direct Marketing Association, services account for almost 40 percent of mail order revenue. While financial services make up the biggest sector of direct-marketed services, there are scads of other options, including photo processing, travel packages, consulting, genealogical research, and real estate.

The only major difference between selling a service and selling a product through mail order will come in terms of inventory. If you're selling tours to Costa Rica, for instance, you're not going to have a stack of tours sitting on shelves in your back room; but if you're selling shirts made in Costa Rica, you probably will have boxes full of shirts waiting to be sold and shipped.

The other thing to consider with service-based mail order is the matter of accessibility. You can sell those Costa Rica tours and all the other services we listed at the top of this section because they can be handled long-distance. You don't need to be close to your customers to perform the service. Some services, however, like lawn care,

Fishing for Customers

Mail order innovator L.L. Bean targets its markets by sending out about 30 different kinds of catalogs per year—pitching special product lines to those most likely to buy them, instead of trying to sell everything to everybody. Check out a few of L.L. Bean's specialty catalog offerings:

- ○ *Corporate Sales Gift Guide*
- ○ *Fly Fishing*
- ○ *Hunting*
- ○ *L.L. Bean Outdoors*
- ○ *L.L. Bean Traveler*
- ○ *L.L. Bean Women's Outdoor*
- ○ *L.L. Home Casual Furnishings*
- ○ *L.L. Kids, Back to School*

require you to be conveniently located. So unless you've got a clever take on how to circumvent geography, you can't market this type of program to those outside of your immediate area.

Bestsellers

What products and services are runaway bestsellers right now? Industry experts agree that computers and their peripherals top the list. Other than that, the answers may surprise you. Take a look at these top-selling mail order categories, courtesy of John Schulte of the NMOA:

- Art, drafting, and printing supplies
- Athletic equipment
- Business equipment
- Children's clothing
- Educational materials
- Fishing equipment
- Global marketing services (especially in Europe)
- Hardware
- Health and fitness products
- Home medical supplies and equipment
- Industrial maintenance and materials handling
- Internet investment brokerage services
- Library and school products
- Men's clothing
- Prescriptions
- Software
- Specialty products and gifts
- Stationery specialties
- Tobacco products
- Videocassettes
- Vitamins
- Women's big and tall apparel

Mail Order Vehicles

As you already know, mail order sales are no longer strictly confined to orders placed via U.S. mail. The savvy mail order maven can choose from a wondrous variety of vehicles through which to market his or her products or services. The Internet

Stat Fact

According to the American Mail Marketing Association, more than 10,000 mail order catalogs are produced every year.

is gaining by leaps and bounds as the vehicle of choice, and television, radio, and classified ads also shine as good sources of revenue. But the tried-and-true catalog sent streaming through the mail along with all those bills, letters, and notices, is still the top-rated method of garnering customers—and, of course, sales.

Mail Order Dinosaur

Traditional catalogs fall into two main categories, *general* and *specialty*. The *general catalog*, like the old-fashioned general store, sells just about everything—from shoes for your feet to tires for your car—in one big package of pages. Except for perhaps the *J.C. Penney* and *Service Merchandise* books, however, this type of catalog has fallen by the wayside. Colossal increases in the costs of paper and postage have made it a mail order dinosaur, too big and too cumbersome to support itself.

And, as yet another blow to the brontosaurus-like general catalog, all the slick and streamlined new specialty catalogs available tend to make the old booster-chair substitute look dowdy and uninteresting in comparison. And who wants to try to generate sales excitement that way?

Specialty Catalogs

Think *Victoria's Secret*, *Sharper Image*, or *Smith & Hawken*, and you're thinking *specialty catalog*. By selling—respectively—slinky lingerie, high-tech toys, and gardening products, these companies have fine-tuned their product lines. Instead of trying to be all things to all customers, they've gone the boutique route, carving out a niche amidst the avalanche of available products.

To be a mail order success story yourself, you must find your own niche, one that nobody else has targeted, and one from which lots of customers will want to buy. We'll talk about how to do this in Chapter 3, but for now let's peruse the pages of current mail order successes to see what's already out there and what might spark a brilliant specialty catalog concept in your mind:

- *Gourmet goodies.* One way to a mail order consumer's heart is through his or her stomach. Gourmet goodies are perennial favorites, from coffees to chocolates to steaks. How about chili peppers, Australian wines, caviar, cherries, or teas? You can even order home-cooked meals to stash in the freezer.

  And if that's not enough, many mail order firms offer goodie-of-the-month clubs in which they send a different type of fresh fruit, fudge, wine—or whatever—to the chosen recipient once a month for a year.

Mail order foods go over great with home consumers, but they're also a terrific draw for corporate types who always need something posh—but not too personal—to send to that special client.

If you're thinking food, keep in mind that some treats, such as fresh meats or seafood, require refrigeration and that most foods need special packaging so they don't arrive squished, squashed, dented, or broken.

- *Getting crafty.* With the new American ethic of getting back to quality time and quality projects, crafting is increasingly popular. Catalogs abound for all types of craft supplies, from cross-stitch patterns to knitting needles to rubber stamps—even handmade vintage wallpapers! You might also consider selling your own finished crafts or those of your talented friends and family members.

  If you're thinking about selling craft supplies, it's wise to take the specialty catalog idea one step further and specialize in one theme, say, stained glass or ceramics, instead of trying to be all things to all crafters.

- *Natural duds.* Apparel is always a popular product category. But just because the biggies like Spiegel, J. Crew, and their ilk dominate the roll call, don't think there isn't room for entrepreneurs. All you have to do is get creative. Think full-figured outfits, maternity wear, natural-fiber duds, easy-dress attire for the

It's News to You

Many mail order mavens have found success by publishing newsletters. If you're an expert on finances, recipes, decorating, health, or any other subject you think there's a market for, you might want to consider making a newsletter your product. You'll have to have good writing skills and think your subject through carefully. Do you have enough material to write knowledgeably about interesting topics and events every month or every quarter? Or will you peter out after one or two issues?

If you think you'll have plenty of material, creating and selling subscriptions to an expert newsletter may be an option for you. Keep in mind, however, that you should have the credentials to back up your expertise. If you've been a computer specialist for a number of years, you can use that as your qualification for writing a software review newsletter. If you're a teacher with many years on the job and various awards, you've got an impressive background to justify your expertise as the purveyor of a newsletter about childhood education. Volunteer jobs and club memberships can also be qualifications if you've been active long enough to garner the experience and kudos needed to qualify you as an expert.

disabled, or baby layettes. The key is (still!) to come up with a special take on clothing, one for which an ample market exists, and go with it.

- *Setting up camp.* The secret to sports and camping catalogs is also specialization. Target your market. Trying to sell paraphernalia for every sport under the sun doesn't work, but catalogs tailored to specific recreational pursuits, such as canoeing, bicycling, equestrian eventing, golf, or tennis can be mail order winners. Companies like Campmor and Wiley Outdoor Sports have discovered that people who like to sleep under the stars among bugs and rocks are terrific targets for mail order camping gear.

- *This does compute.* Perhaps the hottest mail order category in the industry is computer peripherals—software, modems, video cards—all the accessories and assorted goodies that every computer owner and operator must have. With computers multiplying like megabytes and everyone from toddlers to 70-year-olds surfing the Net, it's no surprise that this specialty is the top seller on the Internet.

    When you think computers, think home and business consumers. You might not want to target both, but keep in mind that both groups are viable end users.

- *For more information.* One of the most marketable—and easily attainable—mail order products in the world is the knowledge right in your own brain. We're talking about information, including plans, recipes, formulas, tips, and tricks. If

Bank Robbery Made Easy

Although the mail order industry is open to just about any product or service you can dream up, there are some things better left unsold. Why? Because they're illegal. They include:

- ○ Chain or pyramid schemes
- ○ Firearms
- ○ Lottery tickets
- ○ Master keys to motor vehicles (no car-theft supplies or accessories)
- ○ Materials inciting criminal activity (no books on bank robbery made easy)

you can build a cabinet, repair a watch, prepare a tax form, or cook a knockout tuna casserole, then you have information you can sell.

What are the advantages to selling your secrets? For starters, information is easy to package. Then—important!—it's profitable. You can print a small book or pamphlet for a dollar or less and sell it for several dollars, which gives you a markup of 400 percent to 600 percent over your cost. (We'll talk about markups in Chapter 5.)

Remember that any material you consign to print is yours, and once you've copyrighted it, no one can legally reproduce it without your permission. Of course, you can't liberate somebody else's information either, so make sure that chocolate chip cookie recipe you're so famous for isn't the one that came off the back of the Nestlé Toll House Morsels package.

- *Take it personally.* Except, of course, on those envelopes from the IRS, we all like to see our names in print. Personalized gifts—everything from stationery and monogrammed shirts to baseball caps with your Little (or would-be Big) Leaguer's name inscribed on the bill and children's stories featuring a specific tyke—are perennial mail order favorites.

  Just about anything can be personalized with ink, embroidery, or engraving, but it's not a service you can easily find at retail stores like Wal-Mart. So when you think mail order gifts, think personalized.

- *You are what you eat.* If you're thinking wealth, why not think health? People who haven't got the time or the energy to visit the health food store perk up at a mail order source of vitamins, minerals, herbs, and other health supplements. These customers can also gobble up natural food products like nuts, grains, and gourmet vegetarian goodies.

  When you think health, however, think regulations. You'll need to check in with the Food and Drug Administration to make sure the products you're offering meet with government approval.

- *Bookworm central.* Along with computer peripherals, books are at the top of the mail order hit parade. Not a surprise, when you consider that a) a mail order catalog *is* a book, so people who like catalogs like to read, and b) people who purchase books by mail are doing so to give themselves more time to read. Catalogs for by-mail bookworms encompass everything from New Age and self-help to mysteries and books on tape. There are book catalogs for the

Fun Fact

The perennial *Hammacher Schlemmer* catalog was first issued in 1881, six years earlier than the first Sears catalog. A far cry from its initial print run of 500 copies, the company now prints 12 editions a year and mails catalogs to customers on every continent.

do-it-yourself woodworker, the do-it-yourself attorney, and the do-it-yourself gardener. When you think books, think—as always!—specialization.

- *Fit, not fat.* Americans, ever conscious of their swimsuit profiles, make diet and fitness a prime mail order category. You can market books, exercise equipment, low-fat foods, and weight-loss plans. There is a big red flag here, though: The Food and Drug Administration and the Federal Communications Commission (FCC) have diet products firmly in their sights as potential deceptive advertising hotbeds. So if you dream diet product dreams, be sure your plans include careful consultation with federal regulators.

- *All that glitters.* Everybody loves the sparkle of gold and silver and precious gems, and that makes jewelry a natural candidate for the mail order entrepreneur. (For confirmation, take a look at the hotcake jewelry sales on home shopping channels.) People who might feel intimidated stepping into a high-toned jewelry store at the mall feel more comfortable shopping from home—and also may feel they're getting a better deal.

  When you think jewelry, though, don't confine yourself to diamond engagement rings or gold chains. Think specialty: How about Native American adornments, New Age baubles, or a gem-of-the-month club—a different gem for every flip of the calendar?

- *The envelope, please.* You might think going from jewelry to office supplies is going from diamonds to dullsville. Not necessarily. Every business needs paper, envelopes, pens, staples, and all the other accoutrements of office life—and most businesspeople are so busy that they are drop-to-their-knees grateful for anybody who will deliver to their door.

  As a general rule, mail order office products firms do best targeting companies with 50 or more employees, but you might shine as a purveyor to home-based entrepreneurs. Whatever route you take, keep in mind that people who order office supplies usually need them now, so you'll have to be able to offer a very fast turnaround time.

Direct Mail

Direct mail is really just another name for mail order, but it usually refers to anything that is not a catalog. This includes sales letters (like Publishers Clearing House), brochures, fliers, postcards, and any other sort of printed materials you can send through the U.S. post to elicit a mailed, telephoned, faxed, or e-mailed customer response.

> **Tip...**
>
> **Smart Tip**
> Yet another term for mail order or direct marketing is *direct response,* because your customers (ideally) respond directly to your catalog, radio, or TV spot, or other vehicle.

Instant Access

The Internet ranks as the most exciting mail order vehicle since the invention of the catalog. It's one of the simplest and fastest ways to reach a national or global audience. If you've got a company Web site, everybody in the world who has access to the Internet has almost instant access to your online catalog. Perhaps even better, with your own Web site, you're on equal footing with the big guys. You can easily compete with larger, more established businesses—and even look like one yourself—without spending a fortune. When your site is accessed through the same medium and has the same (or better) graphics, who's to know that your office is in the garage?

More and more mail order entrepreneurs are turning to the Internet as a supplement to their catalogs or are forgoing paper catalogs altogether. Potential customers have come to expect companies to have a Web presence, especially for any computer-related product or service. But even if your company isn't technology-based, a Web site makes sense. Everything from gift baskets to insurance to concrete—

Give It a Shot

The one-shot is a perennial mail order vehicle, so called because you market just one item instead of an entire line, and you therefore have one shot in which to sell it. You might sell, for example, a pair of sunglasses with removable shade lenses and a flashlight attachment so the wearer can see as well at night as during the day. A keen concept, perhaps, but not one that's likely to garner a lot of repeat customers. Once a customer buys one pair, he's unlikely to buy more—he's off your list.

One-shots are typically advertised through sales letters, classified ads, radio ads, and television commercials. You can also find them in the colorful supplements that fall out of your Sunday paper, in magazine ads, and in direct-mail ads.

The advantage to one-shots is that you know immediately whether your ad and product are successful. You don't have to spend a lot of time fine-tuning a whole catalog full of products and then another chunk of time waiting to see if your creative labors are successful. And if your one-shot works, you get a quick turnaround on your investment.

The one-shot method has a serious downside, however, which is that you can't build a mail order business solely on one-shot products. Since each one-shot is liable to vary radically from its predecessors, you have no opportunity to build a solid base of repeat customers.

Stat Fact

Twenty-five percent of the people who purchase mail order products they've seen advertised in TV commercials earn more than $50,000 per year, according to WSL Marketing in New York.

even airplanes—can be purchased on-line, and people who are Net-savvy use the Web the way they would their local Yellow Pages.

Real TV

Another form of mail order is the TV commercial: the one that advertises knives that slice through concrete or the greatest recording hits of your parents' generation and provides the ordering information on-screen. Television advertising can be less expensive than you might guess. The price of TV time depends on various factors, including the size of the market, the length of your ad, the time of day or night your ad airs, the program rating, and how much advertising you buy.

Prices also vary according to whether you're advertising on a local independent station, a network affiliate, a cable channel, or public access television.

Radio Face

Let's face it. Radio commercials also constitute mail order. Advertising on big stations in major markets can be cost-prohibitive for mail order newbies, but you can buy effective and affordable ad time from more intimate local stations for less money than you might think. These smaller stations make up the majority of commercial radio stations in the United States. Their low-power signals limit their geographic reach, but this isn't necessarily a minus. Since the programs on local stations are specifically designed to appeal to their own regional audiences, your advertising can be more closely targeted as well.

Strictly Classified

For some mail order entrepreneurs, a *classified ad* in the newspaper—that tiny inch or so of black newsprint—is a highly effective vehicle. Classified ads usually run from three to ten lines in length, are one column wide, and excel at minimalism: They have no line art, no photos, no graphics of any kind, and the wording is as brief and concise as a Vermont farmer's. So what makes them valuable? For starters, they're very inexpensive yet cover a relatively wide audience. And because they're so inexpensive, they're a terrific way to test new products and markets.

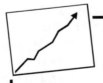

Stat Fact

According to the National Mail Order Association, Internet sales recently netted $2.4 billion in annual mail order dollars. The hottest sellers? Computer products, books, recorded music, gifts, financial services, and general merchandise.

On Display

The *display ad* is a vehicle of a different sort. Because it's larger and usually incorporates photos or some other type of artwork, it's more expensive, but it can be extremely effective if you're advertising a high-end product. You'd use a classified ad if, for example, you were advertising Aunt Polly's famous Macaroni Surprise recipe but a display ad to market a Recipe-a-Month Club that comes with not only the recipe but all also the ingredients for a complete dinner.

Follow the Rules

Now that you've test driven every mail order vehicle, you're ready to roll. But as with operating a motor vehicle, there are rules you must follow. Like the rules for cars, trucks, motorbikes, and buses, mail order's rules are logical and easy to understand. And like the rules for motor vehicles, you can land yourself in a world of trouble if you fail to heed the proper regulations.

So sit back, take another sip of that coffee at your elbow, and let's take a look at the mail order "driving manual."

No Cheating

The Federal Trade Commission (FTC) regulates all companies that conduct business across states lines, which of course includes mail order firms. And the FTC has very strict rules. As a mail order maven, you cannot engage in any sort of false advertising. This means:

- *No taking money under false pretenses.* If you do, you can be convicted of fraud.
- *No fooling.* Your direct-marketing materials are considered illegal if they are designed to fool consumers.
- *No misleading product claims.* You can't advertise that keen gasoline additive guaranteed to give any car 100 miles to the gallon unless that's what it really will do. The majority of mail order mavens, of course, being honest types, wouldn't dream of out-and-out lying about a product. But some people tend to get carried away by their own excitement and end up making claims that aren't quite realistic. Make sure this isn't you.
- *No false medical claims.* When advertising medical or health products, you must

Beware!
Don't undersell youself—or your competitors. It's illegal to price a product at less than your cost if your intent is to injure your business rivals by luring away customers.

have scientific proof that the product will do what you claim. Don't use words like "cure," "banish," or "remedy" unless you can prove through clinical studies that this really is the case.

- *No putting on airs.* Don't use titles like "laboratory" or "manufacturer" or any other description in your company's name unless you actually perform the function you claim.
- *No false pricing claims.* You can't say things like "formerly priced at $5" unless the product really was priced at $5 and you actually did sell a substantial number of units at that price.
- *No fabricated testimonials.* If your ad includes words of glowing praise from satisfied customers, make sure they're real words from real customers, not testimonials you invented yourself.

The Ticking Clock

In 1975, the FTC instituted what was then called the *Mail Order Merchandise Rule* to regulate direct-marketing businesses. The name of the law was later changed to the *Mail or Telephone Order Merchandise Rule*, and it now also applies to orders placed via fax, e-mail, and the Internet. You can find yourself flailing in rough seas if you ignore the Rule's guidelines, but not to panic! Unlike a lot of government legalese, the guidelines actually make sense and are easy to follow:

- You must send ordered merchandise within the time period specified in your ad or, if you don't specify a shipping time, within 30 days. The clock starts ticking on this time requirement when you receive the completed order. An order is complete when you receive your customer's cash, check, or money order or

---

A Little Freebie

Don't mail people anything they haven't asked for. It's illegal for you as a mail order maven to send unsolicited or unordered products to potential customers and then ask them to pay for them. A consumer who receives such a product—whether you sent it inadvertently or on purpose—is under no obligation to return it or pay for it and can consider it a nice little freebie.

The exception to this rule is for charitable organizations that are soliciting donations. They alone can send samples or gifts, so long as they clearly spell out that the recipient can keep the product with no strings attached.

---

have charged the person's credit card account, and have all the information you need to process and ship the order. If the customer doesn't specify essential information, such as size or color preferences, the order is considered incomplete.

- If you don't specify a shipping time and your customer is applying for credit to pay for the purchase, you have 50 days to ship after receiving the order. This is the one exception to the 30-day shipping rule.
- If you can't meet the shipping deadline, you must notify your customer and offer an alternative option: The customer can either receive a prompt refund or agree to a delay. Your notice must include a new shipping date, instructions on how to cancel the order, and a postage-paid way to reply.
- If your customer agrees to a new shipping date and you can't meet it again, you must send a second notice as soon as possible. Unless the customer signs and returns this second postage-paid notice, you must automatically cancel the order and refund the person's money.
- If you can't ship the merchandise on time and you don't notify your customer as required, you must count the order as canceled and send a refund.
- If your customer cancels an order, you must refund his or her money. If the order was paid for by cash, check, or money order, you must return the money within seven business days. If the order was paid for by credit card, you must credit the customer's credit card account within one billing cycle.

The Mail or Telephone Order Merchandise Rule applies to almost everything ordered through direct-marketing sources. The exceptions are: photo-finishing services, magazine subscriptions (after the first issue), c.o.d. orders, seeds, and plants.

The Postal Police

The FTC is not the only government entity keeping an eye on mail order activities. If you're part of the vast majority of good-egg direct marketers, you've got nothing to worry about. But if you should decide to get a little too creative with what's legal and what's not, you're liable to stumble over:

- *The U.S. Postal Service (USPS).* The USPS employs *postal inspectors* who can arrest you if you engage in illegal mail order activities. These postal police can have you sign a statement that lets them stamp "Refused Out of Business" on your packages. If you're

> **Smart Tip** Tip...
>
> To get a complete copy of the Mail or Telephone Order Merchandise Rule from the FTC, call (877) FTC-HELP. You can also visit the FTC online at www.ftc.gov/bcp/conline/pubs/buspubs/mailorder/index.htm and check out *A Business Guide to the Federal Trade Commission's Mail or Telephone Order Merchandise Rule,* which explains how to comply with the rule and gives answers to important questions.

▲

convicted of mail order fraud, you can be fined and/or thrown in the slammer, or you can simply be put out of business.

- *The Food and Drug Administration (FDA).* The FDA does not look kindly on people who make false claims on drug, cosmetics, or food labels, and it, too, is empowered to take action against you.
- *State fraud commissions.* These organizations act as watchdogs on the state mail order front.
- *The Better Business Bureau (BBB).* It's not a government agency, but the BBB has developed an advertising code and responds to complaints about unethical business practices.

You've now mastered Mail Order 101. You know the different types of mail order vehicles, where to go as far as targeting a specialty audience and where not to go as far as illegal activities are concerned. Now let's get on with the fun stuff. Next chapter: Planning Your Mail Route!

Planning Your Mail Route
Market Research

Every business needs consumers for its products or services in order to, as the Vulcans so eloquently put it, live long and prosper. So your first challenge as an aspiring mail order entrepreneur is to identify and research your target market. You'll need to determine who your potential clients will be,

Photo© PhotoDisc Inc.

what regions they'll come from, and what specific merchandise or services you'll offer to draw them in.

This is an important phase in building your mail order business. The proper market research can help boost your business into a true profit center. The more research you do and the better prepared you are before you officially send out your first materials or place that first ad, the less floundering you're likely to do.

This chapter, therefore, focuses on market research techniques and tips for the budding mail order entrepreneur.

Defining Your Market

To be successful in mail order, you must define your own special market, one where a genuine need or desire for your products or services exists and one where the competition isn't overwhelming. Start by thinking about what you know, what you enjoy and what your potential customers need or want. Then match your ideas against these three guidelines:

1. *The products or services you sell must be things you know and are enthusiastic about.* If you're an avid snorkeler or scuba diver and you want to sell products to other divers or market diving-adventure vacations, great! Get in the swim! But if you

hate water, the thought of salt air makes you seasick and you're getting into the specialty because somebody told you it was a good idea, then don't make waves. You will very likely fail. Instead, you need to find something you understand and enjoy.

> **Bright Idea**
> Business-to-business sales—terrific mail order markets—can encompass more types of products and services than you might think. Take a common product and give it a new twist. Instead of selling fine art prints to consumers, for instance, how about art for the office?

2. *You must have a large customer base to draw from.* If you know everything there is to know about flies, you find them fascinating and you have a huge collection under glass, that's swell. But you're not going to find many people who will want to order fly merchandise. If, on the other hand, you're into fly *fishing*, you'll have a huge number of enthusiasts all over the world from which to draw.

3. *You must have a well-defined specialty.* You may have a reputation as a shop-'til-you-dropper, and your friends and family may turn to you as the gift chooser of choice, but it's unlikely you'll succeed with a broad catalog of gift items or preppy clothing. There are already too many really big companies out there doing the same thing, and they're too huge to compete against. But if you choose gifts or clothing for a specialized market—say, handicapped children, seniors, cat lovers, or gardeners—you're moving in the right direction.

Wander and Wonder

Now, if you just can't come up with a line of products or services that's unique but widely embraced, don't panic! There are ways to get ideas:

- *Get creative at gift shows and clothing marts.* Once you've got your fictitious business name (which we will cover in Chapter 4), you're official. You are allowed to enter the hallowed halls of these huge trade shows, which are held periodically at convention centers across the country. Displays by manufacturers, suppliers and wholesalers line aisles crammed with the latest in giftware and fashion apparel. Roam around. Try to get a feel for what's hot, what's not, and how you might put together a line of items that are related in some way—say, dolls for every season or high-fashion clothes for chubby kids.

- *Get crafty at craft fairs and art shows.* Local artists often have terrific wares just waiting to be sold. Use the same strategy described above to sketch out ideas for potential products. How about a line of handcrafted jewelry or a line of art representing the region you live in? Bear in mind, however, that arts and crafts are not mass-produced. If you go with handmade items, make sure your artists will be able to keep up with the potential demand.

▲

- *Bob along at boat shows, home shows, garden shows, and auto shows.* Use your wander-and-wonder strategy to get ideas from all the products displayed.

- *Ask people!* Ask your family, friends, and neighbors what mail order merchandise they buy and what they would like to buy that's not available through mail order. You might hear something that strikes a chord.

The Proverbial Diaper Pail

You've chosen a specialty, you've got a line of products or services, and you've decided that there are plenty of other people out there interested in the same thing. Good! But your work's not done. Now you need to ask yourself some important questions:

- *Is it fashion or fad?* Unless you're going the one-shot route, it's unwise to pin your product line on a fad. If the major rave this year is, for example, happy faces, and your entire merchandise line is happy-faced, it's only a matter of time until the fad fades and your smile is upside down. Make sure your specialty has staying power.

- *Is it Christmas in July?* Stay away from products that are popular in only one season. If you're selling just Christmas ornaments, for example, your sales will shrivel in August. Instead, try selling festive decorations for holidays throughout the year—New Year's, St. Patrick's Day, Independence Day, Halloween, and Thanksgiving. This way your cash flow is steady, and so are your nerves.

- *Is it reasonably priced?* Go with merchandise you can offer your customers at a price they can afford. If you're planning to sell designer diapers at $50 a nappy to people on the Neiman-Marcus mailing list, you might do all right. But if your target market consists of middle-of-the-road young families, you're pricing yourself out of the market and into the proverbial diaper pail.

- *Is it easy to send?* Take shipping costs and perils into consideration. If you're selling refrigerators at rock-bottom prices, your shipping costs may be so high that they put a chill on your bottom line. Or you might be selling Aunt Adele's cookie crescents, which, while lighter than a refrigerator, turn to crumbs when mailed. Think your products through and go with merchandise that's relatively small and light and travels well.

- *Is there room to grow?* Choose a specialty with space for expansion. If you're selling

> **Fun Fact**
> Mail order giant Eddie Bauer invented a goose down jacket in 1936 that was a hit first with Alaskan bush pilots and later with the U.S. Army Air Corps. During World War II, Bauer's downy flight jackets were the only made-for-the-military garments allowed to carry the manufacturer's private label. Imagine how many presold postwar customers that garnered the company!

78-rpm records and 8-track tapes, for instance, and the rest of the world is snapping up CDs, your market will wither faster than you can say Lawrence Welk.

High Concept

Now that you've begun brainstorming products, check out the "Merchandise Planning Guide" on page 38, which will help you choose that perfect specialty for your mail order business. Let's go over the worksheet, item by item so you'll understand how to use it best:

1. *Product or service.* Go back over the first part of this chapter. Then do some brainstorming and choose a product or service that fits the criteria we've outlined.

2. *Complementary products or services.* If you can't think of anything else to go with your initial idea, give it an instant "F" grade and choose another product.

3. *Full line.* As we've explained, unless you plan to leapfrog from one-shot to one-shot, you must choose a product or service you can develop into a full line of complementary merchandise or services. This keeps your customers coming back for more.

4. *Name that target.* In the movie biz, when an idea or concept can be expressed in a short, simple phrase, it's called a "high concept." If you can't give your line a high-concept title, chances are, no one else will be able to, either. And that means you don't have enough to go on.

5. *Special knowledge.* Do you know enough about this specialty to fully develop a line around it and also answer your customers' questions and fill their needs?

6. *Enjoyment.* Do you like this specialty? If you plan to offer word processing services because you've been a secretary for 20 years, but you hate typing, your interest will fizzle before your business gets fired up.

7. *Potential customers.* You must also be able to identify your potential customers in a way that's specific and high-concept. If you're planning to sell clothing, for example, "people who wear clothes" is not a good answer. It's entirely too general to give you a target audience. "Medical professionals who want fashionable work wear" is a great answer. It targets a specific market with a specific need.

8. *How many?* You'll need to know the size of your target audience so you can determine if you've got enough potential buyers out there to make your line profitable. You can get this information from a variety of sources:

   - *The public library.* Reference librarians can be extremely helpful with this sort of thing. All you have to do is call and tell the librarian that you need to know how many medical professionals—or fly fisherman, or disabled children under age 14—there are in the United States. The reference librarian will look up the information and call you back with the answer.

Merchandise Planning Guide

Use this worksheet as a planning guide for each of your merchandise ideas. (Make copies so you have one sheet for each idea.) Answer each question carefully.

1. Product or service: _____

   _____

2. What other products or services will complement it? _____

3. Can you develop this into a full line of products or services? _____

4. Can you put a name to this target line (e.g., classic car parts and accessories, or backpackers' clothing and gear)? _____

5. Are you knowledgeable about this product or service? _____

6. Do you enjoy working in this area? _____

7. Who are your potential customers? _____

   _____

8. How many are there? _____

   _____

9. Where are they located? _____

10. Where do they now get the products or services you plan to provide?

   _____

11. What can you offer that they're not receiving now? _____

   _____

   _____

Or you can go into the library and dig through whole books of demographic statistics yourself, unearthing more facts and figures than you could use in a quadruple round of Trivial Pursuit.

- *The Internet.* A world library at your fingertips! If you're not yet Net-savvy, make becoming so a priority. You'll have access to all sorts of demographics without ever leaving your desk. For starters, check in with the U.S. Census Bureau at www.census.gov (yes, it collects all that data for a reason—here's your chance to take advantage of it). The Census Bureau is part of the Department of Commerce, which has other divisions that may have useful information about your target market. You can visit the Department of Commerce at www.doc.gov.

> **I**f you're not yet Net-savvy, make becoming so a priority.

- *Organizations and associations.* What better places to go for information on your specific market? If you're targeting senior citizens, for example, you could contact the American Association of Retired Persons for a count of its members. For a count of primary school teachers, you'd talk to the folks at state and regional teachers' associations.

9. *Location.* You might think this question is unimportant—after all, this is mail order. Who cares where you are in relation to your customers? You should! This information will help you refine your niche.

- Kate W., for example, based her entire line on her awareness of her alma mater's many alumni football fans living out-of-state—fans who still want team logo goodies. If her research had turned up only a handful of out-of-staters, she would have had to revise her game plan.

- Greer T., the children's boutique marketer, has discovered that her catalogs do better in certain areas of the country. "I do really well in southern states—South Carolina, Georgia, Tennessee, Texas—and also in Missouri and Montana," the Ohio resident says. "My customers there tell me there's nothing in their area for shopping."

10. *Where they get products now.* This is a major consideration. If your potential customers are already purchasing the same sorts of products from other mail order sources—or from shops they're madly in love with—you may want to scratch this line and start over with something else. If, on the other hand, you discover that the products you'll be offering are hard to find, you'll have a definite head start on building a solid customer base.

- Greer, for example, has found that while there are lots of clothing catalogers out there, few compete with the niche she's carved. "There aren't that many specialty catalogs for children in the price ranges I offer," she says.

- How do you find out where your potential customers currently shop? You'll have to ferret this out by conducting market surveys, which we'll explore later in this chapter.

11. *What you can offer.* This is another major factor in developing your niche. Think long and hard about what will make your products different from your competition's. If you're selling books, for instance, what will make your company shine above mail order booksellers like Amazon.com, Barnes & Noble, Doubleday, and Harlequin? If you specialize in children's books, reference volumes, or books on tape, you've got a niche. If you can't come up with anything new, you're thumbing through the wrong tome and you probably won't succeed. "If you try to saturate a market that's very broad, you're just dooming yourself to failure," warns Beth, the gluten-free foods purveyor in Connecticut.

What's My Niche?

Kate, the college football fan's entrepreneur, founded her entire product line on a very special niche—one she takes care to explain to her customers. Each catalog features a personal letter, and Kate used that letter in her first catalog to describe how she started the company as an exclusive mail order service for fans of her alma mater. "I don't mix schools," the former bookkeeper explains, "because everybody

> ### Bright Idea
> One of the largest relatively untouched markets is the older set. While many merchandisers knock themselves out catering to Generation Xers and those irrepressible Boomers, the hale and hearty 60-plusers have been virtually ignored.

likes to know they're a little bit special. The more exclusive or item-specific—or in this case, school-specific—the merchandise is, [the better]. People want their own little niche."

Once Kate had chosen her niche market, she narrowed her sights even more, aiming at a highly segmented target audience. "I think part of the reason we've done so well is that we knew our market—because we *are* it," says the university sports memorabilia entrepreneur. "We knew we were marketing to people who are professionals, who have moved away, been gone for maybe 10-plus years and are older. I'm 40, so I kind of take myself as an average consumer and ask, 'What do I like? What would I buy my husband?' That's a large part of how we select our products."

The Lifeline

In Connecticut, Beth H. has also developed a highly segmented niche market, based on an entirely different set of parameters—foods for people who are allergic to the wheat glutens found in store-bought cakes, breads, and bakery products. While her only intention initially was to provide mixes to people in gluten-free support groups, she soon found herself the recipient of national publicity.

"We were reaching people in all these little places all over the country," Beth recalls, "the Ozarks and West Virginia and places where they thought they were the only celiac in the world and didn't have access to a natural food store.

"Also at that time, in 1993," the former food writer explains, "the natural food industry was made up of a lot of little independently owned stores. They were organic—they didn't want sugar and they didn't want salt. Mine was a separate mission: to make mixes that were good for people who were gluten-free, things that tasted like the products they had to give up when they went on this diet. My mission didn't meet the natural food stores'. But the only place people knew to look for gluten-free products was the natural food stores, which didn't want to carry my products. I knew the end users wanted them. So I started a mail order business."

Armed with her intimate knowledge of what people on gluten-free diets—a very specific niche market—wanted, and of how to provide those products, Beth began selling her mixes, using a simple flier as her direct-mail piece. Soon her business grew. "I began to add other things," the Connecticut mom explains, "because I realized that these people in the Ozark Mountains and West Virginia really desperately needed things they couldn't get. I was, in effect, the lifeline for these people. I started adding more things, like pastas, cereals, and then some soups, and then bread machines—just a whole bunch of products that would make life easier for people."

A Family Feeling

Several states west in Ohio, Greer T. took a much more open-ended market—children's clothing—and gave it a spin, developing her own special niche. "I wanted to open a business that featured fashionable, unique apparel for children and I wanted to incorporate their families, meaning that we also have [matching] clothing for women. We have some unique gift items that generate a family feeling. We wanted to be a one-stop shopping catalog."

As her business grew, the mother of four discovered a sort of subniche—in a way, the same one Beth in Connecticut found—made up of people

> **Smart Tip**
> One of the factors that makes Beth H.'s gluten free foods business a winner is that she's providing products her customers need to order regularly. You don't make one loaf of bread stretch over an entire year. Staple foods, particularly for special diets, are things that get eaten and then need to be purchased again.

> **It can pay to structure your company as an exclusive membership organization.**

41

▲

who live in rural areas. "I think mail order finds its best customers [in less urban areas]," Greer says, "because the people there aren't around metropolises and shopping areas, and they do not have access to a lot of diversity. Here in Canton, we're close to Cleveland, so it's very competitive. We can drive up to Nordstrom's, Neiman, Saks—great shopping. So I think that's the great thing about mail order. You get to those pockets where people want to shop by catalog because they don't have everything available to them."

Snowballing

Another Midwest mail order maven, Mary M. in St. Louis, also took a broad-based market—gifts and home décor—and created a special niche. Although experts recommend finding your niche by focusing on what your customers will need, Mary turned that advice around and began by looking at her suppliers' needs. While remaining true to products that would convey the essence of romance, Mary and her partner Michelle concentrated on handcrafted goods. "We were dedicated to focusing on artisans who were creative," the former romance writer explains. "I have an empathy for artists. I know how difficult it is to sell your work, so that was one of our main goals."

The partners found their artisans through the "tell two friends, who tell two friends" principle. "I founded Missouri Romance Writers right here in St. Louis," Mary says, "and I knew about 100 people. My daughter-in-law, Michell, knew some people, too. One of them has done a beautiful stained-glass kaleidoscope for us. One thing leads to another. A writer friend is doing Victorian lace bags for us. We get people who e-mail us, or I run into them somewhere, and they submit things to us. So it's just kind of snowballed."

Join the Club

While you're brainstorming what your niche will be, why not think club? It can pay to structure your company as an exclusive membership organization rather than an anybody-can-buy retail one. That's what Caryn, the fabric merchandiser in Georgia, did.

"Because we charge wholesale prices and we really work on a low profit," Caryn says, "we felt we needed to sell to people who were truly looking for our product. By having people join our club, either by placing an order or paying a small membership fee, we rule out people who will just keep requesting [catalogs and samples] because they're free. You get people who are serious about your product and want to do business with you, and you have a better opportunity to do business with them. That's why we came up with the idea of having people join. That's worked very well for us.

"Being a mail order company, if you're spending a fortune on mail going out and printing costs, along with so many other costs, and you don't have it coming back to you, you can't stay in business."

How exactly does the club work? Caryn has set up several plans, based on customer desires. "There's no membership fee if somebody places an order," she explains. "That automatically makes them a member. If somebody wants to become a member [without placing an order], we have two different memberships. We have one that is all apparel fabrics, and that is $10 a year. And then we have one that's for people who are only interested in 100 percent cotton fabrics, people like quilters; that's $5 per year. It doesn't cover postage and it doesn't offset much. But if a person's willing to pay a small fee, it does let us know they're serious about our product."

Researching Your Market

Along with determining your special niche in the mail order world, you'll want to go directly to your potential customers to find out how they really feel about the products you plan to offer. Would they buy them? How much would they pay?

Up Close and Personal

One way to research your market is to get up close and personal with a *focus group*. This is an informal gathering between you and a medley of potential customers, usually about five to 12 people. Once you have gotten them assembled and you've distributed some sort of refreshment (always a nice touch), you have a captive

---

No Couch Potatoes

Make sure your focus group consists of people who represent the specific audience you want to reach. If you're targeting physical fitness buffs, don't invite couch potatoes. In this instance, you could cull your group from members of your local gym or fitness center, local college athletes, or members of a nearby running club.

Some market researchers entice participants—frequently lured to a conference room while shopping at a mall or roaming a college campus—with a small payment, maybe $30. If you feel on more intimate terms with your target market—for instance, you're specializing in merchandise for junior equestrians and your own kids are involved in every dressage meet in the county, you might invite those very equestrians and their parents to be your focus group for an evening. In this case, you needn't offer payment because you know these people and you can make it a semi-social occasion. Just make sure you remember the point of the get-together and get your group really brainstorming on your behalf.

Bright Idea

Be sure to collect the names and addresses of all focus group participants. They will be the seeds of your in-house mailing list!

audience to respond to your most pressing marketing concerns.

Mary, the romantic-gifts purveyor, and her partner, Michelle, conducted several focus groups. "We invited some friends and family, and they brought friends with them," Mary recalls. "Michelle had a whole focus group questionnaire, a booklet with questions about our products—which were also for sale. The group filled out the questionnaires, and it helped us figure out what they liked and didn't like, and what would bear price-wise. From that, we developed our Web site, because it helped us pick out the products that would be the most appealing."

Delve into the sample "Focus Group Questionnaire" on page 45 for an idea of how to formulate your own question-and-answer sessions. Obviously, your questions will relate to your own target market. Instead of chocolates, you might be asking about auto parts, craft supplies, or cat grooming products. Keep your questions focused on your objective: finding out which products people find the most appealing and coming up with a pricing structure for your products.

Ask as many questions as you feel your group can comfortably handle (don't try keeping people captive until three in the morning). Hand out the questionnaires, have plenty of pens and pencils on tap, and encourage discussion. You'll learn more than you'd imagine!

Always Flattering

Telephone surveys are another market research tool, although not quite as up close and personal. Some folks are delighted to answer questions—after all, it's always flattering to have somebody seek your opinion. Others in this era of Caller ID are wary of all unsolicited calls and refuse to squander valuable time on telephone strangers. Unless you've got a thick skin, it can be a little difficult to make cold calls to people you don't know and pick their brains. But if you can home in on people in a specific audience and explain why you're calling, you'll have a much better shot at getting relaxed responses.

Where do you get the phone numbers? If you belong to an association or an organization that just happens to be affiliated with your target

Smart Tip

Tip...

You've learned how to conduct a focus group survey with people you know, but how can you get feedback from the general public? A tabletop testing station in a mall or outside a supermarket can be a good way to get responses from the person on the street. Make sure you get the mall or store manager's approval before you set up. Ask participants for answers on the spot. If you give out questionnaires to be mailed back, chances are you'll never see them again.

Focus Group Questionnaire

1. How many times a year do you purchase fine chocolates for yourself? _____

2. How many times a year do you purchase fine chocolates as gifts:
   for your spouse or significant other? _____
   for your children? _____
   for other relatives? _____ what are their relationships? _____
   for clients or co-workers? _____

3. Do you prefer dark chocolate or milk chocolate? _____

4. Do you prefer to choose your own selection (say, nuts, chews, creams, etc.) or would you rather purchase a pre-boxed assortment? _____

5. How much do you usually spend for a one-pound box of chocolates? _____

6. Would you pay more for a box specially wrapped for a gift occasion? _____

7. For which special occasions do you purchase chocolates? _____

8. How much would you expect to pay for this half-pound box of gold-foil-wrapped chocolate stars? _____ *(Here you show the product to your group.)*

9. How much would you expect to pay for an 8-ounce solid chocolate Elvis Presley? _____ *(Here you show the product to your group.)*

10. Would you buy an 8-ounce solid chocolate Elvis Presley? _____

11. How many times in the past year have you purchased something by mail order? _____

12. Were you pleased with your purchase? _____

13. If so, why? _____

14. If not, why not? _____

15. Would you feel comfortable about the freshness of chocolates you received through the mail? _____

16. What would you expect to pay for shipping and handling? _____

17. Please comment on the name Chocoholic Central (love, like, dislike, or hate, and why) _____

18. Please comment on the name For Chocolate Lovers Only (love, like, dislike, or hate, and why) _____

market, you've got it made. You may already have a directory packed with names and phone numbers. If not, you may be able to beg, borrow, or buy a directory from the organization's main office. If your specialty is something more common, like chocolates (who doesn't love chocolate?), you might still start off with the members of your club or group. Your membership will act as the proverbial foot in the door.

If you don't know anybody and you don't belong to any groups, how about a church roster or neighborhood association? Use your imagination!

> ### Bright Idea
>
> If telephone cold calling leaves you chilled to the bone, try hiring a college student. This age group is old enough to sound mature but young enough to bring enthusiasm to the job. Just make sure your ace assistant knows what questions to ask and why you're asking and can take good (and legible) notes.

Get Creative

Direct mail is also a terrific market research tool. You can use the same lists or directories you'd use in your telephone surveys (but don't attack the same people with both phone and mail questionnaires—choose one form or the other).

Keep in mind that people are unlikely to return a mail survey unless you can offer them an incentive. So get creative! Extend an invitation to be put on your mailing list. Make respondents "charter members" of your club, if that's how you're structuring your company. Give them a coupon for 10 percent off your first mailing or catalog.

Take a look at the sample direct-mail questionnaire on page 50. It's been designed as a two-page spread, with a survey page the respondent can tear off and mail back. The reverse side is a stamped and addressed self-mailer. Let's explore the text on the first page:

- It draws in respondents—who are also potential customers—by asking questions that inspire them to read on.
- It enhances customer recognition of the company's name by putting it in a typeface that stands out from the rest of the text and repeating it frequently.
- It asks customers' assistance by stating that the company is being tailored to their needs and desires. Who could resist?
- In bold, italic type that can't be missed, it promises enrollment as a charter member just for filling out the questionnaire. Everybody wants to get something for nothing—or almost nothing—and this does the trick. Plus, being invited to become a "charter member" has a certain cachet; it sounds exclusive.
- It offers a discount certificate for returning the survey. This accomplishes two things: It keeps potential customers anticipating that first mailing and anxious to open it when they receive it, and it motivates people to order something so they can take advantage of the certificate.

- It displays the company's address, phone number, and e-mail address on the certificate, which the customer will retain. Always make sure you've got this information somewhere on each mailing piece you send out. You want your customers to be able to reach you!

Why does the letter read as if the company is already up and running? You've got more credibility as a company with a name and a game plan.

- Now let's look at the questionnaire side of the mailer on page 51. The questions have been designed to help the mail order entrepreneur determine:

- What her customers' decorating likes and dislikes are so she'll know what products and services to offer

---

Netting Names

Some people collect stamps. Others collect coins. Mail order mavens collect names. Here's a list of potential freebie sources to get you started collecting names for your first mailing:

- ❍ Athletic associations or organizations
- ❍ Church groups
- ❍ Client lists
- ❍ Colleagues and co-workers (Large companies often have employee directories.)
- ❍ Condo, neighborhood, apartment, or time-share associations
- ❍ Fraternal organizations (Elks Lodge, Soroptimists, Jaycees)
- ❍ Hobby groups, clubs, and other organizations
- ❍ Networking groups (That's why they exist!)
- ❍ Professional associations and organizations
- ❍ School or university groups (Don't forget alumni associations!)
- ❍ Scouting groups (Boy and Girl Scouts, Campfire Girls, etc.)
- ❍ Sororities and fraternities
- ❍ Your own address book (You've probably amassed more names than you realize.)

You can probably add your own list sources to the ones we've gathered here. Keep in mind, however, that you're wasting your pennies if you send mailings to people on just any old list. You've got to tailor the list to your product.

If you're selling camping gear, for example, go with the scouting group lists—or with the church lists if you know the youth groups do a lot of camping. But don't send to sororities; their members are more likely to be interested in toasting eligible young men than marshmallows.

▲

- What sizes and types of households she will be working with—same reason
- How much her customers are willing to spend on decorating
- Whether her customers will be able to send photos of their decorating problems for her to solve via the Internet with digital scanning or whether they will want to use Polaroids (or neither)

The questionnaire ends with the statement, "Watch for our first mailing—coming soon!" This tells customers that you're not yet ready to roll but keeps them anticipating your grand-opening mailing.

You might think the last part of the mailer, the self-addressed, stamped side (see page 52), isn't worth discussing. But you should take note of these points:

- *Return address.* This is how the entrepreneur will gather the names of people who have responded to her mailing. These names are very important for two reasons: 1) out of all the names on the initial list, they're the ones with the most purchasing potential, and 2) if she used a mailing center to send the questionnaire out to a purchased list, she may not have any names except the ones who respond.
- *Self-addressed, stamped envelope.* Potential customers are unlikely to stick their own stamp on a piece of mail like a survey or questionnaire. Likewise, they are extremely unlikely to take the time to address their own envelope. But if you print the address on the envelope for them and supply the stamp, the only thing they'll have to do after they fill out the questionnaire is mail it.
- *"Dept. 1A" after the street address.* Here's a fundamental mail order secret: There is no Department 1A. This is what's known as a *key code*, and it's used to clue the entrepreneur in to which segment of her list replied to her mailing or ad. For example, say she's compiled her list from two different sources: the members of her alumni association and the members of her time-share association. She puts "Dept. 1A" after her address on the mailings sent to the alumni group and Dept. 1B (or 2A or 3C or whatever suits her fancy) on the mailings sent to the time-share group. This way, she can tell from which group she's received a better response and can decide whether to use that list source again. Pretty nifty, eh!

Shopping the Competition

Now matter how specific and specialized your niche is, you're going to face competition from some avenue. This is OK—a little competition is healthy. If you do your homework properly and structure your niche wisely, your company will shine despite your rivals' qualities.

The market research phase is the time to scrutinize those rivals. What are they doing that is absolutely perfect? What can you successfully emulate? What are they doing that you can do better? What can you offer that will draw customers away from them and to you? You can answer these questions by performing the following research tasks:

- *Go ahead, shop the competition!* Send for all the catalogs you can. Study them. What works? What doesn't? Why?

- *Surf those Internet sites.* Again, study what your rivals are doing and explore what works and what doesn't.

- *Dissect those direct-mail pieces in magazines and your own mailbox.*

- *Put those fingers to work keying in phone numbers of mail order operations.* It's unlikely that you will be put in touch with L.L. Bean or Lillian Vernon (unless you've got a special connection to the Great Beyond), but the owners of smaller mail order companies are usually quite accessible. Ask if you can schedule a time convenient to the entrepreneur to ask some questions. Most will be happy to oblige.

- *Find out exactly who your competition is.* Beth's competition, although indirect, is natural food stores. Kate's is mall-based sports memorabilia shops. What might yours be?

Once you've conducted your market research, you can use the "Catalog Concept Evaluation Worksheet" provided by John Schulte of the NMOA on page 53 to give your catalog idea a final check.

> **Smart Tip** *Tip...*
> In mail order lingo, sending out your catalog or other direct-mail piece is known as *rolling out* your materials.

> **Smart Tip** *Tip...*
> You can use your focus group questionnaire as the basis of your telephone survey—but keep it short and to the point.

Teamwork

Kate, the team logo merchandiser, used her noggin and gained access to the best possible mailing list for her company. "When we first started out," she explains, "we knew a huge market, of course, was the alumni. I became an approved business partner [through the university] so I could work with the alumni chapters around the country."

Kate had to go through an application process, but once her company was approved, she was given lists of chapters to contact—some of which have memberships numbering in the thousands.

Your Own Personal Interior Decorator
OnCall For Pennies!

How would you like to have your very own interior decorator available any time you need her—to redecorate a single room or your entire home, or just to answer all those "little" questions, like what color to repaint the kitchen or how to make the kids' rooms more organized?

Sound wonderful but too expensive? Not so! With ***OnCall Designer***, you can get professional interior design services for as little as $50 per room. And we'd like to offer you a charter membership!

But first, we need your help. In order to tailor our service to <u>your</u> needs and desires, we're asking you to fill out the attached questionnaire and send it back. It's a self-mailer, so it's easy! And to show our appreciation for your help, we'll ***enroll you as a charter member*** of ***OnCall Designer***. This entitles you to:

- ○ *Monthly newsletters packed with design tips and ideas*
- ○ *Fantastic discounts on designer books, kits, and products*
- ○ *10% off your first decorator request*

Sound exciting? It is! When you receive your first mailing, you'll be thrilled with the quality of our products and services—everything you need to give your home that exclusive designer look. Your friends will want to know how you did it!

Ready to get started? It's as easy as 1, 2, 3:

1. Fill out the attached questionnaire.
2. Fold it and send it back in its own mailer to ***OnCall Designer***.
3. Keep the certificate! When you receive your first mailing, you can use the coupon for your 10% discount on the product or service of your choice.

OnCall Designer

This Certificate entitles_____,
a charter member of ***OnCall Designer***, to a full 10% off any product
or service offered in Mailing No. 1.

Enjoy!

123 Décor Drive, Dept. 1A, Art Deco, FL 30000   (305) 555-9800   www.oncalldesigner.com

OnCall Designer

Charter Member's Questionnaire

1. What is your favorite decorating style (country, contemporary, traditional, etc.)?
   _____

2. How often do you redecorate?
   Every year _____
   Every two years _____
   Every time you can stretch your budget _____

3. When was the last time you redecorated? _____

4. Which room or rooms did you do and why? _____
   _____

5. About how much did you spend on this project?_____

6. What are your biggest decorating problems or concerns? (Go ahead—tell us everything!) _____
   _____
   _____

7. How many people make up your household? _____

8. If you have kids at home, what are their ages? _____

9. What is the approximate square footage of your home? _____

10. Is it a house, condo, or apartment? _____

11. How many bedrooms? _____

12. How many baths? _____

13. Do you have a separate family room, office, or den? (Please circle all that apply.)

14. Do you have a patio or deck? _____

15. Would you be interested in tips, tricks, and products for outdoor entertaining?

16. What is your annual household income? _____

17. Do you have a computer with Internet access? _____

18. Do you own and use a digital camera? _____

19. Do you have a Polaroid camera? _____

We appreciate your answers and comments. They'll help us make
OnCall Designer perfect for you. Watch for our first mailing—coming soon!

▲

From:

_____

_____

_____

↑ **Important!** Be sure to fill this out.

To: ***OnCall Designer***
123 Décor Drive, Dept. 1A
Art Deco, FL 30000

- -

Fold Here

OnCall Designer
Your Own Personal Interior Designer!

Tape Together Here

Catalog Concept Evaluation Worksheet

Planning a catalog? John Schulte, chairman of the National Mail Order Association, has kindly provided this worksheet to help you gauge the potential of your catalog idea.

○ *Availability.* Will your customers feel the products you're offering are more readily available from you than elsewhere? _____

○ *Authority.* Why should people buy from you instead of their present source? What gives you the right to say what you're saying and expect to be believed?

_____

○ *Value.* Can you price your merchandise to fit the value considerations of your audience? _____

○ *Satisfaction.* Can you assure customers there will be no hassles when they buy from you sight unseen? _____

○ *Mailing lists.* Do you have lists of known catalog buyers who would be interested in buying the kinds of products you plan to sell at the price points at which they will be offered? _____

○ *Facilities.* Do you have access to facilities suited for a mail order catalog operation? _____

○ *Staff.* Do you have personnel with catalog experience? _____

○ *Money.* Do you have sufficient financial backing to carry a catalog through its unprofitable development period (typically three to five years)? _____

○ *Desire.* Do you really want to be in the catalog business? Enough to stick with it during the whole developmental period? _____

○ *Bright idea.* Have you come up with something that will give your catalog a unique position in the highly competitive catalog marketplace? _____

_____

_____

_____

Packaging Your Business

Choosing a Name and a Structure

You've done your market research. You've decided what you'll sell and how you'll sell it. Terrific! Now you'll need to design a tight, sturdy package for your new company, a structure that will keep it not only lookin' good, but solid enough to weather anything life might dish out. In this chapter, we guide you through that packaging—the features that form the basics of the business—from company name and legal structure to licenses, insurance, and beyond.

Name that Business

Every business, like every child, has to have a name. You should devote almost as much thought to choosing an appellation for your company as you would for your human offspring. After all, you plan to have your business baby around for a long time. You want a name you can be proud of, one that identifies it—and, by extension, you—as worthy of your customers' confidence.

Customers usually form an idea of the type of business they are dealing with from the store's exterior. It's a large warehouse-style building, or an intimate boutique, or a high-tech studio blazing with neon. As soon as they walk through the door, their impressions are strengthened—it's a self-serve emporium stacked to the rafters with office supplies, or a ritzy clothier layered in silks and fine leather, or a trendy gallery pulsing with abstract art. Since your customers' first impression of your store comes from the front page of your catalog or direct-mail piece, you'll have to make sure your name gives the proper first impression. And since your mail order business will be different from everybody else's (because you've developed that special niche), you want to convey your uniqueness to your customers as well.

Biz Whiz

Your business name can reflect your products or services, or even your niche customers—for example, Biz Auto Whiz for a company that insures business automobiles or Perfectly Kids for a catalog that caters to the tiny tot set. Just make sure your company's name doesn't limit you. If the business insurance company decides to branch out to residential sales a few years down the road, its name will no longer accurately reflect its services. And if Perfectly Kids flexes its wings and starts suiting up moms and dads, it will have to change names and risk losing its carefully built customer base.

Sourdough Bread

Companies often go with a name that reflects their geographic location—San Francisco Clothiers or Des Moines Demographics, for example. This is not the best decision for mail order entrepreneurs. By definition, mail order is nongeographic; your products or services can go anywhere. So unless your name is a direct reflection of your products—something your customers will recognize and want because of its regionalism, like San Francisco Sourdough Bread or Louisiana Spices—you'll do better to leave your city, state, or region on the map instead of in your company's name.

Listening Comprehension

Whatever name you go with, remember that you—or your order processors—will be repeating your name every time you answer the phone. Sound out that moniker before you settle on it. Some names look great in print but are difficult, if not impossible, to understand over the phone. M&A Gifts, for instance, may sound like a great name for partners Marty and Andrea, but when spoken it sounds like "MNA" or "Emenay."

Most callers rate about a C-minus in listening comprehension. No matter how clearly you enunciate, they're not going to understand M&A. So save yourself hours of frustration and choose something crystal clear.

For some top-notch name ideas, check out the mail order companies listed as resources in the Appendix. You'll want to choose a name that's as individual as you are, but looking at the names of existing companies can start those creative gears turning.

Potential Roadblocks

Once you've decided on a name, you'll need to register it. "Make getting your trademark your very first top priority," advises Kate in Kansas. "It takes a long time, and there could be potential roadblocks. You want to have your trademark registered before you have a catalog printed and then find out you have to change your name."

She's absolutely right. As we've said, your mail order company is going nationwide, and you need to keep this in mind. There may not be another Perfectly Kids in your

---

What's So Special?

A catch phrase or slogan can be as important as your business name in creating a mail order identity. A well-turned phrase can capture your customers' attention and imagination, as well as clarify your mission and market position. Like the name itself, the right slogan gives prospective customers the color, scent, and flavor of what you're offering and helps them remember what's special about you.

Take a look at these terrific examples:

- ○ "Affordable software solutions direct to you"—*Parsons Technology*
- ○ "America's authority in home fashions"—*Domestications*
- ○ "Where value and selection come home"—*Home Decorators Collection*
- ○ "Offering the Best, the Only, and the Unexpected since 1848"—*Hammacher Schlemmer*

Smart Tip

Want to handle that trademark registration yourself? Contact the U.S. Patent and Trademark Office at www.uspto.gov.

town, county, or even state; but can you be sure there's not another company with the same name somewhere else in the country? And can you picture a worst-case scenario of printing up 10,000 catalogs only to discover that the other Perfectly Kids is suing you for using its name? Or finding out that some other company—which is shabbier and sloppier than yours—is using the same name you have chosen and confusing customers, who think *your* firm is the shabby and sloppy one?

Kate performed her trademark search and registration on her own, with guidance from the U.S. Trademark and Patent Office. You can do it yourself, or you can hire an attorney or a trademark search firm.

Make Someone Happy

Even if you choose not to register your name as a trademark, you'll still need to register it in your local area or state. You do this for three reasons:

1. It ensures that no one else in your local area is using the name and gives you dibs on it.

2. It makes your local authorities happy. Most cities or counties require that you have a *fictitious business name* or *dba (doing business as)*. This way, they can keep tabs on you for tax or other licensing purposes, and you go on public record so anyone who wants or needs to can look up the name of your company and find out whom it belongs to.

3. Most banks won't allow you to open a business checking account—one with your company name, which gives you credibility among suppliers and others—unless you can show them proof that you've registered a fictitious business name.

Suitable for Framing

Unlike the trademark process, obtaining a dba is quick and easy, and you can absolutely do it on your own. The process varies a bit in different regions of the country. In the state of Florida, for instance, you call the office of the Secretary of State and, after a lengthy hold period, are given the opportunity to check on up to three potential business names. When you hit on one that hasn't already been appropriated, the secretary's office sends you a registration form. You mail back the completed form, the registration fee, and a form from your local newspaper verifying that you've advertised your dba for one week. In return, you receive a certificate listing your name—not in neon but on an official certificate suitable for framing.

In other areas of the country, you might simply pop down to your city or county clerk's office, thumb through the roster of business names and complete the registration procedure at the clerk's window.

Eminent Domain

If you plan to have a Web site, you'll also need to register your domain name, that part of a Web address that comes after the "www" and allows people to access your virtual store. Like a trademark, there can be only one domain name per company, so you'll have to think up several versions of the name you want in case your first choice has already been taken.

Here's what you do: Open your Web browser and type in www.networksolutions.com. Now you are in (you guessed it!) the Network Solutions Web site, which is very user-friendly—and fun! Following the easy directions, check to see if the domain name you've chosen has already been taken. If it has, choose another. When you find a permutation that's available, register it online. The cost is $70 for two years of registration or $119 for a two-year reservation (in case you want to reserve a name but you don't plan to use it right away).

> **Bright Idea**
> If your first-choice domain name has been taken, get creative. But not so creative that your domain name has no relation to your company name. If your company is called Pet Pals, for instance, and there's already a www.petpals.com, you would try something like pets.com or 4pets.com.

Laying Your Foundation

There's more to laying the foundation of your business than choosing a name. You'll need to decide on a legal structure, check into zoning regulations and insurance coverage, and line up an attorney and an accountant—all the nitty-gritty stuff that will give your company a solid base on which to build.

On Your Own

To appease those picky IRS people, your business must have a structure. You can operate it as a sole proprietorship, a partnership, or a corporation. Many mail order newbies go with the simplest version, the sole proprietorship. If you'll be starting out on your own, you may choose the same option. It's the least complicated and the least expensive. You can always switch to another format later on if you take on partners and/or employees.

Business Name Brainstorming

List three ideas based on the products or services you plan to provide (e.g., children's clothing, custom menu design, aromatherapy products):

1. _____
   _____

2. _____
   _____

3. _____
   _____

List three ideas based on your special niche (e.g., affordable children's special-occasion clothes, exclusive designs for the small restauranteur, aromatherapy for the office environment):

1. _____
   _____

2. _____
   _____

3. _____
   _____

List three ideas combining a favorite theme with your special niche: (e.g., Tea Party children's party clothes, Table For Two menu designs, The Tranquil Desk aromatic office products):

1. _____
   _____

2. _____
   _____

3. _____
   _____

After you've decided which name you like best, ask yourself a few important questions:

○ Have you said it aloud to make sure it's easily understood and pronounced? (Has it passed muster with your family? Have you had a friend call to see how it sounds over the phone?)

○ Have you checked your local Yellow Pages to make sure the same or a similar name is not already listed?

○ Have you checked with your local business authority to make sure the name is available?

○ Have you started your trademark search?

Home Zoned Home

If you plan to work from home, you need to check into zoning regulations. Since your shop will be virtual, you won't need signs pinpointing your location. And since you'll rarely have customers knocking at your door, you won't need to worry about parking restrictions. But unless you ship from an outside location, you will have UPS or other delivery trucks pulling up to your front stoop every day. It's unlikely, but possible, that a pesky neighbor could take this as a reason to report you to the local authorities. So it's a good idea to play it safe. Find out from your local government whether any permits are necessary, and if so, file them. If zoning regulations prohibit operating a business in your neighborhood, you can apply for a *zoning variance*, a special permit granting you the legal right to run your business at home.

While you're interfacing with your local government agencies, ask about obtaining a business license. This generally involves filling out a simple form and paying a nominal annual fee. Again, it's easier to get it up front than to ignore it and have it worrying you in the back of your mind.

Attorneys and Plumbers

Attorneys are like plumbers—you don't think about hiring one until you have an urgent problem. But as a business owner, you should have a good attorney on call, one who knows small business, and preferably one well-versed in the mail order business. You will want your attorney to check over any contracts you enter into with manufacturers, suppliers, and other vendors and to advise you on the fine points of mail order law. You won't need to call your attorney every week or even every month. But there's no point in waiting until you've got a problem to try to establish a relationship with an attorney and get help.

Along with that on-call attorney, you'll want to look into hiring an accountant. Unless you go with a full-service fulfillment company, you'll handle the day-to-day data entry yourself—tracking customers' orders and payments, generating returns and tracking ad responses. (We'll get into this in Chapter 10.) But you will probably want an accountant to advise you of any special ways you can save money with your business structure, to oversee your operations, and to fill out those tax returns.

And don't forget your insurance agent! Insurance agents can be invaluable sources of information and expertise. If you're going to

> **Tip...**
>
> ## Smart Tip
> Always get a name, department and phone extension when you call someone in government officialdom. This can save you hours of re-explanation if you need to call again. Plus, you'll make a buddy who can probably help with other matters later down the line.

▲

Tip...

Smart Tip

You can find a reliable attorney who specializes in mail order by contacting an organization like the National Mail Order Association (www.nmoa.org) or the Direct Marketing Association (www.the-dma.org), or by asking other mail order entrepreneurs for recommendations.

be homebased, you'll need to find out if your homeowner's package covers your business assets, inventory, and equipment or if you need additional coverage. If you're based outside the home, you need coverage for these same items, as well as your physical location. If you plan to hire employees, you may also need workers' compensation insurance.

Look Before You Leap

We've given you a peek at some important business basics. Remember, however, that other licenses and fees can crop up, depending on what your special niche is and what products or services you'll be selling. Do your homework. Make sure you understand what's necessary in each situation. In other words, look before you leap into that mailbox! Consult with an attorney and an accountant early in the process.

5

Into the Money Bag
Figuring Your Finances

That old refrain, "The best things in life are free," doesn't quite apply when you're starting a business. This chapter, therefore, dips into the murky waters of start-up costs, operating expenses, financing, and budgeting—and, like chlorine, clears them up.

▲

Start-Up Costs

One of the many nifty things about launching a mail order business is that its start-up costs are comparatively low. You've got the option to be homebased, which cuts office lease expenses down to nothing. If you're working with a supplier who will drop-ship, you've got no inventory. And even if you've got inventory, you won't need fancy display cabinets or kicky décor. Your major financial outlay will go toward office equipment, advertising, and your catalog or other direct-mail piece. If you're like many, you've already got the most expensive piece of office equipment: a computer system.

But let's take it from the top. The following is a breakdown of everything you will need to get up and running:

- Computer system with modem and printer
- Fax machine
- Internet/e-mail service
- Web site design and promotion
- Software
- Electronic credit card processing
- Bulk mail permit
- Market research
- Phone
- Voice mail or answering machine
- Call center
- Stationery and office supplies
- Shipping and packaging materials
- Postage
- Initial inventory

Of course, you can add goodies of varying degrees of necessity to this list. For example, a copier is a plus. It's also nice to have bona fide office furniture: a tweedy upholstered chair with lumbar support that swivels and rolls, gleaming file cabinets that really lock, real oak bookshelves. We'll cover office equipment in depth in Chapter 8, which features a sort of shopping bonanza.

But let's consider that you're starting from absolute scratch. You can always set up your computer on your kitchen table or on a card table in a corner of the bedroom. You can stash files in cardboard boxes. It's not glamorous, but it will suffice until you get your own business steaming ahead.

You may wonder why we don't have an allocation for mailing lists and advertising. Good question! The answer is that in mail order, these items—rather than being considered start-up expenses in and of themselves—are calculated into the cost per order, which is used to determine your product prices. Take a look at "Figuring Profits" on page 74 in this chapter and the "Advanced Break-Even Worksheet" in Chapter 12 to find out exactly how this works.

Computer Candidate

A computer system heads the list of start-up expenses. For a basic system—hard drive, monitor, mouse, modem, and printer—you should allocate about $2,500. We'll go over the various permutations in Chapter 8, but this will give you a figure to pencil in for starters.

Fax Facts

Although technically you don't *have* to have a fax machine, just as you don't *have* to have a computer, your life as a mail order maven will run much more smoothly with one. Many customers like to fax orders, and as a savvy direct marketer, you want to oblige. After all, the easier you make ordering, the more orders your customers will place. Having a fax machine allows you to communicate with suppliers and manufacturers quickly, instead of waiting on the U.S. Postal Service. You can purchase a basic plain-paper fax machine for as little as $250 or a fancy multifunctional model for up to $700.

Go Anywhere

A good Internet and e-mail service is a must for the mail order maven. With the power of the World Wide Web at your command, you can go anywhere on the globe instantly—research your competition, communicate with customers, and garner market

Start with a Splash

Although your company is virtual, conducted via mail, phone, and Internet, you'll want to set aside some money for a live grand opening. It's a terrific way to kick off your new venture with a splash and to let everyone know you're open for business. Invite friends, family, vendors, and suppliers, people from your mailing list who live locally, and local news media. If you'll be home-based, get creative with the site for your bash. If your new baby is a golfing catalog, for instance, host your party at a local golf course.

Be sure to have each well-wisher sign a guest book and leave his or her address—free names! Give out catalogs or other sales pieces and perhaps a small freebie from your product line information from worldwide sources—all from the comfort of your own desktop. And it's cheap! Most Internet service providers, or ISPs, charge about $20 to $25 per month and give you unlimited Web and e-mail access.

Internet Explosion

These days, smart mail order entrepreneurs are expanding their catalog operations to the Internet. Four of the seven direct marketers we talked to run a virtual store in conjunction with their paper store or catalog.

Like just about everything else in direct marketing, the cost of setting up and maintaining a company Web site can vary considerably. The entrepreneurs we interviewed all got their sites going in penny-wise fashion by keeping it all in the family. Mary's son set up her site and keeps it running. Beth's husband does hers. Greer's is done by a cousin. And Caryn has mastered the fine art of Web site construction and maintenance herself.

"It took me four months," the Roswell direct-marketer recalls, "and it was truly one of the biggest accomplishments that I've ever done on my own. I was outside screaming at my husband, who was doing some gardening, and he didn't know what had happened.

"You can be successful, but you've got to work at it," Caryn advises. "You've got to commit to spending the time to figure it out."

If you plan to go the Web site route and you're lucky enough to have a computer brain in the family, or if you take the time to become your own computer expert, you can pencil in a zero under Web site design costs.

What can you expect to pay if you outsource your Web site construction? Prices depend on the complexity of your project and how much you're willing do to help the designer, says Roy Fletcher of Fletcher Consulting in Pembroke Pines, Florida. An online catalog with 20 to 30 products and five to 10 variations on each would run in the range of $2,000 to $4,000. You can trim costs by supplying your own text files—giving the designer your product descriptions and other written material on diskette—so that he does not need to charge you for typing all that stuff in. Our price estimate is based on designing a site that features "shopping cart" technology. A shopping cart is the online equivalent of the wire baskets on wheels you find in brick-and-mortar stores. Customers load their virtual carts with purchases, then check out when they're finished shopping. The Web site's system then calculates their total purchases and processes their credit card payments.

Dollar Stretcher

Use your e-mail service to contact suppliers abroad. Why place a pricey international call when you can send an e-mail message virtually for free?

A savvy Web site designer may also be able to advise and assist you with promoting your site on the Internet. Having an advertising strategy for your Web site is a wise move because there's no point in having a Web site if no one knows about it. We'll explore this topic in Chapter 11, but for now, you can pencil in about $300 to $500 for help with designing your Web site. And while it depends on the firm, you may be able to negotiate free domain-name registration and free registration with search

Dollar Stretcher

Web site design and hosting fees may be higher in large urban areas. Shop around. It doesn't matter if you're in Atlanta, Chicago, or Los Angeles. You can hire a Webmaster in Pipsqueak, South Dakota, and work with the person as easily as if he or she were next door.

engines, the sites that direct shoppers to you—and your competitors—when they type in "gourmet chocolates," or whatever it is you're selling.

The Software Skinny

As you know, your computer needs software to give it brains. Software prices can vary dramatically, depending on which programs you buy and from whom. The jury is still out on whether or not you need special mail order software. Kate, who with the help of her trusty computer runs a one-woman office, uses a good general accounting software program. Beth started with a general accounting package but now—with her company's bank of seven computers—relies on a program tailored to the mail order industry. For special mail order software starter packages, you can expect to pay in the range of $300 to $1,600.

Whether you go with industry-specific software or not, you'll also need a good word processing program, a desktop publishing program, and an accounting program. Again, this is a subject we'll discuss in depth in Chapter 8. For start-up purposes, let's say you'll want to allocate about $500.

That's Bulk!

To take advantage of bulk mail rates, which are less costly than consumer ones, you'll need to purchase a bulk mail permit from the U.S. Postal Service. Pencil in a one-time $100 fee for your permit number and then an additional $100 for the annual fee to retain your permit. (You must use your bulk mail permit at least once every two years or you lose your privileges.) To take advantage of the cost savings for bulk mail, you'll have

> To take advantage of bulk mail rates, which are less costly than consumer ones, you'll need to purchase a bulk mail permit.

▲

to sort each piece according to postal regulations. Check out "Fun with Mail Sorting" in Chapter 7 to learn how to do this.

Charge It!

Although you don't have to start off with electronic credit card processing, offering this service will make life much easier for your customers—and, therefore, you. Through the magic of that little electronic credit card authorization terminal, your customers' payments can be processed almost instantly. This means you can ship the merchandise immediately, which makes for happy customers; and you can have the money deposited in your bank account immediately, which makes for a happy you.

Before you can accept credit cards, however, you need to set up a merchant account. Many banks balk at setting up merchant accounts for SOHO (small office/home office) and mail order businesses because they fear a heavy credit risk. But if you shop around, you can locate companies who welcome SOHO and mail order entrepreneurs.

What can you expect to pay for an electronic terminal? Fees depend on which company you go with and, in some cases, the type of business you're building and you personally. We checked out two companies at the two ends of the country.

"Every client is different," says Dennis Varvarigos of Electronic Card Systems in Los Angeles, California. His company scrutinizes:

- *The product or service you're selling.* It will be happier, for instance, if you're marketing cookbooks than if you are selling one-year club memberships. Why? Because it considers the membership, with its finite term, a liability. And this means it'll probably require you to put up a 5 percent reserve.

- *The volume of business you expect to do.* The bank will adjust your rate according to your sales volume.

- *Your own credit history.* You'll get a better rate if you've got a flawless credit record than if you've had credit problems.

So what's the bottom line? Varvarigos quotes the following: Assuming you've got a gold star for credit worthiness, you can expect to pay about 30 cents per transaction, a 2.65 percent discount rate (this is the percent you're charged per transaction), and a $10 monthly statement fee. You'll also be charged $25 to $30 per month to lease the processing terminal. Then, too, there's the $195 application fee and any reserves you may be required to deposit.

Merchant Express, an electronic card processing company based in Merrimack, New Hampshire, is seeking SOHO and mail order entrepreneurs. The company's discount rate is 1.99 percent, with a transaction fee of 30 cents and a $10 monthly statement/toll-free help-desk fee. The application fee is $75, refundable if you don't qualify, and it costs $21 to $35 per month to lease-to-own the processing terminal. Fees are slightly higher for poor or nonexistent credit.

The Check, Man

Merchant Express offers another convenient service, one that lets you accept checks by telephone, fax, or e-mail. With CheckMAN, you enter your customer's checking information into your computer and print a check ready for deposit. Your customer can fax you a copy of his or her check, read you the necessary information off the check over the phone, or send it to you over the Internet. The obvious advantage here is that neither you nor your customer needs to wait for the mail. You get faster payment and your customer gets faster merchandise delivery. All you need besides the software is blank checks printed on special "secure" paper authorized by the Federal Reserve Board, which you can purchase at most office supply supercenters and computer stores.

CheckMAN is not the only check-by-fax software out there, and you don't have to go through Merchant Express, but while their free software offer exists, why not take advantage of it? (Merchant Express is using a terrific mail order sales technique here—giving you a freebie in order to entice you to order their services. Works pretty well, doesn't it? Check out Chapter 10 for more promotional ideas.)

Market Research

As we've explored, the amount you'll pay for market research is a variable. It's almost entirely dependent on your personal style and how comfortable you are with the niche you've chosen. If you're going to be selling books to horse lovers, you know every equestrian within five states, and

> **The amount you'll pay for market research is a variable.**

you absolutely *know* they'll buy the kind of books you'll be offering, you can cut your market research expenses down to nearly nothing. If, on the other hand, you're casting

Market Research Expenses

○ Purchased mailing list of 3,000 names at $50 per 1,000 names	$150
○ 3,000 two-color brochure/questionnaires designed on your computer with your desktop publishing program and copied and trifolded by your local print shop	360
○ Postage, 3,000 pieces at 28 cents each	840
○ Telephone surveys from horse club lists you already have, 100 calls at an average of $1.50 each	150
○ Travel to horse shows to conduct focus groups	200
Total Market Research Budget	**$1,700**

for products to sell and then have to determine how salable they are, you've got a lot of research ahead of you.

So let's say you're somewhere in the middle. You're planning on a catalog featuring everything for the horsy set, from currycombs to muck rakes to T-shirts, but you're not quite sure which products will sell. The chart on page 69 shows what your market research budget might look like.

You will, of course, want to modify this budget to suit your own needs (especially if you're allergic to horses), but this should give you a good idea of how to start your own plan.

Phone Fun

We assume that you already have a telephone, in which case you already know all about phone bills. You should, however, install at least two separate, dedicated lines for your business. You'll want one line for handling phone calls and another for your fax machine and ISP (Internet service provider, remember?), unless you plan to transmit all your information and conduct all your research late at night or in the wee hours of the morning. Computers and fax machines use phones the way teenagers do—when they're transmitting, no one else can possibly get through. So unless you want to risk having callers receive a busy signal or empty ring—which is fatal for a business that takes telephone orders—you'll need to have a separate line.

Costs, of course, depend on how many fun features you add to your telephone service and which local and long-distance carriers you go with, but for the purpose of start-up budgeting, let's say you should allocate about $25 per line. You'll also need to add the phone company's installation fee, which should be in the range of $40 to $60. Check with your local phone company to determine exactly what these costs are in your area.

The Mechanical Receptionist

You won't always be available to answer your phone. So what, other than having the phone surgically attached to your ear, can you do? You've got three ways to go here: the trusty answering machine, the phone company's exciting voice mail service, or a *call center* to answer your phone and process your orders.

All three phone options have pros and cons, which we'll discuss in Chapter 8. For estimating start-up costs, let's figure an answering machine will cost about $40 to $150 and voice mail will run about $6 to $20 per month. The call center pencils in at $200 to $300 for the initial deposit, with an additional fee of $250 if you decide to have the center set up your mail order software.

My Calling Card

Company stationery is as important to your mail order image as a well-answered phone. Even though your customers may see only a catalog or Web site or specially designed direct-mail piece, you'll still need stationery for your dealings with suppliers, vendors, manufacturers, and bankers. To help build that solid, established identity that will make other businesses eager to work with you, you'll need professional-quality letterhead, envelopes, and business cards.

You can purchase blank stationery, including business cards, and print everything up yourself inexpensively with a desktop publishing program. Or you can have a set of stationery and business cards printed for you at a copy center like Kinko's or Office Depot. Either way, you should allocate about $200.

Floating Pencils

Don't forget about basic office supplies: pens, pencils, and paper clips, plus a stapler, a letter opener, tape, and those all-important printer cartridges. You'll also need blank paper for designing ads and catalogs and for printing out invoices, receipts, and return vouchers. If you figure that you're purchasing all of this brand-new for the business (as if you didn't have scads of pens and pencils floating around the house), you can write in about $150.

Shipping and Packaging Materials

You're also going to need shipping and packaging supplies. This is another start-up category where you'll have to get down to the nitty-gritty on your own, depending on your particular products or services. If you're selling subzero refrigerators, for instance, the cost of shipping and packaging supplies will be considerably higher than for someone who's selling dried flowers.

Keep in mind that we're talking not only boxes or crates but also that snappy bubble wrap, shredded paper to replace those environmentally uncouth Styrofoam peanuts, mailing labels, tissue paper, and—unless you *are* shipping subzero refrigerators—gift wrap and ribbon.

For businesses dealing in merchandise more manageably sized than those you need to deliver with a forklift, figure in about $350.

The Mane Event

How much initial inventory should you purchase? You can use the results of your market research as a guideline. Let's say your surveys show that 90 percent of your respondents are really interested in the horse mane conditioner. You plan on an initial catalog mailing of 5,000. Now, let's say you get a 1 percent response. That means 50 people order from your catalog. And if 90 percent of them go for what seems to be the main event—the mane conditioner—you'll need to have at least 45 bottles on hand. If your cost for the conditioner is $3.25, then you'll probably want to pencil in $162.50 (that's $3.25 x 50 bottles) for your initial inventory for that product.

Sample Start-Up Costs

Costs	Chocoholic Central	OnCall Designer
Rent	$N/A	$1,200
Mailbox rental	20	N/A
Office equipment & furniture	4,213	10,237
Market research	1,650	3,000
Credit card processing (electronic terminal)	96	110
Lettershop	N/A	600
Software	300	800
Licenses	150	150
Bulk mail permit	200	N/A
Phone	90	115
Call center	N/A	450
Utility deposits	N/A	150
Employee payroll	N/A	2,000
Grand opening	100	50
Legal services	375	525
Miscellaneous postage	50	10
Internet service	20	20
Web site design & promotion	N/A	4,500
Stationery/office supplies	50	150
Insurance	500	600
Shipping materials	350	500
Inventory	3,000	7,000
Miscellaneous expenses (add roughly 10% of total)	1,116	3,047
Total Start-Up Costs	**$12,280**	**$35,214**

Start-Up Costs Worksheet

Costs	
Rent	$
Mailbox rental	
Office equipment & furniture	
Market research	
Credit card processing (electronic terminal)	
Lettershop	
Software	
Licenses	
Bulk mail permit	
Phone	
Call center	
Utility deposits	
Employee payroll	
Grand opening	
Legal services	
Miscellaneous postage	
Internet service	
Web site design & promotion	
Stationery/office supplies	
Insurance	
Shipping materials	
Inventory	
Miscellaneous expenses (add roughly 10% of total)	
Total Start-Up Cost	$

You'll also need to consider your supplier's order cycle. If you've got a six-week window between the time you place an order and the time the order arrives, you'll be looking at a trough full of trouble if even 51 customers immediately want the mane conditioner. In this case, you'll want to stock a few extra bottles, just to be on the safe side. Of course, if your supplier can have fresh bottles out to you within a reasonable time after you call for help, you can cut your initial stock count closer to the bone.

Dollar Stretcher

Manufacturers or suppliers will often give you a much better per-unit price when you order a larger amount of product. For example, you might pay $3.25 per bottle for up to 50 bottles of mane conditioner but only $2 per bottle if you purchase 100.

What's a reasonable amount of time? It depends on your company's strategy. If part of your sales strategy is sending out merchandise within 48 hours of the customer's order, you're going to need fresh stock from your supplier a lot faster than if you've promised your customer delivery within four to six weeks. Now, make like a banker and scrutinize each of your products this way. Then add up your total cost for initial inventory.

All that Jazz

Other expenses you'll need to plug into your start-up expense chart include business licenses, business insurance, legal advice, utility deposits, and all that jazz—the costs intrinsic to any company's beginning. To give you an idea of what to budget for, two hypothetical mail order companies, Chocoholic Central and On-Call Designer, have kindly provided their start-up costs for review on page 72. Chocoholic Central plans to be a homebased company with no employees except its owner, who will keep all operations in-house. OnCall Designer will make its base in an office in an industrial park near the airport and employ one full-time assistant in addition to the owner. OnCall will take advantage of a call center, a Web site designer, and a lettershop.

You can use the work sheet on page 73 to list your own start-up costs. If you copy a couple of extra sheets, you can work up several options, compare them all, and decide which will be the best for you.

Figuring Profits

Now that we've determined how much it's going to cost you to get your business up and running, let's turn to the fun part—figuring out how much you can expect to make. This, of course, means figuring out how to price your merchandise or services.

Warning: This section contains actual math problems. If you suffer from acute math phobia, you may be tempted to take this book and toss it out the window. Don't!

There's a big difference between having to calculate when two trains traveling at different speeds on the same track will meet and figuring out how much money you can make in your mail order business. So sit back and enjoy!

Chocolate Success

Before you can begin to calculate your profits, you have to set up a pricing structure. About the easiest way to figure out what to charge is by calculating your *cost per order*. Let's say you're selling gift boxes made of pure, decadent chocolate, and you've decided to place a small display ad in the regional issue of a national magazine. After haggling hot and heavy with the magazine's salesperson, you negotiate a cost of $1,100 and place your ad. It's a success! Five-hundred chocolate lovers call and e-mail in frantic requests for your product. Now you can figure that your cost per order is $2.20. Here's the formula you use:

$$\frac{\text{Ad cost}}{\text{Orders received}} = \text{Cost per order}$$

Now plug in the numbers:

$$\frac{\$1,100}{500} = \$2.20$$

This is valuable information, but you still don't know how much to charge for those sinful chocolates. So let's go one step further—or back. Through terrific negotiating earlier in the game, you've convinced the manufacturer to give you the chocolate boxes for $5 each. So we tack that cost onto your cost per order, using the formula below:

$$\text{Cost per order} + \text{Cost per item}$$
$$= \text{Product cost}$$

Now, lets plug in the numbers:

$$\$2.20 + \$5.00 = \$7.20$$

Gee, now that box is more expensive. Not to worry! You now know exactly how much your product will cost you, and you can start playing with how much you'll charge your customers. If you apply a 400 percent markup (meaning you multiply your cost by 400 percent), you'll price each box at $28.80.

We'll bump that up to $28.95 because:

- People feel more comfortable with retail prices at "something and 95 cents" than at an oddball number like 80 cents.

- People tend to perceive a price like $28.95 as $28, which gains you an extra 95 cents per item without damaging your customers' view of your price.

Now, if you sell one box to each of your 500 ad respondents, you'll gross $14,475, which we determined with this formula:

$$\text{Product cost x Orders received}$$
$$= \text{Gross profit}$$

Using the numbers from our example:

$$\$28.95 \times 500 = \$14,475$$

Doesn't sound gross at all, does it? But keep in mind that in accounting, "gross" means your profit before you deduct your expenses. (Remember, if you eat all the chocolate, you won't have any profit at all!)

Tweaking Figures

Where did we get the 400 percent markup? By tweaking our figures until we came up with a price that:

- Meets our customers' expectations of what a box made of gourmet chocolate should cost (too incredibly high or too implausibly low, and we lose our customers)

- Is comparable to competitors' prices for the same or similar goods

- Adequately covers our expenses and provides a healthy profit

The norm in the mail order industry is a mark-up of 300 to 400 percent on each product to cover the cost of advertising, mailing, and product manufacture or purchase. This is an excellent rule of thumb, but keep in mind what we said in the previous paragraph. You have got to take a variety of factors into consideration before coming up with your final price.

Incredible Discipline

You may have other expenses to figure into your cost per order. Let's say you've exercised incredible self-discipline and not eaten your way through your inventory. And you've decided to place a classified ad instead of a display ad. And you've decided to make it a two-step ad. (Remember, this means the customer calls or writes for your catalog or brochure.) Now you've got to calculate not only the cost of your ad but also the cost of printing your catalog or brochure and the cost of mailing that printed material.

Take a look at "How to Price a Chocolate Box" on page 77. Here we've taken 400 orders (which is not the same as the number of inquiries—you may have gotten 450 people to request a brochure, but only 400 of those have actually ordered). We've spent $200 on printing up an inexpensive brochure, and we've spent $166.50 on sending our

How to Price a Chocolate Box

1. Figure your cost per order:

Add:	Cost of ad	$ 240.00
	Cost of printing	200.00
	Cost of mailing	166.50
Divide by:	Number of expected orders	400
Equals:	Cost per order	$ 1.52

2. Figure your total product cost:

Add:	Cost per order	$ 1.52
	Cost per Item	5.00
Equals:	Total product cost	$ 6.52

3. Figure your markup price:

Multiply:	Total product cost	$ 6.52
	Markup	300%
Equals:	Markup price	$ 19.56

4. Arrive at your final product cost:

You can use the last dollar amount in Step 3 above ($19.56) or round up to a more common retail price like $19.95.

5. Figure your gross profit for this advertisement:

Multiply:	Final product cost	$ 19.95
	Number of expected orders	400
Equals:	Gross profit	$ 7,980.00

Product Pricing Worksheet

1. Figure your cost per order:

Add:	Cost of ad	$_____
	Cost of printing	$_____
	Cost of mailing	$_____
Divide by:	Number of expected orders	_____
Equals:	Cost per order	$_____

2. Figure your total product cost:

Add:	Cost per order	$_____
	Cost per item	$_____
Equals:	Total product cost	$_____

3. Figure your markup price:

Multiply:	Product cost	$_____
	Markup (usually 300 to 400%)	_____
Equals:	Markup price	$_____

4. Arrive at your final product cost:

You can use the last dollar amount in Step 3 above ($_____) or round up to a more common retail price like $_____.

5. Figure your gross profit for this advertisement:

Multiply:	Final product cost	$_____
	Number of expected orders	
Equals:	Gross profit	$_____

material out first-class mail (37 cents each) to the 450 people who requested brochures. (You must have a minimum of 200 pieces of mail to take advantage of a bulk mail permit, and we've opted to send out brochures as fast as inquiries come in instead of waiting until we've got 200 saved up.)

Dollar Stretcher

Shoulder as many direct-mail campaign tasks as possible on your own. Delegate as many more as you can to knowledgeable (and willing) family members. The less you out-source, the more money you save!

Once again, we've arrived at an oddball final product cost of $19.56, so we've bumped up our price to $19.95. Our customers will perceive this as $19, and we'll perceive it as an extra $216 in profits.

You'll also have other expenses to account for (pardon the pun!). We'll discuss fixed and variable expenses in the next section, "Operating Expenses." These include costs like telephone bills, inventory, and supplies.

Blip in the Time Line

Now, you may have noticed a blip in the time line here. We're figuring how to price your product based on orders you haven't yet received. Heck, you haven't even placed your ad!

But, you have done your market research (right?), and you've carefully calculated that you can expect at least the number of orders we've plugged into our computations. If you get more orders than your 400 minimum, your cost per ad goes down and your net profit goes up. (Conversely, of course, if you get less than 400 orders, your net profit goes down.)

Check out the "Product Pricing Worksheet" on page 78. Make copies so you can experiment with various advertising costs, expected numbers of orders, and product prices.

Operating Expenses

We've gone over your start-up expenses, your product costs, and your product pricing. Now we need to talk about operating expenses, those other fees that make up the backbone of every mail order operation. These, subtracted from your projected gross profits, will tell the true tale of how much you'll be making.

We're going to assume once again that you'll be homebased, so we won't worry about expenses for office rent or utilities. We do, however, need to consider the following:

- Phone
- Mailbox rental
- Call center (if you decide to use one)
- Postage (not for shipping your materials or merchandise but for paying bills and corresponding with manufacturers, suppliers, and customers)
- Web hosting (so your Web site, if you choose to have one, has a server to keep it up and running)
- Shipping and packaging materials
- Stationery and office supplies
- ISP (Internet service provider)
- Loan repayment

Dial Toll-Free

As we discussed in the start-up section of this chapter, high-quality phone service is a must in the mail order business. Six of the seven entrepreneurs we interviewed for this book offer customers a toll-free number. The sidebar "A Toll Order" on this page will help you estimate what such a service would cost you each month.

A Toll Order

Another of the many start-up decisions you'll need to make is whether or not to provide customers with a toll-free number for ordering. Shoppers often expect to reach catalog sales companies through toll-free numbers, so if you choose not to offer this service, you could be cutting yourself off from potential sales. If you expect that most of your sales will be through standard mail or the Internet, you might want to stick with your own area code, at least until you build up some working capital.

What can you expect to pay for your toll-free number? We checked with two long-distance carriers, AT&T and MCI, and found costs of 11.3 cents and 12 cents a minute, respectively. Of course, there's a catch: AT&T tacks on a $5 per month service fee, which the company waives for the first six months, while rival MCI gives you its rate only as long as you spend at least $25 per month on MCI services.

So let's figure it out: If you go with the higher rate of 12 cents a minute and you receive 30 calls a day at an average of 5 minutes each, you'll be paying $18 per day or $540 a month. Compare prices carefully before you decide on a carrier.

Or you can go the call center route. If this is your choice, expect to pay a minimum of 60 cents to $1 per minute or $75 to $100 per month

Whichever route you take, you'll still have routine phone expenses, the same as any other business. Start with a base rate of $25 per line—one for your business, which is separate from your home phone, and one for your fax machine and e-mail. Then add in estimated long-distance charges based on where your manufacturers, suppliers, and advertising venues are located, how often you expect to call them, and what sort of rate you've negotiated with your long-distance carrier.

Mailbox Rental

If you're going to be homebased, you'll probably want to rent a box from a mail center like Mail Boxes Etc. so your company has the benefit of a street address but your customers, should they be in the neighborhood, don't pop in on you uninvited. Expect to pay $10 to $20 per month for this service.

Bloomin' Postage

Since you're adding your shipping charges to the cost of each order, you might think you can scribble out the "postage" line on your operating expenses worksheet. However, as with phone expenses, you'll have all the routine mailing costs every other business has—mailing payments to manufacturers, suppliers, advertising venues, and other creditors, as well as sending correspondence to customers and vendors. What kind of correspondence? Information dealing with returns, complaints, compliments, and other customer service issues, as well as the catalog requests you'll send to suppliers. (After all, they're dealing in mail order, too.)

As your company grows, your postage expenses will bloom, too, but for your first year of operation, you should be able to keep it to a minimum. If you figure on an average of two pieces of mail per day at the first-class rate of 37 cents per piece, you can pencil in about $20 per month.

> ### Smart Tip *Tip...*
> For information about mailing and shipping rates, visit the U.S. Postal Service online at www.usps.gov, or go directly to the "U.S. Postal Service Rate Calculators" page at www.usps.gov/business/calcs.htm.

Web Host

Now, if you've got a Web site, you'll need a Web host, which is not a dapper chap in a tuxedo standing at the door with a tray of champagne cocktails but the computer or computers that handle all the traffic to your Web site. While you can manipulate your Web site all you want from your home/office computer, it takes a much, much

▲

larger server to handle the complexities of Web traffic, and that's why you need a host. Some Web site designers provide hosting and updating services, Roy Fletcher of Fletcher Consulting explains, for about $150 to $600 per month—again depending on exactly what your needs are. If you feature Web specials that change every other day, your costs will be in the higher range, but if you make only a couple of merchandise or price changes a month, you can expect to pay lower fees.

If you want strictly hosting, and you'll make any changes and additions (or deletions) yourself, you can expect to pay in the range of $10 to $75 per month for a Web host.

Keep on Shippin'

As we explained in our start-up costs section, your costs for shipping and packaging supplies will depend on your product line. Do your homework! Once you've determined your line, you can get estimates from companies that supply shipping and packaging materials.

Bagging Evidence

Once you've made your initial outlay for office supplies and stationery, your fixed expenses in this category should be fairly low. Staplers last a long time, you can reuse paper clips, and unless you're planning some violent activity with your letter opener and scissors for which the police will bag them as evidence, you shouldn't have to buy another set.

Your main expense will be paper: paper for your printer and fax machine, fine-quality paper for stationery, and envelopes. Be economically and environmentally smart: Reuse your printer paper. Instead of practicing hoop shots into the trash with all those versions of letters, price sheets, and other printed materials that you decided you didn't like, set the pages aside. When you've compiled a tidy stack, load them back into your printer and print on the blank side. Save your "good" paper for the final draft that goes out in the mail. You can expect to pay $4 to $6 per ream for multipurpose paper.

Olé! Online Service

What praises have we not already sung for the Internet service provider? As we've said (repeatedly), this is a must for mail order entrepreneurs. It's also, in most cases, a fixed expense. ISPs generally charge a flat rate of $20 to $25 for unlimited monthly service, which gives you access to the World Wide Web and to e-mail.

Paying the Piper

We've set aside a fixed expense called loan repayment. If you don't borrow money to start your business, you won't need to bother with this one. If, however, you finance your start-up costs in any fashion, you'll need to repay the piper. Here's where you pencil in whatever your monthly fee is.

Putting It Together

To give you an idea of what to budget for our two hypothetical companies have provided their projected income and operating expenses for review on page 84. You can use the worksheet on page 85 to pencil in your own projected income and operating expenses. You may have many more expenses than the ones discussed here, such as: travel to trade shows or crafts fairs and hotel and meal expenses; employees and the worker's compensation and payroll costs that go with them; auto expenses; subscription fees for professional publications; butler and maid service (dream on!); and pizza delivery or Chinese takeout costs. We've put rent, utilities, and employee payroll costs on our worksheet because they're a common feature of financial projections and you should be familiar with them. If they won't apply to your business, of course, you won't need to worry about them.

Once you've added up your projected monthly operating expenses, you can subtract them from your projected gross monthly earnings and—*voilà*—you've got a projected net monthly income total.

Romancing the Bank

Now that you've done all the arithmetic, you can determine just how much you'll need to get your business up and running. And as a bonus, you can present all these beautifully executed figures to your potential lender to show that your business is a good risk and that you'll be able to repay the loan without difficulty. To make the best possible impression on your banker, assemble your start-up materials in a professional-looking folder along with your desktop-published brochure or price list. The more businesslike your company looks, the better.

You might want to consider financing through your bank or credit union. In this case, your projected start-up cost and income figures are extremely important. The bank will want to see all of this, neatly laid out and carefully calculated. You'll also want to present all the statistics you can gather about the bright future of the mail order industry.

Projected Income and Operating Expenses

	Chocoholic Central	OnCall Designer
Projected Monthly Income	$4,900	$19,600
Projected Monthly Operating Expenses		
Rent	N/A	1,200
Utilities	N/A	75
Mailbox rental	20	N/A
Phone service (including toll-free number)	640	1,100
Call center	N/A	1,350
Credit card processing (electronic terminal)	31	45
Employee payroll	N/A	2,000
Miscellaneous postage	20	40
Insurance	90	90
Web hosting	30	300
Miscellaneous expenses (stationery/office supplies)	10	50
Shipping & packing materials	50	100
Loan repayment	N/A	200
Internet service provider	20	20
Total Operating Expenses	**$911**	**$6,570**
Projected Net Monthly Income	**$3,989**	**$13,030**

Projected Income and Operating Cost Worksheet

Projected Monthly Income	$
Projected Monthly Operating Expenses	
Rent	
Utilities	
Mailbox rental	
Phone service (including toll-free number)	
Call center	
Credit card processing (electronic terminal)	
Employee payroll	
Miscellaneous postage	
Insurance	
Web hosting	
Miscellaneous expenses (stationery/office supplies)	
Shipping & packing materials	
Loan repayment	
Internet service provider	
Total Operating Expenses	$
Projected Net Monthly Income	$

Signed, Sealed, Delivered
Daily Operations

By this time you're probably wondering what exactly a mail order maven does all day. Slit open envelopes full of checks, take a spin down to the bank, and then sit back and sip piña coladas? Spend all day with an ear pressed to the phone, scribbling down orders? Or sit on the floor surrounded by cardboard boxes and packing peanuts?

Photo© Adobe Image Library

The answer is a combination of all of these—minus the piña coladas—plus a whole lot more. In this chapter, we'll take a peek into the mailbag of a direct marketer's daily life and explore the ins and outs of mail order operations.

The Juggler

One of the great joys of running a mail order business is that you can arrange your workload around any schedule you choose. Some mail order entrepreneurs work best in the early morning; others pace themselves throughout the day. The hours they spend and the time frames within which they structure those hours are as individual as each entrepreneur.

"Most of the time I liken myself to a juggler with six balls in the air," says Beth H., the Connecticut gluten-free foods seller. "If I have more than six, I'm liable to drop one; if I have less than six, it's kind of boring."

A typical day for Beth includes meeting with the printer to go over the latest version of her catalog (for which she does all the graphics, copywriting, and layouts), rushing home to care for her puppies, and then spending an afternoon stint in her office. But that's not all. "I'll probably be here until about 3:50 P.M.," says the entrepreneurial mom, "then I have to pick up my son from school and get him back to my office for an hour for a snack and homework so he can go to swim team [practice].

"After that, we'll go home and have dinner. And I'll probably work a little tonight after I help with his homework. So that's the way my day goes. I start at home, usually spending an hour on the Internet answering mail and working on projects I really have to concentrate on. Then at night, I'll test recipes.... It's pretty wild."

Kate W., the on-the-go team logo merchandiser, runs her mail order business from her home in Kansas. "I start working early, and I work pretty late at night," the former bookkeeper says, "but I do like to be around for my family. We warehouse our inventory. I get around during the day to make sure the inventory is there, but I do my actual work from home.

"Most of the business we do is via an 800 number," Kate explains. "We have a service that handles all our calls. For cost reasons, I couldn't hire somebody to answer [the phone] 24 hours a day, seven days a week—which I believe you have to do in mail order. They take most of the calls, but I try and take the bulk when I can. They handle all of the incoming calls, and then everything is faxed to my office.

A typical day starts with Kate checking the fax machine to see what orders the call center has taken and forwarded to her. She enters everything into her computer, which generates sales invoices. Then she processes credit cards. Next, she fills the orders and gets them ready for shipping.

"After that," Kate says, "we'll go and pick up the mail. If there's something I really want to get out, we make a late-night run and go straight to the UPS distribution center. We'll run packages up there until 8:00 at night. One of our policies is to turn orders around within 48 hours. Generally, unless it's really busy, we'll do it in 24.

"So first I do all the paperwork. As soon as it's done, I go fill all the orders and ship everything. Then I come back and start again. It's a long day sometimes.

"Last year for the holidays, we were shipping 25 to 30 packages a day. Again, that's just me, processing them in the morning and shipping them in the afternoon."

If your eyes roll back in your head at the prospect of such whirlwind days, don't panic. As we've said before, you can organize your day in whatever way suits you, your family, your lifestyle, and your energy level.

Kate admits that she doesn't actually have any days off but says there are ways to compensate. "If I know I need to be gone the next day, I'll get it all done the night before," she explains. "It's a whole lot more flexible when it's just you."

Three-Armed Skeleton

If you took an X-ray of any mail order company, you'd see three distinct arms:

- Sales and marketing
- Order processing and fulfillment
- General management and administration

In most start-up companies, however, these three arms are all attached to one body—the owner's. As a mail order entrepreneur, you'll have days where you're not only using (or wishing you could use) a third arm but also wearing a dozen different hats: product development director, advertising campaign director, graphic designer, copywriter, and marketing manager. You'll also be in charge of (and sole employee in) the order processing, customer service, and fulfillment departments. This is all in addition, of course, to your administrative tasks as bookkeeper, accountant, file, and mailing list manager, and supplier liaison.

Don't lose your head(s)! You won't always be doing all of this at one time, and most of it is—or should be—a lot of fun. Remember, if you've done your homework and chosen a specialty and a target market that you relish, then everything else is—if not always a snap—a pleasure.

Mailing Lists

One of the mail order maven's key tasks is to get that catalog or other vehicle to its ultimate destination—the customer. Classified or display ads will reach their targets through whichever newspapers or magazines you place them in. Radio and TV spots will hone in on prospective customers through the broadcast venues they're placed in. But what about catalogs and direct-mail pieces? How do you get a catalog or direct-mail piece aimed at dog lovers in the mailboxes of puppy-philes and not those of cat fanciers, tropical fish fanatics, or professed pet haters?

You know the answer: through mailing lists, those Santa-sized rosters of names, addresses, and phone numbers. But did you know that there are companies out there called list brokers that exist solely to rent mailing lists? The savvy mail order maven not only knows this but also takes advantage of these lists to whisk catalogs straight into the hands of target customers.

List Seekers' Secrets

A good list broker has hundreds of lists of *qualified buyers* and can pull out just about any criteria, or *selects*, you're interested in: for instance, people who own dogs, earn over $50,000 per year, live in the Midwest, have high-school-age children, and have purchased something by mail order within the past six months.

So if your catalog is aimed at dog lovers, the list broker can provide you with a mailing list compiled from dog magazine subscribers, kennel club members, and purchasers of other pet-related merchandise. And if your

> **Tip...**
>
> **Smart Tip**
>
> A *qualified buyer* is somebody with a reputation for having bought by mail order already, for demonstrating an interest in the area you've targeted and for having the income to pay for your merchandise.

direct-mail piece is targeting ladies who would like church-themed children's clothing patterns, the list broker might pull your list from parochial-school parent associations, quilting club rosters, and church groups.

List brokers get their lists from virtually every wellspring you might imagine—magazine subscription lists, the customer lists of mail order businesses, club and organization membership rosters, professional and political association membership lists, financial ratings lists, school directories, and more. And they're always on the lookout for new lists.

> **Tip...**
>
> ## Smart Tip
>
> You can request an nth name selection for your list, which means you get every nth name, say every seventh or 10th, instead of every name from "A" through "D." This way, you get more of a cross section of names.

Mailing lists are big business in the direct-marketing world. Their costs can vary tremendously, depending on what sort of list you're renting and how many selects, or variables, you want. First, you'll need to decide whether you want a *compiled list*, made up, for example, of people who by age and income might be Hawaiian cruise prospects, or a *response list*, made up of people who have actually purchased Hawaiian cruises already—those qualified buyers we have mentioned.

Because the compiled list is not as specific, it is cheaper. You can expect to pay an average of $50 per 1,000 names, says Daren Cicchillo of Lighthouse List Company in Fort Lauderdale, Florida. The response list, on the other hand, may cost as much as $120 per 1,000 names, plus $5 to $10 extra for each select you choose (age, income, geographic region, etc.).

Business-to-business names can be even more expensive, Cicchillo says, because fewer people offer them, so they're harder to come by. Expect to pay $75 to $200 per 1,000 names for this type of list.

Most brokers will insist that you rent a minimum of 3,000 to 5,000 names. Why do we say "rent" instead of "buy"? Because the list broker who provides you the names can charge you each time you request another use. You're only allowed to use the names once—and brokers have ways of making sure you comply with this rule. That's the bonus on the broker's side. The plus on your side is that because the broker keeps the list, he or she is responsible for its care and maintenance. The list broker is the one who goes through and weeds out all the *nixies*, the return-to-sender names who've moved and left no forwarding address. The broker is also the one who compiles and recompiles the lists based on any criteria you specify.

Additional Profit Center

Of course, while you're renting lists from someone else, you can start compiling your own lists based on the customers you've already mailed to, breaking them down into those who have ordered, those who are still potentials, those who have ordered a certain dollar amount or live in a particular region, or whatever suits your needs.

Then—and this is really key—you can rent your list to other direct marketers. The money you make from renting your list is a sort of gravy on top of the "real" earnings from your mail order sales and is referred to as an *additional profit center*.

You can use the list broker as an intermediary, just as you would a real estate broker to rent or sell property. You can rent your list directly to other mail order companies without going through a broker, or you can swap lists with other mail order mavens.

A list broker usually charges about 20 percent of whatever you earn from renting your list. So if you charge $50 per 1,000 names and you rent 10,000 names to another company, you've made $500. You give the broker $100 and count the other $400 as profit.

How do you know the broker isn't going to give your hard-earned names to a company that's in direct competition with you? The industry has built in some fail-safes. One is that the broker isn't going to get very far with a reputation for selling out his customers. Another is that the broker will ask the list renter for a sample of his or her mailing piece. If it's too competitive with yours, the prospective renter doesn't get the list.

You protect yourself from someone else stealing your list or using it for more than the one-time rental by *salting*, or *seeding*, it. You mix a few fictitious names and addresses in with all the legitimate ones—addresses you know will come straight to you. How do you accomplish this? Rent a few post office boxes to use as your addresses. (Commercial mail centers like Mail Boxes Etc. will give you a post office box with a street address so it looks more like a residence, for added plausibility.) Or you can salt the list with the names and addresses of people who will be certain to report any received mail to you. (How about your mom? Moms love to help out with this kind of thing.) If you or one of your seeded addresses gets mail from a company that isn't

---

Beverly Hills 90210

If you're selling products geared toward a specific socioeconomic group, you might identify a target ZIP code and make that one of your selects or list criteria rather than just indicating the city. This way, you can be assured that those catalogs touting caviar in mother-of-pearl saucers, for instance, go to upper-crust neighborhoods instead of blanketing boroughs where no one can afford your merchandise. This is a good strategy in large metropolitan areas like Los Angeles and Atlanta, where Beverly Hills and Buckhead have their own high-falutin ZIP codes. In small towns where everybody lives in the same ZIP, however, this tactic doesn't work.

supposed to be using the list, you can sue the business for damages.

When you *swap* lists, you choose a buddy mail order firm, one whose interests are compatible with yours but not the same, say a company that sells dog food while you're selling dog health insurance. This way, they're not treading on your turf or vice versa, yet you can both feel fairly confident that the dog owners on both lists will be interested in both companies' products. Then you exchange lists, either as a one-use deal or as a permanent trade, and you—and your swap partner—get free names! And since list rental makes up about one-third of your mailing expenses (the other two-thirds are printing and postage), you've suddenly "found" money you can put to other uses.

> **Tip...**
>
> **Smart Tip**
> You can swap lists with a direct competitor! Just make sure the list is composed of people who haven't purchased from you in more than six months. You never know—receiving a catalog from your nemesis might inspire your customers to take another look at your merchandise and become regular purchasers.

Close Encounters

Your personal, exclusive mailing list, which you can rent to other companies, is one additional profit center. But there are more. And they, too, can add to your earnings without increasing your fixed overhead (like rent and utilities) or at least pay you enough to defer your mailing and postage costs. Give these profit centers a spin:

- *Piggyback products.* There are other mail order entrepreneurs out there who will gladly pay you to have their advertising materials or samples tucked in with your merchandise.

- *Add the advertising.* If you're mailing a newsletter, book, or other published information, other mail order mavens will pay to advertise within your printed copy.

Your best bet for both of these profit potentials is to find businesses compatible with your own target market. If you sell gifts and apparel for UFO enthusiasts, for example, your customers would probably love a brochure from a mail order bookstore specializing in books about close encounters of the alien kind. If your catalog caters to home brewers, you might include promotional material from a gourmet pretzel and popcorn company.

Keep in mind that these piggybacked products will reflect on your own company. Even though they have somebody else's name on them, your

> Make sure everybody who mans your phones is familiar with your products or services and has enthusiasm for them and for your company.

customers will associate the products with you and may even want to hold you accountable if they don't like what they get. You'll want to be sure your piggybacked products:

- Match the type of merchandise you're selling
- Meet your own high quality standards
- Increase your customers' enthusiasm for your products

How much should you charge? Your fee should be a percentage of your normal shipping cost. Your list broker can fill you in on all the details and can even help sell the service for you.

Thanks for Calling!

You've placed your ads or media spots or purchased your mailing list and sent out your catalog or other materials. Now, it goes without saying that a significant part of your day will be taken up with order processing. This is good! It means your customers have found you and you're making money. But it also means that you—and your order takers—need to put your sunniest face forward at all times, especially when you're taking orders over the telephone. Since your customers' visits are all virtual, their first—and lasting—impression of your company will be the one made by that voice on the other end.

Some mail order entrepreneurs like to field all calls in-house so they have seat-of-the-pants control of their order processing. Others delegate the ordering process to an outside service. Unless you like being awakened by 3 A.M. phone calls or you plan never to sleep again, using an outside service is probably your best bet, especially if you're starting out as a one-person operation and you want to offer 24-hour availability. This is also a good option if you're going to start out part-time. The service can take orders while you're at your day job, and then you can fill them when you get home.

Whether you answer your phones yourself or have someone do it for you, what you or your customer representatives say and how you or they say it can make the difference between a sale and a changed-mind, and between a ho-hum one-time customer and a customer for life. A lackluster or uninformed response can spell see-ya-later to a sale. Make sure that everybody who mans—or womans—your phones is familiar with your products or services and has enthusiasm for them and for your company.

> **Bright Idea**
>
> When you take your customers' orders, ask for their birth dates and keep track (something several software packages can do). Then, as each customer's birthday rolls around, send a birthday card and a small freebie. It's a great way to help customers remember you!

Scenario for Success

You'll want to carefully think through the way your order line is answered, basing your responses on your merchandise or service and your company's philosophy. To get you started, you can use the following "script" as a scenario for phone order success.

1. *Greetings!* Even if you've spent a sleepless night cleaning up after a sick child or pet (or both), your car just gave its last gasp and your coffeemaker is spitting out watery dregs, you should always answer the phone in a cheerful, friendly tone. Be sure to give your company's name. Aim for something like: "Books by Jove. This is Maria. How can I help you today?"

2. *The key code please.* If the caller wants to place an order, ask for the key code or source code, if you have one, from the catalog or order card. This code, which is printed somewhere on your sales material, tells you what ad, sales letter, or catalog the customer is responding to. A key code like MWC02, for instance, might indicate that the catalog was your Christmas 2002 version mailed to customers in the Midwest.

3. *Product verification.* Verify what your customer is ordering. When the customer gives you the item number for the product, you can say something like, "That's the set of six holiday bookmarks." Make sure your customer agrees, so you know you're both talking about the same item.

4. *Quantity, size, and color.* Find out how many of the product the customer wants. Then ask for size and color preferences—assuming, of course, that these questions apply to the product. Repeat this information back and let the customer confirm it.

5. *Ad identification.* Ask how the customer learned about your company. If it was through an advertisement, ask where the person saw it. Take notes. This will be an important aid in future marketing efforts.

Checking It Twice

Unless you want the UPS man to deliver your customer's package to the wrong address, make accurate order entry a priority. Double-check names, addresses, and phone numbers with your customers and take the time to enter them properly. All it takes is one wrong digit to land that order several states away from its intended recipient.

And such an error, while entertaining in the way a slip on a banana peel is entertaining, can cost you hundreds of dollars in terms of customer dissatisfaction, merchandise replacement, and reshipping fees.

▲

6. *And what else?* Ask if your customer would like to order anything else. Don't forget to cross-sell and up-sell!

7. *Customer ID.* Ask for your customer's name, address, and phone number. Read it back to make sure you've got it correct. If you're shipping by UPS or FedEx, you'll need to make sure customers provide a physical street address like 123 Main Street. Most shipping services can't deliver to a post office box.

   Remember, too, that people like to order products as gifts and have the merchandise shipped directly to the gift recipient. Be sure to ask if the shipping address differs from the billing address. (You might also ask if the giver would like a card enclosed—a terrific personalized touch!)

8. *Payment.* Phone orders are typically paid for by credit card. Find out whether your customer is paying by Visa, MasterCard, American Express, or Discover (or whichever cards you plan to accept). Then take the account number and the expiration date.

9. *Shipping.* Let your customer know when the order will be shipped and about how long it will take to arrive.

10. *One more time.* Repeat everything back to your customer one more time, so you're both sure it's accurate.

11. *Thank you!* Be sure to thank your customer for ordering from you and invite him or her to call back any time you can be of assistance in the future. Wish the person a pleasant day. You want your customer to feel good about having called your company and look forward to placing another order. Remember, the repeat customer is where you earn your money!

The Captive Audience

There's more to taking an order by phone than meets the ear. Once your customer has displayed interest by taking the initiative to call you, you've got a semi-captive audience. Now is an excellent time to increase your sales:

- *Up-sell.* Offer your customer a special on two or more products of the same type. For example, if the person is ordering one box of Decadence Chocolates, offer a second box for 10 percent off (or whatever works for you). If a holiday's in the offing, suggest that a box of Decadence Chocolates makes a memorable gift. (Or if customers tell you the first box is being purchased as a gift, tell them they owe themselves a box, too!)

- *Cross-sell.* Offer customers a product related to the one they have just ordered. For customers who order the Decadence Chocolates, suggest a canister of Amaretto Almond Dream Coffee to go with it. You can say something like (assuming, of course, that it's true), "We get a lot of orders for the coffee because it goes so well with the chocolates," or, "All of us here in our shop go nuts over the Decadence and Amaretto Almond Dream combo; it's our favorite coffee break treat."

The idea here is to help your customer on to an increased order. It's the same concept as the salesperson in the exclusive clothing store who suggests that snazzy tie or scarf or belt to go with the suit you're trying on. Your customer will appreciate it. After all, who doesn't like a little personalized service?

Talking Football

Answering the telephone can be more than just a method of taking orders. It can become a valuable marketing tool.

"We listen to our customers a lot," Kate W. says. "I handle the phones often. This is good and bad, because when I take the phones, first [my customers and I] talk about their [team] room—because almost everybody has one—and they tell you everything that's in there. Then you have to talk about football and what happened in the last game. And then you get to the order.

"So it costs me more to take the calls, but it is fun and I keep that one-on-one communication with the customers. They tell me all the time what they want. If we don't have it, we try to find it. This year it helped us a lot. We selected some of the products based on what they told us. They'll tell us, 'We couldn't find this anywhere,' and that's how we know what to buy.

"If I wasn't handling the calls at all, I wouldn't have a clue what they're telling my order representatives. But because I need to know that right now, and I want them to know there is a Kate out there who wrote the letter in the front of the catalog, I try to take as many calls as I can."

The Game Plan

The mail order maven's day consists of more than answering the phone. There's also processing the mail and opening all those fascinating envelopes full of customers' orders and payments. This may sound like a no-brainer operation, but, like taking phone orders, it requires organization and attention to detail. And, like taking phone orders, it's something for which you should have a game plan mapped out.

Why? Because turnaround is everything. Today's customers, used to life in the fast lane, expect speedy service. So the faster you process their orders and get the merchandise delivered, the happier your customers will be.

There are some really excellent mail order software packages on the market (see our Appendix for information), and we strongly suggest you purchase one. For the price of a newbie-level program (as little as $299), you get far more than your money's

▲

worth. These programs can track your customers and your advertising by key codes, advertising venues and dollars garnered (which means they do some of the testing calculations for you). They can process credit cards and keep track of shipping, inventory, and sales taxes—all the things that can get really messy and take hours of time when you do them by hand, time you could be spending on other tasks.

Into the Bank

Take a look at the following scenario, which is based on the fact that you've taken our advice and purchased mail order software. Again, you may want to do a lot of this the hard way, with ledgers and spreadsheets, and if you do, that's OK—at least until your business grows to the point where it's no longer feasible.

Your mail- and order-handling strategies will differ slightly from this scenario, depending on your lifestyle. (That's one of the perks of running your own business!) But the following guidelines will get you going:

- *Open sesame.* Open and sort your mail. You're going to get a lot of it! Yes, you'll have customer orders, but you will also have bills, inquiries, returns, solicitations, and trade publications—not necessarily in that order. You should have a designated place for each mail breed: a box or file or drawer. Just make sure you don't stash things where they'll never see the light of day again, or you will forget they ever existed.

- *Sort again.* Now you'll want to sort your customer orders by payment type, separating the credit cards from the checks from the money orders. Place any faxed or e-mailed orders in the proper stack.

The Master List

While you're tallying orders, you can put your customer information into your computerized database. This will give you instant access to your customers' names, addresses, telephone numbers, and order information. If they've filled out any demographic information on the product reply card you've cleverly incorporated—such as age, income, and interests—you can add it in. Remember, all this stuff, including the all-important clue of how your customer found you (display ad, direct-mail piece, etc.), is vital. You absolutely, positively must have a master list of all your customers. Each time someone new places an order, his or her name and information goes on the list. This is how you build your own mailing list, the one you'll use over and over again—and the one you'll rent to other mail order entrepreneurs.

- *Into the computer.* Enter customer and order information for all credit card payments into your software program. Don't forget to enter the key code—remember, this is how you track the success of your advertising campaigns. (See "Key Code Roundup" in Chapter 10 for more details.)

- *Check it out.* There are two schools of thought on handling checks. Some mail order mavens insist on waiting until checks have cleared before mailing out merchandise. Others, operating on good faith, send out the product as soon as they receive the order. Greer T., the children's clothing merchandiser, holds check-paid orders for ten days to allow the checks to clear. Beth H., the gluten-free foods specialist, sends her products out right away, whether they've been paid for by check or not. "We've had a couple of checks bounce," she says, "but not anything big."

  You'll have to decide for yourself how to handle this issue, based on the feedback you get from others in your target industry, the cost of your merchandise, and your own faith in your fellow humans. If you decide to wait until the checks clear, put them in a pending file—again, one where you won't lose track of them. If you go ahead and ship, enter the checks on your bank deposit slip and then enter the orders in your computer. The customary waiting period for checks to clear—especially if they are out-of-state checks—is two weeks. If you haven't received a returned item slip from the bank by that time, you can assume they're OK.

- *Money orders.* These are easy. Since money orders are basically the same as cash, you don't need to worry about getting them authorized or cleared. Enter them on your deposit slip and then enter the orders in your computer.

> **You should have a designated place for each mail breed: a box or file or drawer.**

- *Into the bank.* Tally up your bank deposit slip, slide it along with the day's checks and money orders into that snazzy vinyl pouch the bank gives you when you open your account, and make that deposit.

- *Into the bank, part two.* Your credit card charges are automatically entered into your bank account electronically through your computer's software.

Fulfillment

Fulfillment in mail order lingo means getting orders in customers' hands—fulfilling their wishes. And as we've explained, the faster you fulfill, the more dedicated your customers will be. If you're the type of person who can't be torn away from the wrapping paper and ribbons at gift-giving times, then every day for you will be Holiday

Packing Slip/Receipt

CHOCOHOLIC CENTRAL

123 Cocoa Court
Truffle Bay, FL 30000
Toll-Free (800) 555-4000
Fax (305) 555-4242
Internet Orders: www.chocoholic.com

Bill to:

Charlie Coffee
458 Cafe Circle
Cookieville, IL 60000 USA

Ship to:

Cindy Coffee
17 Latte Lane
Port Indulgence, TX 70000

Your order of October 11, 2002 (order no. 101155579) from (312) 555-8214, shipped October 12, 2002

Qty.	Description	Product No.	Our Great Price	Total
1	Decadence Chocolate Assortment	12651	29.00	29.00
1	Almond Amaretto Dream Coffee, 1 Lb Canister	12656	12.00	12.00
2	Chocoholic Central Coffee Mug	11175	7.50	15.00
1	Chocoholic Central T-Shirt, Size Sml	211822	14.00	14.00
			Subtotal	70.00
			Shipping & Handling	9.90
			Order Total	79.90
			Paid via MasterCard	79.90
			Balance Due	0.00

Thanks for shopping **CHOCOHOLIC CENTRAL**. Please call on us again soon. And may all your dreams be sweet!

CHOCOHOLIC CENTRAL

Our Return Policy:

You may return any product in its original condition at any time for a full refund of the merchandise cost. We can only refund shipping costs if the return is a result of our error. Just fill out the return information on this packing slip and include it with your return. Please wrap the package securely. Send it to:

Chocoholic Central
Returns Department
123 Cocoa Court
Truffle Bay, FL 30000 USA

For your protection, please use UPS or Insured Parcel Post.

Reason for Return:

_____

_____

_____

_____

_____

_____

_____

_____

Questions, Suggestions, or Problems?

If you have any questions about this order or any Chocoholic Central product, please contact us by phone at (800) 555-4000, fax at (305) 555-4242 or e-mail at orders@chocoholic.com.

Thanks for shopping CHOCOHOLIC CENTRAL. Please call on us again soon. And may all your dreams be sweet!

Central. If you're the other type, one who'd just as soon give that gift in a brown paper bag, read up anyway because this is an important part of your daily operations.

Now, you'll need to create an invoice, or packing slip, a receipt, and a label for each package. If you're clever, you can make an all-in-one packing slip and receipt. Each one should show:

- Billing and shipping addresses
- Date your customer placed the order
- Date you shipped the order
- Order number
- Phone number or e-mail address from which the order was placed
- Name or description of each product
- Quantity, size, and color, if applicable
- Price of each product
- Shipping cost
- Total cost, including shipping, for all products in package
- Method of payment (credit card, check, money order, etc.)
- Your thanks (This is important!)
- Your return form, which includes your return policy (This should be printed on the other side of your packing slip.)

Check out the sample packing slip/receipt and return form on pages 100 and 101. You will, of course, keep a copy of this form for your files. It will give you just about all the information you'll need if you, your customer, or your accountant has a question. The only thing you may need to refer to separately will be a credit card number, and you'll have that on your credit card receipt.

You can design and print a similar form with a desktop publishing program on your computer, have one made up at a local printer or let your mail order software do it for you. (Some programs will generate a packing slip/receipt and shipping label in one smooth move.) Or you can purchase invoice/receipt forms from an office supply store. Go for the ones that come in duplicate: One copy goes to the customer, and one copy goes into your files for inventory and accounting purposes.

How often do you wear your fulfillment cap? It all depends on your sales volume. Most mail order mavens are proud of their quick turnaround and take pains to ship packages within 24 hours of order placement. If this is you—and it should be—you'll probably be shipping every day.

> **Tip...**
>
> **Smart Tip**
>
> If your merchandise can't go out to the customer right away, send a postcard indicating that you've received the order and are processing it. This builds good customer relations and keeps your customer from worrying that you never got the order.

Pack It Up

If you love the product development and advertising aspects of mail order, but you're all thumbs when it comes to taping packages, you might consider using a *fulfillment house*. This is an outsource company that does everything from packing and shipping those orders to answering your phones, processing customer credit card payments, and depositing your money in the bank for you. Some fulfillment houses will also manage your mailing lists, print your materials, and mail them out.

Smart Tip

In the fulfillment biz, a company that handles packing and shipping is called a *pick and pack* operation.

The big plus here, of course, is that instead of wearing all those hats at once, you've got somebody else to take over a portion of the work, leaving you to concentrate on the creative genius and number crunching stuff. The big minus is that you're no longer in complete control. You can't know exactly how the fulfillment house's representatives are handling your customers at all times, and you miss all the customer feedback that can be so crucial when you're first starting out.

Still, a solid relationship with a good fulfillment house can solve a lot of headaches. You'll want to carefully screen the company, which includes screening their customer service people to make sure they are compatible with your company's philosophy.

Your Back End

One key to making multiple sales in mail order is developing a good back end. Yes, it sounds like some sort of hard-body weightlifting regimen, but your back end really is your list of repeat customers. Your prospects, those you've mailed material to but who have not yet bought anything, are called your front end.

So how do you develop that firm back end? By developing follow-up merchandise to sell to your first-time buyers. People who have an interest in one product will generally be just as fired up over the next one and the one after that, provided they're all in the same category.

The home handyman who buys that set of all-occasion screwdrivers, for example, will also want the holiday hammer collection, the drill bit of the month, and the wrist-saver wrench. Not to mention the build-it-yourself books, the tool box assortment, and the carpenter's apron.

And there's your back end!

The Professional Look

If you're handling your own orders but outsourcing your packaging and shipping operation, you can automate fulfillment into a system where your orders go to the fulfillment house once a day, once every few days, or once a week. You tally requests for particular products on a large tracking sheet and attach shipping labels preprinted with your customers' addresses. Then you affix a code number to each label, indicating which product goes to which customer. This way, the center knows not only how many of each product it needs, but also who receives what. The fulfillment house's turnaround is faster, and this makes your company look all the more professional.

Working with Suppliers

Most mail order entrepreneurs deal in tangible products that have to come from somewhere. If you're selling services or information from your own mind, such as recipes, how-to guides, or newsletters, your inventory is on tap: It basically consists of the knowledge you put on paper for your customers to access. But if you're selling gifts, books, tools, or shampoo, you've got to buy them so you can resell them. This brings us to suppliers.

Let's Shop!

Depending on your inventory selection, you may need a handful of suppliers—or dozens. Sometimes they'll contact you through their sales representatives. More often, particularly when you're in the start-up phase, you'll have to locate them through trade shows, trade journals, wholesale showrooms, and conventions, as well as some less traditional sources. Follow along as we take a spin through the realm of mail order suppliers:

- *Manufacturers.* Most mail order mavens buy through manufacturers' sales reps or through independent sales reps who handle the wares of several different companies. Prices are usually lowest from these sources, unless your location makes freight shipment a problem. Larger cities like Los Angeles, Chicago, and New York have permanent gift marts that house manufacturers' showrooms. As a mail order

> **Bright Idea**
> Craftspeople and artisans often have mailing lists of their own. When you take them on as suppliers, ask if you can use (or reasonably rent) their lists. Or how about a list exchange? Their customers will see their wares showcased in a new light—your catalog—and you'll get new names.

Promises, Promises

Drop-shipping is great," says Mary M., the romantic-gifts merchandiser in St. Louis, "although you do pay a little bit more sometimes." Besides the extra cost, the former romance novelist cautions, there are other items to consider when working with a drop-shipper.

"Make certain he can deliver the product in good condition, as you promise your customers," Mary advises. "Because if you give the guarantee—which we do—of 100 percent satisfaction, meaning that no matter what, even if the customer doesn't like the product two months down the road, we'll take it back, then you have to have vendors with quality goods behind you. So that's an important thing to look for. Know what the vendor's rules and stipulations are before you make those promises and before you drop-ship anything."

entrepreneur, you can shop 'til you drop any time during business hours. Just make sure you have your business cards and wholesale license with you to verify your status as a retailer.

- *Distributors.* Also known as *wholesalers*, *brokers*, or *jobbers*, these people use quantity discounts to buy from two or more manufacturers and then warehouse the goods for sale to retailers. Although their prices are higher than the manufacturer's would be, they can supply you with smaller orders from a variety of sources. (Some manufacturers won't break case lots to fill small orders.)

- *Independent craftspeople.* These people will often offer exclusive distribution of one-of-a-kind creations when you attend gift fairs or trade shows. While small crafts operations are generally limited in their production capacity, they can supply some of your best buys.

- *Import sources.* Mail order mavens often buy foreign goods from a domestic import wholesaler. Some mavens travel abroad at least once a year in search of new and exciting goods. Check out Entrepreneur's business start-up guide *Starting Your Own Import/Export Business*, for the scoop on importing your own merchandise.

- *Trade shows.* In most industries, major suppliers display their wares at seasonal trade shows in an attempt to out-wow each other and attract retailers with new products. Although you can buy all year long from the sources we've already listed, the trade show is the shindig of the year, the main event in every retailer's buying cycle. Almost every major city hosts one or more trade shows that may be relevant to your mail order business. Contact your local chamber of commerce or convention bureau for the shows in your city or state. You can

▲

also check out the *Tradeshow Week Data Book*, which is published annually and lists important data on all trade shows in the United States. For details about this book or information on other *Tradeshow Week* publications and resources, visit www.tradeshowweek.com.

- *Closeout sales.* When manufacturers go out of business, they stop a production line, which results in closeout sales that savvy retailers take advantage of. You can buy closeout lots at great savings that you can pass on to your customers. You can often purchase thousands of items for a fraction of a dollar apiece—and sometimes you can purchase the dies and molds, too, so you can start your own production line if you like. This is a terrific way to obtain *proprietary* or ownership rights to a product. Sources for locating closeouts include newspaper classifieds, going-out-of-business sales, and government auctions. You can also buy from wholesalers, who can offer you credit. But make sure you don't pay so much for the materials or the new manufacturing that you lose your profit margin!

- *Business and trade magazines.* Make it a point to read and research magazines in your target market—this is where lots of new products are advertised. If you're specializing in giftware, for instance, look in the classified sections of giftware magazines, where suppliers, importers, and manufacturers advertise. If you're not sure which magazines cover your industry, ask your local librarian.

- *Drop-shippers.* As you know, a drop-shipper is a manufacturer or other supplier that sends out its products for you when you receive an order. For instance, you run an ad in a magazine for a $10 garden spade. When you receive an order from a customer, you send $5 (or whatever percentage has been agreed on) to the drop-shipper, along with the name and address of your customer. The supplier then sends the spade to the customer. It's not all that easy to find a supplier willing to drop-ship. You'll probably pay more for the product, and you won't get the same profits as if you keep the spades in inventory at your own facility. But if you can find someone willing to make this arrangement with you, it leaves you free to put your money where it will earn you the most—in advertising and marketing, instead of tied up in inventory.

- *Catalog houses.* The catalog house is an attractive proposition. It's also an extremely risky one that you should probably pass right by. A catalog house sells you preprinted catalogs filled with items it will drop-ship to your customers, with your company name imprinted on each catalog and order form. This seems good: You forgo the heavy expenses of catalog preparation and printing, as well as the cost of maintaining inventory. You mail the catalogs to prospective buyers, and when the orders and payments come in, you send those orders—and up to 50 percent of the retail price, plus shipping—to the catalog house, which then drop-ships the merchandise to your customer. The problem here is that by the time you pay for the mailing list (which is how you get your first customers), the shipping, and half the merchandise revenue, you don't have enough left to call an income. Plus, you don't have that all-important niche in the market—you're "copying" somebody else's success.

While you're shopping for suppliers, remember that as a mail order entrepreneur you're only as good as your merchandise. Reliable suppliers will steer you toward hot-selling items, which—if everything works the way it should—will increase your sales. But don't let anybody pressure you into a sale. Analyze all advice before making a purchase.

When all your supplier searching pays off and you're able to offer an exclusive item, one that only you are contracted to sell, make sure your catalog or advertising copy tells your customers so. They'll get the thrill of getting a "your company" original, and they won't be tempted to think they might find that item for less money somewhere else.

Zero in on Merchandise

Adding new products is a terrific way to keep your customers coming back—and buying. But how do you decide what new goodies to offer?

Kate W., the Midwest team-logo merchandiser, took a careful look at what her customers wanted and then built up her merchandise line accordingly. "We decided that, instead of going with products that are available to someone in Florida or California, we would offer the things that are not so accessible, the novelties," says Kate. "That's really what we've built our business on: the gifts, collectibles, and memorabilia. In our first year, that's all we had in the catalog.

"This year, in an effort to expand the line, and because we got so many requests, we started to add a little bit of apparel. Again, I had a niche market that I felt was not being adequately served—and that's women's apparel. You can find men's stuff everywhere. But where can you find a cute little polo for a gal?

"They're starting to make them, but over the years women just wore solid reds or something like that because they didn't have the cute stuff men had. So we do a whole line of stuff exclusively for women, made for them and cut for them. And that's done very well this year.

"We always try to zero in on our market and then be very specific with it," Kate says. "We try to [come up with] exclusive things, design them ourselves and have someone make them for us."

Greer T., whose catalog is filled with unique apparel for children and their moms, finds her merchandise at clothing markets in Dallas, New York, and Chicago. Talk about shopping 'til you drop! She enjoys comparing what's offered in retail stores with what's

Smart Tip

Inventory control does not mean just counting. Take physical control of your inventory, too. Remember that inventory is money.

available at the markets because it's a chance to see what's popular and then set her own trends. "They have thousands of different vendors," the Ohio resident says. "You make appointments and then you go see the different things they have to offer. That's the fun part!"

Customer Service

No matter how smoothly your company is run, you're going to get some customers who complain. It's human nature. Your job is to:

- Be as perfect as possible so you get as few complaints as possible

- Treat complainers with tact and understanding

- Remember that the customer is always right—even if you don't agree

Most people just want to vent. Let them tell you what they're unhappy about, and they're fine—so long as you let them know that you understand the problem and you plan to solve it. Sooner or later, of course, you'll run into the rare crank who refuses to be mollified. This will test your patience and your nerves, but it's only a test. Don't take those harsh words to heart. Eventually, you will also run into the rare creep who's trying to test your policies by intimidating you into an unfair return or refund. Don't let yourself be railroaded. As long as your policies are clearly spelled out and meet FTC guidelines, you're in the right. But use your own judgment. Some people will be customers for life if you give in on something a little out of the ordinary. It's up to you.

> **Fun Fact**
>
> Mail order pioneer Sears experienced more than a few customer service growing pains, according to the company's Web site. "For heaven's sake," the site reports an early customer complaining, "quit sending me sewing machines. Every time I go to the station I find another one there. You have shipped me five already."

Charted Territory

What kind of customer service issues will you encounter in mail order? Well, for starters, you're going to get a certain number of returns. It's part of the charted territory of mail order and retail. The reasons for returns are as varied as human nature:

- People change their minds.
- They order the wrong size or wrong color.
- They give gifts that aren't quite right (or are entirely wrong).
- They order so late that they no longer need the product by the time it arrives.

- They receive the wrong merchandise, or it arrives in less than pristine condition.

No matter what your customer's reason is, however, you will have to deal with it—preferably in a win-win manner. You should have a return policy already in place and clearly stated in all your advertising material. If you've decided on a no-return policy, you must spell it out in your advertising and/or catalog so that, hopefully, the customer already knows this when ordering. If you've got a limited-return policy, you must clearly write this out in your advertising and ordering materials.

Stick to your policy, but remember that you want to keep your customer happy. If bending the rules a bit might make the difference between a repeat customer and one who chooses never to use your company again, you know what to do.

"Sometimes [the reason for the return] may be something you don't feel is your fault," advises Caryn O., "and you feel you shouldn't have to make it up to them, but you've got to do it anyway because it will make the customer happy. And that's what you've got to remember constantly."

Many Happy Returns

What's commonly included in a limited return policy? You might accept returns only on certain products, within a certain time period (say 30 days), with certain tags still attached, or (often in the case of CDs or software) with the product packaging unopened.

Think carefully about how you structure your return policy. More and more retail stores are allowing customers to try out products and then return them within 14 to

---

Customer Appreciation

The other side of the customer service coin is customer relations. The better relationship you have with your customers, the more likely they are to buy from you on a regular basis.

Kate W. holds an annual customer appreciation promotion, a special catalog mailed exclusively to people who have purchased from her the previous year. She puts together selected merchandise and offers it in the spring, her slow season, at great prices.

This is smart business. Kate's promotion thanks customers in a splashy manner that encourages repeat sales and customer loyalty, while bringing in revenues during an otherwise lackadaisical season.

30 days. If you go for a policy like this, you could be asking for a lot of unusable, returned stock. On the other hand, you can garner a reputation as a friendly, here-to-please company that customers will want to buy from.

And you can always offer those "test-driven" products at a discount, earning yourself happy customers of a slightly different bent. Also, check with your vendors; you may be able to send your returns back to them.

Beware!

Banks may charge you up to $30 each for *charge-backs,* which are refunds to customers for merchandise returns or disputes.

Tried and True

Over the years, mail order mavens have adopted these tried-and-true methods of processing returns:

- *Instruct customers to ship products back in the original packing materials within 30 days.* This ensures that a) you won't receive returned merchandise years later, and b) you know the merchandise came from your company instead of somebody else's.

- *Offer an exchange program in which the customer phones in his or her concern, and you immediately ship out a replacement product.* When the customer receives the replacement, he or she puts the damaged original into the same box the replacement came in, with the same packing materials, and sends it back to you with shipping prepaid by you.

- Some companies offer an open return policy, like Lands' End. They'll take back anything for any reason any day of any year. You'll have to think carefully about whether you can financially handle a program like this.

7

Special Delivery
Inventory and Shipping

It's difficult to be successful in the mail order business without having a good handle on inventory and shipping. After all, we're talking about two things that are absolutely essential to your business: what you sell and how you get it to your customers. In this chapter, we'll explore the ins and outs of managing your stock and discover the secrets to efficient packing and shipping.

▲

Inventory

You might think all there is to inventory control is buying merchandise. But like the groceries in your refrigerator and pantry, you have to know what to buy, when to buy it, and how much to buy. If you stock up on 40 loaves of sourdough sauerkraut, raspberry bread because it's on sale, but your family won't eat it, you've effectively mangled your monthly food budget and lost your customers. They're over next door, having supper with the Pinkelmans. On the other hand, if you come home with only two double chocolate macadamia dream cookies and you've got a family of five, you're going to be seriously understocked and you will, again, have lost your customers, who are down at the corner bakery ruining their dinners with somebody else's desserts.

Catch-22

Your inventory must serve two functions:

1. If you're working with a multiple-product line, it should provide your customers with a reasonable assortment of the products you offer.
2. It should cover the normal sales demands of your company.

Now we arrive at the Catch-22 of retail inventory operations. To accurately calculate basic stock, you must review actual sales during an appropriate time period, such as a full year of business. But you don't yet have previous sales and stocking figures to use as a guide. So you will have to use the information from your market research—and your intuition. Keep your ear to the ground and your eyes on your customers' buying habits. Keep good records. Stockpile all this information in your brain's own inventory for future use.

Greer T., the children's apparel merchandiser, agrees that inventory is difficult to predict. "It's hard to say how much you're going to need and what's going to sell better," she says. "I buy a certain minimum amount, [but] there are certain items in our fall catalog that we're [already] at the point of being sold out on. That's the game I think all stores play."

Chocolate Zeppelins

Another factor you'll need to consider in calculating your basic stock is lead time, the length of time between when you reorder a product and when you receive it. Warning: math ahead. Let's say, for example, that you're selling chocolate zeppelins. You know that once you call and place your order, it takes four weeks for the vendor to deliver more zeppelins to you. This means your lead time is four weeks. So if you're selling ten zeppelins a week, you'll need to reorder before your basic inventory level falls below 40 zeppelins.

If you wait until you're out of zeppelins, you'll also be out of luck, because you'll have to put all those lovely customer requests on back-order and risk losing sales and customers. You'll also lose cash flow. And then you can pronounce "lead" as "led," as in lead-headed. Or hearted.

One way you can protect yourself from inventory shortfalls is by incorporating a safety margin into your basic inventory figures. You can figure safety margins by anticipating external delays or problems. For instance, you might order extra quantities of seasonal merchandise that you know sells quickly, or, if you deal with a vendor located in a winter-blizzard zone, you could order extra products before shipping delays set in.

Nightmare on Inventory Street

A word of caution: Some mail order entrepreneurs get so excited about a new product that they order entirely too many at one time. Excess inventory creates extra overhead, and that costs you money. Inventory that sits in your garage or warehouse doesn't generate sales or profits.

Newbie mail order entrepreneurs sometimes add financial insult to injury by marking overstocks at reduced prices, hoping for a quick sale. This solves the overstock problem but plays havoc with your bottom line, because that product you've written into your financial plan as selling at $100 is now pulling in only $50. It's not holding up its share of the weight.

You may be tempted to bounce back from this nightmare on Inventory Street by getting timid with your next orders. Don't do this, either. When you reduce normal reordering, you risk creating a stock shortage, and that's not healthy for your bottom line.

We've told you everything *not* to do, but what makes a good inventory plan? Try the following:

- Do as much research as you can before ordering so that you can order as realistically as possible.
- Order only what you feel confident will sell.
- Establish a realistic safety margin.

The October Lull

As a mail order maven, you'll probably find that your business is seasonal. "Definitely," says Kate W., the team logo merchandiser. "The holidays—and I think this is true throughout the retail industry—is of course your absolute busiest season. We did [most] of our business just at the holidays. Thanksgiving through the Bowl games, which is the first of the year, we did easily 50 percent, maybe even higher. The other real big hot period is at the beginning of the football season, usually August and September.

"Then there's October. It's awfully strange, and I am glad somebody explained it to me, because last year I was really worried. In collegiate sales it's called the 'October lull,' and you slow down a little bit. After the real busy August and September, you get to sit back and catch your breath. By then you know what's really hot and what's not, so you know what inventory you need to bring in. And you prepare yourself for the holiday rush."

Autumn rates a gold star on Greer's seasonal calendar, too. "Fall is the biggest market," the children's clothing expert says. "Back to school—definitely. We got our catalog out in early August, so we've had a great September and a great August response rate. October, November, and December should do very well for our fall catalog."

And there's more to a "good season" catalog than just higher numbers of orders. There are also price differences. "There are higher-end products for your fall catalog than for your summer catalog," Greer explains, "so you tend to make more money on your products at that time. A coat sells for something like $150, while your most expensive summer dress would be something like $100. You sell more coats and more expensive items in the fall."

In Connecticut, Beth H.'s gluten-free foods also sell seasonally. "I think probably the fall catalog is the best one for us," the former cooking teacher says, "but I'm not really sure. We don't have a particularly slow time, although we do have a couple of months that are slower than the others."

And in St. Louis, Mary M. finds that her romantic gifts sell best during the winter holidays. "Around the holidays, the last quarter, is usually your busiest time," the former romance writer advises. "In the summer, you want to start acquiring the merchandise you believe you're going to need. You keep that on hand. The rest of the year is a little slower, so you have that flexibility. But the last quarter—you definitely need to stock up."

Shipping and Handling

You've got your inventory squared away. Now you need to think about how you're going to get it to your customers. Fulfillment—speeding that package from your garage or warehouse to your customer's door—is perhaps the single most important thing you can do in your operation aside from effective marketing. Failure to provide prompt fulfillment will result in more complaints, cancellations, refusals of c.o.d. payments, and nightmares than just about anything else in the mail order entrepreneur's world.

So exactly how will you get those packages to your customers? You've seen the TV commercials. Your main choices are the U.S. Postal Service (USPS), United Parcel Service (UPS), and Federal Express (FedEx). Most mail order

---

Fun Fact

According to United Parcel Service, each company driver delivers up to 500 packages per day.

---

mavens use UPS for packages because it's generally cheaper than FedEx, faster than the post office, and has better tracking capabilities for those nightmarish lost items than the post office. It pays to comparison shop. Both FedEx and UPS offer various discounts when you set up an account, so be sure to ask—and don't forget to negotiate!

Take a look at your loss ratio when deciding whether to spend a little and ship U.S. Post or spend more and ship UPS, advises Tony Romano of All USA, an Illinois-based call center and fulfillment service. If the product you're sending costs less than $50, go ahead and ship first-class or priority mail. If it's more than $50, spend the extra dollars to send it UPS and get tracking capability.

For those packages that don't necessarily require tracking, it's smart business to offer your customers a choice of shipping services. You can tell them, for instance, that you can have their package out to them by U.S. priority mail with an expected—but not guaranteed—delivery time of three business days. Then you can offer second-day service by UPS or overnight by FedEx at an extra cost. Give the customer options. This way people know you're working with them, in terms of both price and speed. What a great company!

Out of Your Hands

Understanding how the relationship between your business and shipping companies affects customers will go a long way toward keeping your shipping operations on an even keel. In short, your customers will hold you responsible for any delay in receiving their merchandise, even if the delay is caused by the shipping company. So be prepared to be sympathetic to complaining customers—and stern with the USPS, UPS, and FedEx.

"One of the difficult things about a mail order business," says Caryn O. in Georgia, "is that you can work your tail off, but once you give [the merchandise] to a shipping company, it's out of your hands. For instance, we use UPS a lot. You have done everything, you take an order, you get it out, it's great, everything's fine. And then UPS loses it or takes extra time getting it there. You can have a very distraught, unhappy customer when you've done nothing wrong.

Fun Fact

According to FedEx, its drivers—in the United States alone—cover more than 2.5 million miles per day.

▲

"You have to understand that the shipping company is almost a part of your company," the textiles merchandiser explains. "It's an extension, and even though you're not related, your customer doesn't see it that way. All they know is that they don't have their package. They don't care when you got it out. They want to know where it is now.

"You have to stay on top of things like that," Caryn says. "We're constantly in very close contact with UPS. If UPS causes a problem for our member, we make UPS call and apologize. We fight for our members and do everything we can to make it up to them and make them happy."

Pass the Popcorn

There's a method to everything, including packing and shipping. Here's a list of smart tips for shippers to help you help yourself and your customers.

- Take a tip from the box boy down at the supermarket. Place heavier or larger items on the bottom of the box and lighter ones on top.

- After you've got each piece of merchandise in the box, place a piece of cardboard on the very top. This way, if your customer gets carried away with his penknife while slicing open the box, he won't slash his brand-new goodies as well.

- Use shredded newspaper or actual (unbuttered!) popcorn instead of Styrofoam peanuts. Your customers will appreciate your concern for the environment, and if you get hungry while packing, you can eat your materials!

- Indicate which end of the box should be opened first or face up. Sometimes breakable merchandise will make an entire cross-country trip in one piece, only to smash on the customer's floor because he opened it wrong side up.

- Make sure your shipping label is clearly visible to the deliverer. Some shipping companies will refuse to deliver a package if any part of the address is obscured or too small to read.

- Absolutely do not ship to a P.O. box. Most shipping firms cannot deliver to a post office box. Make sure your order takers ask for an actual street address.

- Include all invoices, receipts, thank you letters, new catalogs, and other printed materials in one envelope with the customer's name on it, placed on top of the merchandise. This saves your customer the time and frustration of having to dig through packing materials to find these things.

Smart Tip Tip...

Let your customers know you are recycling old boxes and newspapers. It makes you look good, and it helps your customers think environmentally, too.

- Reuse boxes. It's not only ecologically sound but also economically smart. When you reuse a box, make sure all old labels, addresses, and postage markings are covered up. Stick another label on top so the delivery man doesn't mix up whom your package is intended for.

- Design packing models so your shippers (and you) know how products fit into boxes, how merchandise is folded, stacked, or tissue-wrapped, and how packing materials are used. Weigh each packing model on a scale and make sure it doesn't go even one-eighth into the next pound. This cuts postage costs, reduces returns from damaged goods, and adds to your income by creating happy repeat customers.

Bulk Mail

Bulk mail is one of those interesting things in life that can be either a boon or a bust, depending on how much mail you're sending out, how fast you want it to get there and how much work of the tedious variety you're willing to put in.

Wrap It Up

One way to lavish your customers with attention is in the way you package your merchandise. "When we send fabric," Caryn O. says, "we wrap it in tissue paper so it arrives looking neat and [attractive]. Our customers are spending a lot of money for a product they've got pictured in their heads. They don't look at it and see a piece of gray flannel—they see it as the beautiful outfit it's going to become. We want to make it presentable, so when they open the box it looks like what they expected."

And this attention to detail works. "We get a lot of compliments," the Georgia fabric retailer explains. "Our customers tell us, 'Thank you. I love how my fabric arrived; it shows how much you care about it.'" And how much she cares about them.

▲

The obvious advantage of bulk mail is cost savings. Where a first-class stamp for a one-ounce letter goes for 37 cents, the same letter sent bulk rate will cost about 28 cents. This sounds great. But—and here we get to a whole list of buts:

- If you're just starting out, it may cost you almost as much to send bulk rate mail as first-class. First you have to purchase your *bulk mail permit*, which will set you back $200 (a one-time fee of $100 and an annual fee of $100). Then you add up your postage: If you send 3,000 pieces at 28 cents each, you'll spend $840. Add your $200 permit fees, and you've got a cost of $1,040. Compare that with the first-class rate of 3,000 pieces at 37 cents each, which adds up to $1,110. The bulk rate is cheaper, but:

> **Tip...**
>
> ### Smart Tip
> The UPS Package Lab is staffed entirely by engineers with four-year degrees in package engineering. (Bet you didn't even know there was a degree in package engineering!) They'll design packing models and even special packing for your products—for a fee. For a price quote, contact UPS at (800) PICK-UPS.

Leave the Mailing to Us

If you want to mail your materials at the bulk rate but you don't want to spend all those hours sorting by ZIP code and state, you might check into the services of a *lettershop*. This is a company that lets you leave the mailing to it—not only sorting and stamping or metering your pieces but also folding, inserting, and stapling. A good lettershop can advise you on what mailing rate is best for the job you're doing, what type of label or on-the-envelope printing to use, and even what type of mailer might be best. Some lettershops specialize in big corporate jobs, while others are mom-and-pop operations geared toward entrepreneurs with small business.

Lettershops generally charge by the type of service provided, says Don Golden of Action Communications in Boca Raton, Florida. There's a minimum fee for each type of service—for instance, inkjet-printing envelopes, inserting letters into envelopes, or sorting the finished product. Expect to pay a minimum of $100 to $300 per type of service, plus postage, which you pay to the shop so it can pay the post office.

Golden, whose firm works with large mail order companies only, suggests you check with the Mail Advertising Service Association, MASA, for information on reputable lettershops in your area, then call those shops to find out if they're geared toward your mail level. Don't forget to check references!

- You've still got to buy a rubber stamp and stamp each piece with your permit number and postage. Or rent a postage meter and shoot each piece through the meter. Or pay your printer to imprint each piece with your meter number and postage.

- Then you have to sort. And sort. And sort again. Check out "Fun with Mail Sorting" on page 121 to learn exactly how this is done.

- Then you have to take your mail trays to an official U.S. Postal Service bulk mail center.

Smart Tip

Your local print shop may offer *lettershop* services, handling not only insertions, stapling and folding but also bulk mail processing. And since you're giving them your printing business, you may be able to negotiate a cost-effective package deal.

The more pieces you send, the more cost-effective bulk mail becomes. If you're sending 6,000 letters, your cost is $1,680, compared with the first-class rate of $2,220—a $540 savings. Some mail order software programs will handle the sorting for you, which makes this even more appealing. (For Haven Corporation's Mail Order Wizard, for instance, you can purchase a bulk mail supplement called Mail List Monarch, which costs an additional $495.)

Endless Permutations

Not all bulk mail fits neatly into the one-ounce-for-28 cents category. The U.S. Postal Service has an entire 126-page *Quick Service Guide* devoted to endless permutations of mail sizes, weights, and categories, each with its own rules and regulations. And although the post office seems to have made a genuine effort to make this book user-friendly, it's not. There's a major learning curve, here. Of course, the folks down at your local bulk mail center are usually very friendly and will guide you through anything you need to know, but it's not as simple as licking a stamp and sticking it on your letter.

One issue to consider is the time factor. If you're anxious to get those letters to your customers, you might not want to go bulk mail. Bulk items can take up to two weeks for delivery, while first-class letters get the first-class treatment—usually two to four days for delivery.

Bright Idea

How about outsourcing your bulk mail sorting to a center for the disabled? Such an organization would be glad to take on the work, and you can usually negotiate a very reasonable fee.

You should also be aware that bulk rate letters are less likely to be opened by potential customers than first-class, stamped ones because they're perceived as junk mail. This is not to say that all bulk rate items get tossed—they don't. If your presentation is clever and well-conceived

▲

Smart Tip

Tip...

Who says the post office doesn't give immediate satisfaction? There's no waiting period on bulk mail or first-class mail permits. You can use them the same day you apply.

(see Chapter 10 for tips and tricks), you'll probably reach your target customers anyway.

What's the bottom line? How you handle your mailings is completely up to you. You decide which are the biggest issues—cost, labor, time, or customer perception—and what benefits you're actually gaining. To help you compare your options, we've provided a chart, "Bulk vs. First-Class Mail," on page 122. Don't forget that you can outsource your bulk mailings to a lettershop, fulfillment center, or printing house. You won't need a permit, and you won't need to spend time sorting and resorting. Be sure to check out these alternatives before making a final decision.

Have Your Cake

If you want a discount mailing rate, but you need the speed of first-class mail, you can more or less have your cake and eat it, too, by sending your pieces first-class presort. Here your cost is 30.5 cents per one-ounce piece. You must presort the same as you do for bulk mail and you have to purchase a first-class permit at an annual fee of $100. And where you need only mail 200 pieces to take advantage of the bulk mail rate, with first-class presort you have to send a minimum of 500 pieces.

If you like, you can buy both a bulk mail permit and a first-class permit and have the option of using either method at any time.

Fun with Mail Sorting

To take advantage of bulk mail prices, you have to presort your envelopes according to U.S. Postal Service guidelines. To get an idea of just what's involved, take a look at this nutshell explanation of how to sort standard mail, or, as the Postal Service calls it, the "packing and traying sequence." The people at the post office will provide you with rubber bands, trays, and stickers. They'll also give you help, so don't hesitate to ask for it.

	Five-Digit ZIPs	Three-Digit ZIPs	State-by-State	Leftovers
Sort	Sort all letters with identical five-digit ZIP codes.	Sort all letters with identical three-digit ZIP code prefixes.	Sort all letters going to the same state.	Sort all letters going everywhere else.
Bundle	Bundle into packs of ten or more with rubber bands.	Bundle into packs of ten or more with rubber bands.	Bundle into packs of ten or more with rubber bands.	Bundle into packs with rubber bands.
Label	Affix a red label "D" to top envelope.	Affix a green label "3" to top envelope.	Affix a pink label "A" to top envelope.	Affix a tan label "MXD" to top envelope.
Tray	Put bundles in trays; no partially filled trays permitted.	Put bundles in trays; one partially filled tray per destination permitted.	Put bundles in trays; no partially filled trays permitted.	Stick all leftover bundles in this tray.

Bulk vs. First-Class Mail

Issue	Bulk Rate	First-Class
Permit fees	Costs $200 (one-time fee of $100 and annual fee of $100)	No permit needed.
Cost for a 1-ounce letter in a #10 (business-sized) envelope	28 cents	37 cents
Stamping or metering	Buy a rubber stamp and imprint each piece with your meter number and postage. OR Rent a postage meter and shoot each piece through the meter. OR Pay your printer to imprint each piece with your meter number and postage.	Apply stamp.
Sorting	Mail must be sorted by five-digit ZIP codes, by three-digit ZIP codes, by state and by mixed parcels, and then set into trays. (See chart on page 121.)	No sorting necessary.
Mail drop-off	Mail must be delivered to a U.S. Postal Service bulk mail center.	Drop mail in any corner mailbox or take it to any post office.
Delivery time	10–14 days	2–4 days
Customer appeal	May be considered "junk mail" and discarded unopened.	Looks like mail from a "real" source and has a greater chance of being opened and read.

Sorting through
Business
Equipment

Your office will be your command center, the heart of your business, and the proper equipment will contribute greatly to your success. With the right tools, your operations will run smoothly, speedily, and efficiently; without them, your company will be like a small and rickety biplane delivering merchandise while your competition soars along in jumbo jets.

Photo© Adobe Image Library

Die-hard shoppers may be tempted to rush out and buy every item brand-spanking new, but this might not be necessary. Some or all of the equipment you'll need may already be sitting around in your home, just waiting to be put to use.

We've provided a handy checklist (see "The Mail Order Maven's Office Checklist" on page 141) to help you determine what you'll need, what you already have on hand and which of those in-stock items are ready for business. After you've read this chapter, run through the checklist and evaluate your stock. Is your computer mail order ready, or is it an antique that won't be able to keep up the pace? Does your answering machine take and receive clearly audible messages, or does it tend to garble crucial information? How about that printer? Can it produce professional-looking materials in short order, or does it take ages to spit out a solitary page?

> **Your computer will be the command center of your office setup.**

Let's get started on our business equipment shopping spree. What you'll be looking for, generally, are the middle-of-the-road models. Ready? Go!

Computer Glitterati

Your computer will be the command center of your office setup, coordinating your invoicing, accounting, word processing, database, and desktop publishing activities—

not to mention co-starring in all Web site activities and e-mail correspondence. It may be your most important start-up purchase. If you already own a computer, you will want to make sure it's capable of handling the tasks you'll assign it.

Now, while it is technically possible to start off without a computer system, if you opt for this method, you're asking to do things the good old-fashioned—and really hard—way. All the entrepreneurs we talked with have at least one computer, which they rely on to perform a variety of tasks.

With a good system as your silent partner, you can single-handedly perform more functions than you might believe possible. Just for starters, you can:

- Create your own catalog pages, display ads, and other direct-mail pieces
- Generate stationery, invoices, packing slips, certificates, and order forms
- Track orders
- Track inventory
- Perform accounting functions and generate financial reports
- Maintain databases of repeat and potential customers
- Access research materials and other resources online
- Sell via an online or "virtual" catalog
- Process credit card payments
- Communicate with repeat and potential customers via e-mail

Your new computer should have the Windows 95 or higher operating system. To run your software properly, you'll need 32MB to 48MB of RAM, plus at least a 3GB hard drive, a CD-ROM drive, and a 56Bps modem.

The leading light among computers sold in today's market is the Pentium-class PC, fully loaded with Windows XP, a modem, and usually enough peripheral software to keep you on a hyperactive learning curve for weeks. You can expect to pay $1,500 to $3,500 for a name-brand computer (not including printer), with prices increasing as you add on goodies.

Squint-Free Hours

Monitors are generally sold separately. You'll want an SVGA high-resolution color display and a screen large enough to make long-term viewing comfortable, say 17 inches. Remember that a few extra dollars spent upfront will save hours of squinting in the long haul. You can expect to dish out $300 to $400 for a solid, midrange model.

Snapshots

If you plan to produce your own Web site or your own advertising materials (or both), you'll definitely want a digital camera. With one of these wondrous tools, you simply snap a photo of your product, hook the camera up to your computer, move your mouse around a bit, and presto! —you've got the picture of your product right in your desktop publishing program. Expect to pay $400 to $700 for a good-quality digital camera.

Once the photo is in your computer, you can manipulate it in all sorts of interesting ways, acting as your own photo-finishing expert. You can crop it, expand it, zoom in or out on various features, blur the edges for that shot-through-gauze look, make it look like a watercolor, pastel, or oil painting, ad infinitum. This stuff is not only great for business purposes, it's a heck of a lot of fun! Some digital cameras, like Kodak's, come complete with photo-finishing software. Or you can purchase any number of programs, from Broderbund's Print Shop Deluxe, priced at about $50, to Adobe's Photoshop, which costs about $600.

Scanner, Anyone?

You may also want to consider buying a scanner, a nifty gadget you can purchase for $200 to $300 that imports or "pastes" graphics from just about any printed medium, including books, photographs, original art, advertising pieces, or postcards, into your desktop publishing program. But remember, you can't use anything someone else holds a copyright on, whether it's graphics, art images, or text, without permission. So make sure you've obtained permission to use any copyrighted material before you scan it into your catalog or other direct-mail piece.

Spare No Expense

To give you an idea of how much you can expect to budget, the "Equipment Expenses" chart on page 127 lets you check out the costs of software, equipment, and supplies for our two hypothetical mail order companies, Chocoholic Central and OnCall Designer. Chocoholic is a homebased newbie with no employees except its owner. The fledgling company's equipment includes an inexpensive computer system, an LED printer, and a SOHO (small office/home office, remember?) version mail order software package.

OnCall Designer, up and running for three years, makes its base in an office in an industrial park near the airport and has one full-time employee in addition to the owner. OnCall boasts a top-of-the-line computer system for its owner, an inexpensive computer for its employee, a laser printer, a combination fax/scanner, a copier, top-of-the line mail order software, and various publishing and marketing software programs.

Equipment Expenses

Furniture, Equipment, & Supplies	Chocoholic Central	OnCall Designer
Computer system (including printer)	$2,000	$4,000
Fax machine	250	700
Software	650	2,100
Phone system	70	160
Answering machine	40	130
Uninterruptible power supply	125	250
Surge protector	34	34
Calculator	15	50
Copier	N/A	700
Desk	200	600
Desk chair	60	200
Printer stand	N/A	70
File cabinet	25	200
Bookcase	70	70
Printer/copier paper	25	50
Packing/shipping supplies & equipment	350	500
Blank business cards	6	12
Letterhead paper	30	30
Matching envelopes	35	35
#10 blank envelopes	3	6
Address stamp or stickers	10	10
Extra printer cartridge	25	80
Extra fax cartridge	80	80
Mouse pad	10	20
Miscellaneous office supplies	100	150
Total Expenditures	**$4,213**	**$10,237**

Purring Printers

A good printer is a must. You'll want to produce all sorts of advertising materials, invoices, receipts, packing slips, mailing labels, thank you notes, contracts, statements, and sundry other materials, and they all need to look polished and professional. The materials you produce will be a direct reflection of your company. Shaky, faint dot-matrix printing looks amateurish. Sharp, bold graphics and print give your business an aura of confidence and success.

You also want a printer that's fast. There's nothing quite like the frustration of waiting for material to trickle out of a slow-going printer. One page per minute can seem like one page per hour.

Fortunately, really hot printers are much less expensive now than ever before. You can purchase an LED, which virtually simulates the higher-ticket laser printer, or an inkjet, many of which can produce all the wonderful colors of commercial artwork. Color-capable models print more slowly than their black-and-white colleagues, but if you'll be doing lots of marketing materials like brochures and newsletters, color should be a consideration. You can expect to pay $200 to $1,000 for a color inkjet or laser printer.

Just the Fax

The fax machine, as we've discussed, is a must for the mail order maven. Along with e-mail, it's the method of choice for communicating quickly and clearly with customers, manufacturers, and vendors—including importers and exporters around the globe. (And don't forget faxing lunch orders to that deli down the street.)

A fax machine can be purchased for about $700 as part of a multifunction device, a peripheral unit that serves as a fax, copier, printer, and scanner. These devices can be slow when used as a printer so be sure to check before you buy. Also, make sure the fax machine you purchase will print on plain paper. Most of the documents you receive will be keepers—correspondence, invoices, and the like—that will need to go into your permanent files. The ink on thermal fax paper fades to near invisibility in a short time, thus negating any archiving attempts. A plain-paper fax machine will cost about $250.

> **Tip...**
>
> **Smart Tip**
>
> Sending information to suppliers by fax is more businesslike than calling with a list of figures. It's also far less expensive. And if you're working with importers, the fax machine can place a call overseas at any hour of the day or night and transmit your message faster than you can—it doesn't have to spend time on formal greetings or chitchat before getting down to business.

Software that Sorts!

The mail order entrepreneurs we interviewed for this book held mixed views on whether, as a newbie, you should spend your money on special mail order software or whether you can start off with a good general accounting program. Industry experts, however, feel you should definitely go with specialized software. Here's why:

- The biggest advantage to industry-specific software is, of course, that it's tailored to the needs of a mail order company. You don't need to spend time tweaking some other program to "force" it to do what you want, or compromise on your needs.

- Sooner or later you're going to grow enough to really need the industry-specific stuff. Why not start off with it so there's no big switch midstream when you may not have the time to change gears?

- A starter package, which you can upgrade later, is not really that much more expensive than the nonspecific programs.

- If you use a call center to handle your order processing, and you and the call center use the same mail-order-specific software, you can get instant feedback any time you like. "Order processing information appears in your system as if you had input it," says Tony Romano, owner of All USA, a call center in Westchester, Illinois.

> **Tip...**
>
> **Smart Tip**
>
> No matter how user-friendly a software package is, there will be times when you'll need hand-holding. So when you shop, be sure to ask what sort of technical support comes with the software.

Mail order software prices can vary dramatically, depending on how many fancy add-ons you go for and what customer volume you anticipate. Start-up entrepreneurs can expect to pay anywhere from $299 to $1,595 for a system that handles order entry, inventory, customer and list management, order fulfillment (labels, invoices, etc.), and ad tracking. How could you go wrong?

Basic-model mail order software packages often contain only a few of the functions listed on our "Mail Order Software Checklist" on page 131. While you can routinely expect functions like order entry and mailing list management, other goodies—such as credit card processing and bar code printing—are usually sold as add-ons.

When you're evaluating software, eliminate packages that don't completely satisfy your needs. If you'll want to field order status inquiries over the phone, for instance, you can exclude software that can't do the job.

In selecting your software, you'll also need to consider potential performance issues. Some programs can handle mailing lists containing literally millions of names. Others choke on 3,000 labels. The same goes for the number of orders per day. Some systems hum along with thousands, while others peak at 50 to 100. Good program vendors can tell you if their product will work for you now and in the future based on your company estimates.

Item counts and item identification systems can be tricky, too. Find out how many products the program can handle and how it copes with size, color, style, and other issues unique to your operation. What happens if somebody orders more items than will fit on one invoice or packing slip? Can the program sail sunnily along, or does it glitch up and force you to create multiple orders?

Can the program generate reports that will be specific enough for your needs? If you want to see summaries of all men's sweater orders or determine your most popular boot sizes, now's the time to think about it.

More food for thought: If you will handle perishable products like foods, find out how the software will track in-and-out dates. Will it automatically warn you of pending problems?

Can the order processing software be gracefully interrupted midorder? If the answer is yes, this feature will allow you to enter mailed or faxed-in orders during telephone lulls. What you don't want is for customers to have to wait while you finish entering a mailed-in order.

Remember that mailing lists—the manna of your business—need to be as clean as possible. With soaring printing and postage costs, you can't afford to send three or four identical catalogs to the same address. Make sure the software can eliminate duplicate names. Then find out if the following apply:

- Can you identify big spenders as well as inactive names? If you rent names from somebody else, can you merge them easily with your own list?
- Can you track the use of rented names and identify their sources?
- If you decide to sell or rent your own lists, can the software export this data to a diskette?

Software for Other Stuff

A dazzling array of software lines the shelves of most office supply stores, ready to help you perform just about every general business task. You can design and print your own checks, develop professional-quality marketing materials, make mailing lists and labels, and even act as your own accountant and attorney, all with the help of various software programs.

Mail Order Software Checklist

Use this checklist to help determine which software program is best for you. First, make copies so you've got one for each candidate. Then go down the list and decide which items are must-haves and which ones you won't need—at least in your first year or two. Most systems let you upgrade as you grow. Check off your must-haves. Cross out the don't-needs, if you like. Then compare!

Software Candidate:_____

❏ Maintains and updates mailing lists, including address correction and merge/purge, which means combining duplicate list entries into one and purging invalid entries, such as those for people who have moved and provided no forwarding address

❏ Helps salespeople with telephone order processing and answers order status inquiries

❏ Automatically creates invoices

❏ Computes postage shipping charges

❏ Profiles customers by capturing information like past purchases and average order amount

❏ Tracks inventory and notifies you when it's time to reorder

❏ Tracks in-and-out dates of perishable products

❏ Automates credit card approvals

❏ Tracks in-house credit accounts

❏ Holds orders pending receipt of payment

❏ Creates shipping paperwork

❏ Prints labels, packing slips, price tickets, and shelf labels

❏ Creates and reads bar-code labels

❏ Tracks and fills back orders

❏ Issues FTC back-order notifications

❏ Sends personalized letters and order forms

❏ Analyzes and reports sales trends

❏ Handles discount arrangements

❏ Handles sales commissions

❏ Tracks success of ads and catalogs

❏ Uses multiple printers (to eliminate paper swaps)

▲

You Better Shop Around

Your software is probably going to be your closest partner—after your call center, if you decide to use one—so choose carefully. The list of software helpmates is lengthy, with a variety of capabilities and prices available.

Some packages are set up based on customer volume and product limits. Haven Corporation, for instance, offers everything from the WizKid, capable of handling up to 80 products and a mailing list of 5,000, to the Wizard, which can handle 5,400 products and a mailing list of 4 million. The WizKid goes for $795, while the big-budget-sized Wizard is priced at $7,495.

Core Technology's Mailware comes in the SE version (designed especially for the SOHO) and a standard version, priced at $299 and $799, respectively.

Most software companies will send you a demo version on diskette or CD if you call and ask. So take that test drive before you plunk down your money.

Most new computers come preloaded with all the software you'll need for basic office procedures. If yours doesn't, you may want to look into the following types of programs:

- *Word processing.* You'll need a word processing program, which allows you to write correspondence, contracts, sales reports, and whatever else strikes your fancy. A good basic program such as Microsoft Word or Corel WordPerfect will cost $60 to $220.

- *Accounting.* You may also want an accounting program such as QuickBooks (which is recommended by many mail order mavens who prefer not to start with the industry-specific stuff) or Microsoft Money to track your business finances. These are a sort of checkbook on a CD and make record-keeping a breeze. You assign categories such as office supplies and business travel to the checks you write, and at tax time you print out a report showing how much you spent for what. Your accountant not only thanks you but also gives you a discount for not having to wade through all your receipts. You can expect to pay $49 to $199 for your virtual checkbook.

- *Desktop publishing.* For those polished marketing materials, you'll want a desktop publishing program, such as My Marketing Materials by My Software. It's user-friendly, with a lot of depth and a lot of breadth, multiple formats and multiple layouts. And it's customizable. You can expect to pay $29 to $49 for this type of program.

- *List management.* You can purchase a list management program like Parsons Technology's Ultimate Mail Manager, which includes U.S. Postal Service certified technology for ZIP code accuracy, for about $60.

The Power Touch

If you're going to be a one-person order-processing department, with one ear to stick to the phone, one voice to answer with and two hands to take orders, you've got a problem. If your advertising methods have been effective, you'll discover early on that you can't handle the call volume. Impatient potential customers often hang up if placed on hold for too long, causing you to miss sales.

As that one-person department, your options for handling multiple calls boil down to the following:

- Contract with a call center.
- Purchase a two- or three-line phone, and put callers on hold.
- Purchase a phone with "power touch" capability and "memory call" service.

With power touch, you get the junior version of the big companies' on-hold messages. Say you are taking one customer's order and another customer calls in. A red light blinks on your phone. You push a button and your second customer hears the familiar litany: "Your call is important to us. All of our customer representatives are busy. Please hold for the next available representative." (Or words to that effect.)

This is great—except that if a third customer calls in, he gets diverted to voice mail (via memory call service) and is asked to leave a message. And people often don't want to leave a message. Or they leave before you can get back to them. Or they find something else to order from someone else.

Still, this option may work for you if you will have a limited or spread out call volume, or if you will have close-knit customers who will leave a message. If you think power touch might be your ticket, expect to pay about $240 for the phone itself and an extra $7 per month for the memory call service.

Call Center

Another solution to the problem of making sure all your calls are answered is to contract with a *call center*. The call center lets you handle any call volume. It gives your customers the ability to place orders 24 hours a day, seven days a week. And it gives your start-up, one-person company the ambience of a major mail order operation.

Bright Idea

If you decide to start out answering your own phone, interview call centers anyway. Find one you like, then ask how long it takes to get set up and what you'll need to provide so that when you're ready to outsource, everything will be in place.

Once you establish your toll-free number with a long-distance carrier, you can arrange for the call center to handle calls using one of several options:

- *Answer your call overflow with alternate-destination routing.* The call center takes over if your phone goes unanswered after a set number of rings or if your line is busy.

- *Answer after hours with time-of-day re-routing.* The call center takes over at a preset time each evening and then releases calls back to you at a preset time each morning.

- *Answer all the time.* The call center handles all your calls, leaving you free for other tasks. According to Tony Romano of All USA, most start-up mail order mavens choose this option, requesting that only customer service calls be routed to them.

What's the bottom line? Try negotiating for these options:

- *Price per minute.* A typical order, Romano explains, takes about 3 to 3½ minutes to process and is billed at 60 cents to $1 per minute, based on the complexity of your orders. If your catalog is very specific, for instance, and your customer can easily say, "I want size small in red" and be done with it, you'll be charged less per order than if the order processor has to guide the customer through each step and explain things along the way. Price-per-minute is the standard call center billing method.

- *Price based on call type.* You might set up a program with the call center where you pay different fixed amounts based on whether the incoming call is for an order, a catalog request, or some miscellaneous objective.

Weird Hours

What's the prime shopping time for catalog purchasers? Later than you might think. "Most of our evening calls come from moms whose kids are finally asleep and they've found a moment to shop," says Caryn O., the fabric merchandiser. "Those kinds of people shop anywhere from 9 P.M. to midnight."

That's why Caryn's phones are answered by order processors from six in the morning until the witching hour. For those wee hours in between, when her company receives the least number of calls, she relies on an answering machine.

In Overland Park, Kansas, Kate W.'s phone is answered 24 hours a day, either by an answering service or by Kate herself. "As a catalog shopper myself," the former bookkeeper explains, "I shop at weird hours, after everybody's gone to bed. Eleven or 12 at night is when I sit down and go through my catalogs. So having 24-hour service was the first thing we decided on."

Line of Defense

A good call center will work with you at every step along the way. "We're your first line of defense," says call-center owner Tony Romano. "And we are a partnership."

When you contract with a call center, you'll provide order processors with a list of questions your customers may ask and what the answers should be. Then, as the call center works with your customers and products, it will likely provide you with a list of questions to answer—things that will help the order processors better serve your customers. The call center will also share hints, tips, and tricks of the trade to help you develop the best product codes and the best catalog copy.

Take advantage!

- *Price based on up-selling or cross-selling.* Here you're billed the same rate as in a price-per-minute setup but with an additional "commission" to the call center based on the revenue from each order. Why would you want to pay extra? The bonus rate acts as an incentive or motivator for the call center to up-sell and cross-sell.

Other fees you can expect to pay, Romano advises, are:

- An initial deposit of $200 to $300
- A monthly minimum of $75 to $100, or the actual per-minute amount, whichever is higher
- A setup fee of $250 if you choose to have the call center enter all your products into the software, assign product codes, and perform any other functions needed to get your operation computer ready. If you choose to set up your own program, the setup fee will be waived.

Take a Message

Even if you go with a call center, you'll still need a "substitute you" to answer your office phone. You won't always be at your desk—sometimes you'll be at the post office or UPS outpost, attending trade shows, or interfacing with vendors and suppliers. During these times, you'll need somebody or something to answer your phone. A Murphy's Law of business life is that people most often call when:

- You're not in your office.
- You're sitting down to a meal.
- You're in the bathroom.

Beware!
Don't "enhance" your answering machine message with background music or a cutesy script. It's not professional. Keep it short and simple. Give your company's name—spoken clearly and carefully—and ask the callers to leave a short message and a phone number. Thank them for calling and assure them that someone from your office will return their call as soon as possible.

Another business life law is that an unanswered phone is extremely unprofessional. And in mail order, it can be deadly.

Your call center's order processors will deal with customers, not with your manufacturers, suppliers, and other behind-the-scenes types. So you need to think about who—or what—will act as your secretary when you're not available. One solution is voice mail, the phone company's answer to the answering machine—with a few nice twists.

Like an answering machine, voice mail takes your messages when you're not in the office. If you have call waiting, a feature that discreetly beeps to announce an incoming call while you're already on the phone, and you choose not to answer that second call, voice mail will take a message for you. With voice mail, as with many answering machines, you can access your messages from a remote location.

Voice mail costs depend on your local phone company and the features you choose, but you can expect to pay $6 to $20 a month.

Fancy Gizmos

If you choose not to go with voice mail from your local phone company, you'll need an answering machine. Unless you want to put your business greeting on your home machine and risk having your kids erase the messages left for you, you should purchase a separate machine for your office.

The models on the market now are digital, which means they don't have audiotapes to get knotted or broken. There are also all sorts of fancy gizmos complete with Caller ID, speakerphones, cordless phones, and 15 kinds of memos, but a good, basic model capable of answering your business line can be purchased for about $40. For a snazzier model that can answer two lines, you can expect to pay about $150.

Hello Central

Now for the telephone itself. You will probably have three telephone lines coming into your home, two of which will be for your office. Therefore, unless you've opted for the power touch contraption, you'll want a two-line phone so you can put one on hold while you're answering the other. You can divide up the three lines any way you like: You might put your home line and your business line on the two-line phone, leaving the third line for your fax machine and modem.

Or you might put the business and fax-modem line on the two-line phone, leaving your home line in the kitchen or den. The idea behind either of these choices is that you can call out on your home or fax-modem line (when it's not in use) and leave the business line for incoming calls.

Smart Tip *Tip...*

Is talking on the phone getting to be a pain in the neck? Switch to a headset, which will increase your productivity.

Whichever option you choose, you will want the telephone itself to have two lines that can be put on hold. This way business callers can't hear you explaining to your children why they cannot have a nose ring when they call you collect from the mall.

A speaker is also a nice feature, especially for all those on-hold-forever calls to your banker, attorney, insurance company, and the like. Your hands are free to work on

Read All About It!

Make sure your brain is as well-equipped as your office. One of your first steps in your new venture should be to read everything you can, not just about the specifics of international trade but about starting a small business and about marketing and sales techniques. Blitz the bookstore. Make an assault on your public library.

Your own business library should contain a plethora of reference manuals. For starters, check out the following:

- ○ *Building a Mail Order Business: A Complete Manual for Success* (John Wiley & Sons) by William A. Cohen, Ph.D.
- ○ *Home-Based Mail Order, A Success Guide for Entrepreneurs* (McGraw-Hill) by William J. Bond
- ○ *How to Start a Mail Order Business* (Avon Books) by Mike Powers
- ○ *How to Start and Operate a Mail-Order Business* (McGraw-Hill) by Julian L. Simon
- ○ *Start Your Own Homebased Business*, Entrepreneur's business start-up guide (Entrepreneur Media Inc.)
- ○ *Successful Sales & Marketing*, Entrepreneur's business start-up guide (Entrepreneur Media Inc.)

Don't stop with these. Immerse yourself in your subject. The more you know, the better mail order maven you'll be. Read all about it financial data or your latest advertising materials, your shoulder remains un-hunched, and you're free to move about the cabin while you listen to Muzak and wait your turn.

You can expect to pay about $70 to $80 for a two-line speakerphone with auto redial, memory dial, a mute button, and other assorted goodies.

Laugh at Lightning

You should invest in a UPS, or uninterruptible power supply (not to be confused with UPS, the shipping service), for your computer system, especially if you live in an area where lightning or power surges are frequent. If you're a computer newbie, you may not realize that even a flicker of power loss can shut down your computer, causing it to forget all the data you've carefully entered during your work session, or—the ultimate horror—fry your computer's brains entirely. With a UPS in your arsenal, you won't lose power to your system when your house's power flickers or fails. Instead, the unit flashes red and sounds a warning, giving you ample time to safely shut down your computer.

If you'll be spending a lot of time online and connecting to the Internet through the standard dial-up method, using your computer's modem and your telephone line, you want to be sure that your UPS includes phone line protection. You can expect to pay $125 and up for one of these power pals.

Lightning Strikes Again

A surge protector safeguards your electronic equipment from power spikes during storms and outages. Your UPS will double as a surge protector for your computer hard drive, or CPU, and your monitor, but you'll want protection for those other valuable office allies: your printer, fax machine, and copier. These devices don't need a UPS because no data will be lost if the power goes out; a surge protector will do the job for a lot less money. If you've got a fax machine, be sure the surge protector also defends its phone line. You can expect to pay in the range of $15 to $60.

Cool and Calculating

What do calculators and telephones have in common? A numbered keypad and an important place on your desk. Even though your computer probably has an onboard calculator program, it helps to have the real thing close at hand. You can do quick calculations and then check your work with the paper tape. Expect to pay under $15 for a battery-operated model and $25 to $50 for a plug-in job.

Stress Buster

Unless you plan to walk or bicycle to the post office every day as a form of exercise and stress relief, getting a postage meter is a good idea. Depending on the model you choose, you can not only stamp your mail but also fold, staple, insert, seal, label, weigh, sort, stack, and wrap it. Phew! The fancier and faster the machine, the more expensive it will be to rent, lease, or purchase. It used to be that you'd have to lug your postage meter down to the post office and

> **Smart Tip** Tip...
>
> Presorting bulk mail takes time, but it will save you money. You can also outsource sorting.

stand in line to get it reset. Not anymore! Now you reset your meter by phone or computer. What's the cost for all this technology? It depends on what you get, but as a ballpark figure, you can expect to rent a postage meter/electronic scale combo for anywhere from $24 to $117 per month.

If you're really into automation, you can also purchase letter-folding and letter-opening machines, which can process up to 4,000 sheets per hour and 600 envelopes per minute, respectively. You probably won't need this type of speed immediately (and if you go with a lettershop, you won't need it at all), but you should know that these gizmos are available.

Paper Cloning

A copier is an optional item, probably the least important on the list, but as you grow, you may find it a worthwhile convenience. Keep in mind that you should never send a piece of paper out of your office unless you've kept a copy. You can always print two copies of every document you generate on your computer, keeping one as a file copy. Copiers range from $250 to $600 and up.

Step into My Office

> **Smart Tip** Tip...
>
> Want to keep your equipment costs way down? Consider launching from a business incubator, where services, facilities, and equipment are shared among several businesses.

Office furniture is also optional. It is important that your work environment be comfortable and ergonomic, but if you're homebased, it's perfectly acceptable to start off with an old door set on cinder blocks for a desk and an egg crate for your files. When you are ready to make the move toward real office furniture for that oh-so-professional look, you've got a stunning array of options to choose from.

We shopped the big office supply stores and found midrange desks from $200 to $300, a computer work center for $200, printer stands from $50 to $75, two-drawer letter-size file cabinets (which can double as your printer stand) from $25 to $100, and a four-shelf bookcase for $70.

▲

Chairs are a very personal matter. Some people like the dainty secretary's chair for its economy of space; others want the high-back executive model. There are chairs with kangaroo pockets and chairs with pneumatic height adjustments. Prices range from $60 to $250.

Pick and Pack

The last item on our shopping extravaganza list—and probably the least important for the start-up entrepreneur—is a *pick and pack*, or fulfillment service. If you choose this option, you'll have the packing, wrapping, and shipping stuff done for you. And you'll have the warehousing done for you as well, since the service will have to maintain your inventory at its site in order to access it.

To take advantage of this type of service, according to Tony Romano of All USA, you're looking at $1 to $2 per box, depending on the size and type of product, plus the cost of the boxes and shipping materials. You'll also have to set up an escrow/drawing account with the fulfillment service for postage and delivery fees.

Tip...

Smart Tip

Not using a pick and pack service? A hand truck, otherwise known as a dolly, can be a back saver when you need to cart around large packages for shipping or storage. Dollies come with a variety of features, from safety straps to cushioning, and they will cost you anywhere from $45 to $300.

The Office Supplies Mini Shopping List	
Computer/copier/fax paper	$_____
Blank business cards	_____
Blank letterhead stationery and matching envelopes	_____
File folders	_____
Return address self-stamper or stickers	_____
Extra printer cartridges	_____
Mouse pad	_____
Miscellaneous office supplies (pencils, paper clips, etc.)	_____
Extra fax cartridges	_____
Total Office Supplies Expenditures	$_____

The Mail Order Maven's Office Checklist

Use this list as a shopping guide for equipping your office. It's been designed with the one-person home office in mind. If you've got partners or employees, or you just inherited a million dollars from a mysterious foundation with the stipulation that you spend at least half on office equipment, you may want to make modifications.

After you've done your shopping, fill in the price next to each item and add up the total. This will tell you about how much you can expect to spend on the equipment you need.

High-Priority

❏ Windows XP-based Pentium-class PC with
   SVGA monitor, modem, and CD-ROM drive $ _____

❏ Laser or inkjet printer   _____

❏ Fax machine   _____

❏ Mail order software   _____

❏ Word processing software   _____

❏ Desktop publishing software   _____

❏ Accounting software   _____

❏ Phones, two to three lines with voice mail or...   _____

❏ Answering machine   _____

❏ Uninterruptible power supply   _____

❏ Zip drive (if not included in computer)   _____

❏ Surge protector   _____

❏ Calculator   _____

❏ Postage meter/scale   _____

❏ Office supplies (see "Office Supplies Mini Shopping List," p. 140) _____

Not on the Critical List

❏ Digital camera   _____

❏ Scanner   _____

❏ Copier   _____

❏ Postage meter   _____

❏ Dolly   _____

❏ Desk   _____

❏ Desk chair   _____

❏ Filing cabinet   _____

❏ Bookcase   _____

Total Office Equipment and Furniture Expenditures $ _____

Return Address
Your Business Location and Employees

Every business needs a base—a safe, secure spot in which to create and implement plans, carry out operations, and deal with customers and their orders. Every business, as it grows, generally reaches the point where it needs employees to help it achieve long-term success. In this chapter, we will explore the secrets of choosing the perfect location and hiring the best employees.

Choosing a Location

As we've explained, one of the perks of running a mail order business is that it lends itself ideally to the homebased entrepreneur. Mail order doesn't require a high-traffic or high-visibility location, so you don't need to set up shop in a trendy part of town. Because all your business is virtual, you won't need a mahogany-paneled office with a lobby and conference room in order to impress or entertain clients. The only space requirement is an area large enough for your desk, your chair, your filing cabinets, and perhaps a bookshelf.

The home office is convenient: You couldn't get any closer to your work unless you slept with your computer and your telephone. It's economical: You don't need to spend money on leased space, extra utilities, transportation costs, or lunches down at the corner grill.

Working at home is not, however, mandatory. You may want to leave your laundry, your dog, and your loving-but-noisy family at home while you go off to an office space that's quiet (except for those ringing phones), clean, and yours alone.

The Home Office

If you choose to be homebased, you can locate your office work space anywhere in the house that's convenient, but ideally, you should have a dedicated office, a room that's reserved just for the business. You can locate this room in a den, a FROG (finished room over garage), the garage itself or a spare bedroom. Keep in mind that whatever space you choose will be your workstation and command center.

Bright Idea

Some homes, especially older ones, have walk-in closets that are large enough to turn into a cozy little office—some even have windows. If your closet is of the sliding-doors, runs-along-one-wall variety, take out the clothes and stash them somewhere. Remove the doors, and you've got a dandy office nook! If you decide to turn your closet into an office, make sure it has adequate ventilation and light.

If a dedicated office is not an option, you can also station yourself in a corner of the kitchen or at the dining room table. If you've got a boisterous family, however, a cubbyhole in your bedroom is liable to be much more conducive to quiet, clear thinking than a nook in the family room with the TV blaring at all hours. Also remember that yelling into the phone over cartoon *kerblam*s and *pow*s will not give your customers confidence in your company's soundness and reliability.

Kate W., in Overland Park, Kansas, bases her business in her home. She starts early and works late into the night, but even so, she's around for her family. In

Roswell, Georgia, Caryn O. also maintains a home office, although most of her business operations, along with her 10 employees, call a large warehouse "home." "I keep a home office," the textiles merchandiser explains, "where I do my scanning [onto the company Web site]." Along with a great many other tasks. "In the morning, between getting my [daughter] off to school," Caryn says, "I'm on the Internet answering e-mail. Then I'm off to work. Then I leave at a certain time to get my daughter off the bus. When I get home, I am back on the computer answering e-mail and scanning in or deleting fabrics from the Web site. And I'm always in contact with the people at the warehouse."

The Tax Man Speaketh

A big advantage to the home office is the ability to wear two hats—to be at home with your family and be at work at the same time. Another advantage is the ability to count your home business as a tax write-off. The IRS will graciously allow you to deduct money from your income taxes if you're using a portion of your home as your income-producing work space. You can deduct a percentage of expenses

> **Smart Tip** Tip...
>
> Check out Entrepreneur's business start-up guide *Start Your Own Home-based Business,* for more information on tax laws affecting homebased businesses.

equivalent to the percentage of space your home office occupies. If, for example, you're using one room in an eight-room house, you can deduct one-eighth of your rent or mortgage plus one-eighth of your utility bills.

There is, of course, an "if" involved here. You can only use this deduction if you're using a space in your home solely as your office. If you have turned your spare bedroom into your office and you don't use it for anything but conducting your business, then you qualify. If, however, your office is tucked into a corner of the kitchen, and you're still feeding people in there, you don't qualify for the home office deduction (unless you can convince the IRS that you order Chinese every night and the refrigerator is actually a file cabinet.)

Organized and Efficient

If you prefer to have your coffee and croissant—and your office—in your home, it's important to remember that you're still a professional. Your work quarters, like yourself, should be organized and efficient. If at all possible, designate a separate room with four walls and a door. Aim for pleasant, quiet, well-lit surroundings. You're going to be spending a lot of time in this space, so you want it to be comfortable.

If you can't carve out a dedicated space, by all means take over a corner of another room. But consider it your permanent office. Clearing your work materials off the dining room table before meals is a definite drag.

Beware!

Be sure to print and file hard copies of all e-mail correspondence sent to you and all missives you send to others. Keeping everything on your computer's hard drive may seem like a swell paper-saving idea, but if your computer crashes, you will lose everything (including, temporarily, your mind). The same goes for computerized databases of customers, manufacturers, and the like.

Appropriate a desk or a table large enough to hold your computer, keyboard, phone, pencil holder, stapler, etc., and still have enough room left to spread out your working papers. A charming 19th-century cherry wood secretary looks great but probably won't allow enough space for your files—and you and your computer. Don't skimp on elbow room.

Your main realms of activity will be advertising, order processing, administration, and shipping. Make sure you have enough space to store currently running and already-tried ads and catalogs, as well as files for current and potential advertising venues, manufacturers, suppliers, and customer service issues. Whether you use the fanciest hanging file folders in mahogany drawers or simple manila ones in

Prestige Address

You've decided on a home office. Now what about your address? Mail order mavens have mixed views on this issue. Some feel that since customers do occasionally decide to pay a surprise visit, it's best to rent a post office box and preserve your privacy. Others believe that a post office box instead of a street address gives customers the idea that you're a fly-by-night operation.

One way to maintain your privacy and keep a "real" address is to rent a box from a company like Mail Boxes Etc. You use the rental facility's physical address and add a "suite" number to distinguish your box from those of the facility's other patrons. Your customers, however, won't know the difference.

The only drawback to this system, of course, is that you have to pop over to the facility every time you want your mail, whereas if you stick to your home address, the postman brings it to your door. (Mail centers will provide you with a key so you can check your box after hours.)

Another plus for the mail center option: When you have inventory shipped to you, UPS will quote and guarantee delivery dates if you have packages sent to a "business" address. But if they come to your home office, they consider it a residential delivery and will not guarantee dates.

The Home Office Worksheet

Use this handy worksheet to locate and design your home office.

List three possible locations in your home for your office, which should include a work area for you and enough space for your desk, computer, and telephone:

1. _____

2. _____

3. _____

Make a physical survey of each location:

- ○ Are phone and electrical outlets placed so that your equipment can easily access them? Or will you be faced with unsightly, unsafe cords snaking across the carpet?
- ○ Measure your space. Will your current desk or table (or the one you have your eye on) fit?
- ○ Do you have adequate lighting? If not, can you create or import it?
- ○ Is there proper ventilation?
- ○ What is the noise factor?
- ○ Is there room to spread out your work?
- ○ Optional: How close is it to the coffeemaker? Refrigerator? (This can be either a plus or minus, depending on your current jitter factor and waistline.)

Next, list three possible home locations for your inventory:

1. _____

2. _____

3. _____

Again, make a survey of each location:

- ○ Is it climate-controlled? Will you need climate control?
- ○ Is there adequate lighting, ventilation and space for you to easily access your inventory?

The Home Office Worksheet, continued

○ Will you need to construct special shelving or add other storage space? If so, make notes here:

_____

_____

_____

Finally, take a look at your packing and shipping space options. Make a list:

1. _____

2. _____

3. _____

Ask yourself:

❏ Will you have an adequate, well-lit work space?

❏ Is there room to stash and easily access packing, gift-wrapping, and shipping materials and tools?

cardboard boxes, you must be able to access this information quickly and easily. It's no fun digging through the back of the clothes closet or running out to the garage every time somebody calls with a question.

You'll also need enough space to package your products for shipping. It doesn't matter if it's the kitchen table or a special workstation in your office, so long as there's adequate room to spread out your materials and wrap that package professionally.

And don't forget your catalogs, brochures, or other mail-out materials! You will need easily accessible boxes or shelves where you can keep these items safe, clean, and tidy at all times.

Growing Pains

As your business grows, you may decide to move into a commercial office space. Because the mail order business doesn't rely on client traffic or a prestige address, any area that appeals to you and your pocketbook is up for grabs. Rents in high-traffic areas like malls or trendy downtown shopping districts can be astronomical, so don't set your sights on them. Instead, try going the office/warehouse route in an industrial park. If product storage, rather than room for people, is your only problem, you might consider keeping your home office and renting space from a self-storage facility, as Kate, the team logo merchandiser, has done.

Beth H., the gluten-free foods specialist, houses her company, along with her ten employees, in an industrial park. The site features office space with an adjacent warehouse.

If storage is not a concern for you, but you want an office away from home, you might look for commercial space in other areas—but not in the retail arena. You don't need the high visibility, or the higher rent that goes with it.

Greer T., the children's boutiquer, has put this maxim to work in the location of her combined mail order/retail operation "I'm in more of an office area," the Canton, Ohio, mom explains. "It's kind of off the beaten track. It probably hinders me that I'm not in a mall area. But it helps me because I don't have the big overhead or the big mall lease."

Freeze or Melt

The biggest factor in your decision whether to have a home or away office—other than you and your family's personal preferences and lifestyle—will be inventory storage. Take these questions into consideration:

- How large will your products be?
- How diverse are they?
- Will they require special handling or storage?
- Can they survive in a spare bedroom or the garage, or will they need controlled conditions?

If you're selling Foods from New England's Shores, for example, you won't get very far storing Maine lobster or cod in the garage (unless it's an unheated one in the dead of winter). You'll need refrigeration. And if you're selling candles in New Orleans, you may want to think twice about storing them in your garage in the summer (unless you're going for the naturally melted look).

Your Cargo Bay

Commercial mail order facilities usually range in floor size from 2,000 to 5,000 square feet and are divided into office and inventory storage spaces. Obviously, the more storage space you have, the more inventory you can house. But don't overextend your "cargo bay" and skimp on the area allocated to humans—you'll still need a command center for your shipping, receiving, order processing, and administrative work.

Whether your office is in an artist's loft, over a bagel bakery, or in an industrial park, you'll need the same basic setup as in a home office, with plenty of room for

Bright Idea

Contact a realtor for help finding office and warehouse space. Besides giving you the lowdown on the local rental market, your realtor may have a mailing list you can beg, borrow, or rent inexpensively.

all those files, plus your desk, chair, minimalist visitors' furniture, and a desk and chair for any employee(s) you may hire. And let's not forget the electronics. Whether in a home or commercial office, your computer should occupy a place of honor, away from dirt, drafts, and blinding sunlight. Ditto for your printer and fax machine.

In a commercial office, you'll also want that altarpiece of American offices, the coffeemaker. And if you can provide a tidbit or two—a plate of cookies, for example, when you know those rare visitors (like manufacturers' reps) are arriving—you'll go a long way toward cementing ties. Everyone appreciates a treat!

Alternative Officing

If commercial office space is not your bag, you might consider a less conventional approach. You can rent a house or an apartment (providing you check the zoning laws first). If you already live in an apartment, you may choose to rent another unit in the same building to use as your office. You can walk to work. And the landlord may give you a package deal—or a finder's fee!

You might work out a rental arrangement with a colleague in another type of business who has extra space and needs a little extra income. How about an artist who needs lots of work space but can't quite afford that midtown loft? (Make sure you make arrangements for partition walls or alternate work hours so your ringing phones don't drive your officemate nuts.) Or what about a newbie real estate agent who'd like help with her office rent in exchange for office space? (Ringing phones in the background make realtors look good.)

You could always rent your own space over a downtown storefront. How about over a coffeehouse or donut shop or bagel bakery? What better incentive to get to work in the morning?

Hiring Employees

Depending on how much growth you envision for your business, you may never need employees. But you may expand to the point where you can't do everything yourself—the point where you'll need to consider taking on assistants. Employees are another of those funny facts of life that seem to bring with them as many cons as pros.

One of the many perks of the mail order business is that you can accomplish a great deal without ever hiring anyone.

When you hire help, you're not a swinging single anymore. You've got responsibilities. Suddenly there's payroll to meet, workers' compensation insurance to pay, state and federal employee taxes to pay. And work to delegate.

Some people are born employers, finding it easy to teach someone else the ropes and then hand over the reins. Others never feel quite comfortable telling someone else what to do or how to do it.

One of the many perks of the mail order business is that you can accomplish a great deal without ever hiring anyone. You can easily start out as a one-person show, handling all the tasks of your fledgling company yourself. You won't need help immediately. But as your company flourishes, you may one day find that: a) you need more hours in a day, b) you need science to make great strides in the field of cloning, or c) you need to hire help.

One Singular Sensation

Most of the work in a mail order business can be more or less compartmentalized into three areas:

1. Sales and marketing
2. Order processing and fulfillment
3. General management and administration

As a newbie mail order operator, you will probably have all three areas handled by one person: you. You'll have to be, as the song says, one singular sensation—capable of wearing a lot of hats and tap dancing your way through every routine in your company. You'll need to:

- Conceive and direct extensive marketing campaigns that will garner sales
- Design and produce ads, brochures, catalogs, or other direct-mail pieces
- Write ad, brochure, or catalog copy
- Manage order taking
- Fulfill orders
- Keep the books
- Rent and maintain mailing lists
- Handle customer service
- Deal with manufacturers and suppliers
- Seek out new inventory where no mail order maven has gone before

In addition to all this, you'll be expected to eat, sleep, bathe periodically, dress yourself, and carry on a normal family and social life. And as your company grows, you may eventually discover that you can't do it all yourself (except—hopefully—for the eat, sleep, bathe, and dress parts).

When you reach the point where you're walking around with coffee jitters and bags under your eyes from multitasking, you may want to outsource some of your responsibilities.

You can, for example, contract with:

- A copywriter and an artist to do advertising and catalog development
- A fulfillment house to warehouse your products and process orders
- A list maintenance service to keep your mailing database in pristine condition

Or you can keep all your operations under your own roof and still retain your sanity by hiring help.

Your Helpmates

We've gone the archetype route here, giving you a thumbnail sketch of the different team members you may want to hire. Keep in mind, however, that these are sketches. Your company will be as individual as you are, and the people you choose to hire will also be individuals. If you do your hiring right, using your analytical and intuitive skills and communicating your enthusiasm for the company, your employees will be more than worker bees—they'll be team members, every bit as creative and dedicated to your company as you are.

Sales and Marketing

Your sales and marketing people may arguably form the most important areas of the firm. Why? Because they'll be responsible for planning advertising campaigns, designing ads, catalogs, and other printed materials, compiling and maintaining lists, and actually selling your merchandise to customers.

Here are the sales and marketing areas in which you'll want to hire those special somebodies:

- *Planning and management.* These are your hybrid pocket-protector/market innovators, responsible for analyzing the market, developing a marketing plan, and supervising the plan's implementation.

> **Bright Idea**
>
> How about a college intern as an advertising or marketing whiz, copywriter, or graphic artist? You'll benefit from the student's fresh ideas; the student will benefit from the resume-building on-the-job experience.

They'll do this by creating surveys, analyzing statistical data from government and private research sources, charting the courses of customers' spending habits, analyzing trends, and testing all campaigns.

> **Bright Idea**
>
> Since every company will have computer problems at some point, look for an employee who can handle not only the "usual" role you're seeking to fill but who can double as your resident computer guru as well.

- *Graphic design.* These are your artistic types, the ones with the weird postcards and clip art tacked all over their work areas and the really fun ideas for designing your materials and giving them that visual edge. They also do all the production stuff, working with photos, clip art, and original graphics, and putting them into desktop publishing software to be printed en masse at a print shop.

- *Customer service.* These people should be mellow and able to take cranky people in stride without dishing back but also sharp enough to think on their feet because they'll handle customer complaints, returns, and other problems. They should have the authority to make decisions about what to replace or repair and whom to reimburse.

- *Sales.* Friendly! In most mail order operations, sales refers to the inside salespeople who actually take orders over the phone and—don't forget!—do cross-selling and up-selling. These people often find their jobs overlapping with those of the customer service reps because they sometimes field complaints, so they should also be trained in how to handle various customer service issues as well.

The ideal setup would be to have at least one employee for each of the four areas described above.

Order Processing and Fulfillment

While we have said that sales and marketing are "arguably" the most important parts of your operation, your success in the mail order business also depends on having an efficient order processing and fulfillment system. If your customers don't get the product they thought they were ordering, or they don't get it when they expect it, or it arrives smashed or dented—or any other nasty permutation of the above—your company will not go very far, despite a brilliant marketing campaign.

When you think hiring here, think:

- *Warehouse manager.* This is your inventory and shipping expert, the one in the comfortable khakis with the pencil tucked behind his or her ear and the omnipresent clipboard (and computer printouts). Your manager will schedule workers, assign duties, keep a log of shipped merchandise and incoming returns, and—under your aegis—hire and discipline staff.

▲

- *Packers and shippers.* These are your T-shirt-and-sneaker types, bobbing along to music wafting out of the radio, the ones who make everything arrive in one piece and looking like a special gift.

Administration and Management

Now we arrive at the internal operations branch of your mail order business, the people concerned with all those accounting, record-keeping, and personnel matters. Here's who you'll be looking at:

- *Accounting manager.* This button-down type will handle supply and inventory invoices, make sure large orders handled by contract are paid to you in a timely manner, and make sure your bills are paid to others on time. Your accounting genius will also handle customers' bounced checks and charge-backs (remember, this is when the customer returns something paid for by credit card), and balance your books.

- *Recordkeeper.* Here's another archetypal button-downer, responsible for maintaining accurate ledgers of customer purchases, archiving retired paperwork, and scanning existing paperwork for errors. This person will work with your accounting manager but might also report in some degree to your marketing manager.

- *Human resources or personnel.* Whichever name you call it, the person in this department is your no-nonsense, by-the-book (but fun) type who looks out for the health, welfare, and morale of your employees. This person oversees health insurance administration, advertises your employ-

For a small but growing mail order business, a one-person personnel department will usually do the trick.

Legal Beagle

For the most part, attorneys are an outsource item, on call as you need them. But as your company grows and can afford an on-staff lawyer, you might consider hiring your very own in-house legal beagle to sniff out potential problems. He or she can advise you on all aspects of mail order law, review all advertising materials and sales letters, oversee safety checks on merchandise, and, of course, represent the firm should an irate customer decide to go the lawsuit route.

As a bonus, it's sort of like having a doctor in the family—you can run to your in-house attorney with questions any time you like!

ment opportunities, and sometimes hires staff, and devises and administers employee benefits like movie tickets and ride-sharing plans. (Choose someone with fun ideas!) Your personnel manager is also responsible for payroll, including keeping track of those sick and vacation days. For a small but growing mail order business, a one-person personnel department will usually do the trick.

Your Kind of People

Now that we've got all the archetype, stereotype, boilerplate personnel stuff out of the way, let's go back to what we said earlier about hiring *your* kind of people, your very own invaluable team members—people who are individuals.

Moms and Dads

When Caryn, the fabric merchandiser, began her hiring program, she decided to make her company as personal for her ten employees as it is for her. "My company is made up of moms and dads," the Georgia resident says in no uncertain terms. "My family is always number one—that's the most important thing over anything. I felt that the one thing I could give to other people was to allow them the same thing that I allow myself: for their family to be number one. So if I have a mom or dad whose kid wants them at a school event or is sick, or their spouse is getting an award and they want to be there—they can do it.

"Yes, they'll be missed at work," Caryn admits, "but somebody else will take over for them and take up the slack. That's the kind of people I want working for me because those are the values I think are so important."

Moms and Teens

Beth, the gluten-free foods provider, also employs a staff of ten—and among them, who else but moms? "What happens," the former cooking teacher explains, "is that most of the people are not full-time. They're part-time, so we rotate. We employ moms in the morning until about three in the afternoon. Then we have coverage from maybe one to five with people who don't have to get home right away to their families."

Who are these afternoon people? They're teens, recruited from the high school right around the corner from Beth's office. "It's perfect," the Connecticut mom says, "because when they're off from school, they want to pick up some extra money, and the moms aren't available because they're home with the kids.

"I recruited almost every one of the moms from my son's class," Beth reports. "Little by little they each ended up knowing other people [who spread the word]. There are four or five of us who have kids in the same class."

That same family feeling has helped Beth recruit and retain her teens, too. She started out by contacting the high school guidance office. "We had a really great crop of kids," the former food writer says. "If one person was leaving or one person came to work for us, they would bring a friend. So for a long time we were able to keep going with just friends of friends."

After a while, however, everybody went off to college. "We started to run out of friends of friends," Beth explains. "But we don't have a lot of summer openings because our kids come back then."

Holiday Help

You may want to start, as Beth has, with part-time help, someone to work four hours in the morning or afternoon, or perhaps two or three days a week. Or you might want to start off with somebody full-time. Some mail order mavens take on help during their busiest season and take all the reins back in their own hands the rest of the year.

Kate W., with two and a half years of operation under her belt, had in October already interviewed temporary help for the coming holiday season rush. "Last holiday season I thought we were busy," the football fan says, "and that's the volume we did this summer. With 15,000-plus catalogs out there this year, I really expect to have the holidays a lot busier. I don't like to do the computer stuff, so I'll either do the phones or the packing. There's too much for one person to do in a day."

Whether you hire full-time, part-time, or seasonally, there are no rules except the ones you make. Which is another of the wonderful perks that come with running your own business.

All Together Now

Another alternative to hiring employees is to put your family to work. We've already seen how some of the mail order mavens we interviewed use family computer gurus to set up and maintain Web sites. Why not take your family operations even further?

Teenage children can help out with data entry and can certainly pack and ship products. So can a willing spouse. When you have on-call help in the family, you have the advantage of no employee taxes or insurance, although—at least in the case of teens—you'll probably still have to pay your workers. Helping mom or dad or a spouse with the family business gives everybody a warm, fuzzy feeling of pitching in and can be a great togetherness booster.

That's certainly what Caryn has found. "You come into my house," the Atlanta-area merchandiser says, "and walk into the room that's my home office, we've got 50 to 70 fabric bolts in there at any one time and samples, and the kids are matching things up. My kids have even gotten involved in their own way, one with crafts, one with other things. We all get into it; we all talk about this stuff and about new ideas all the time."

The Sampler

Hire new team members as you need them, but not until they're really a necessity. There's nothing worse for you as an employer—or for your employee—than a position without enough to do. It leads to boredom, anxiety, and financial pressures. But when you really and truly need someone, go ahead and hire.

"We have one person now who just handles samples," says Caryn. "That's a new department. When we got on the Internet, there were so many customers who wanted samples because they saw them on [our Web site]. We were so inundated with sample requests that now we've got a full-time position."

Caryn didn't start out with a sample-request filler or any of her other nine employees. "We started small," the Roswell, Georgia, mom recalls. "Actually, my first employee was the person I hired to take care of my son, who I brought to work with me. He was just a little baby. I always kept him with me, and he had a playpen there.

"That's why I say this is truly a family that lives the business," the fabric expert explains. "Everybody knows the business and can do anything for it. We're all committed to it. From there, as we felt we needed somebody and it made sense, we hired."

Insuring Your Gems

Once you find those gems of employees, you'll need to think about caring for them. Workers' compensation insurance laws vary from state to state; check with your insurance agent for details in your area. Workers' comp covers you for any illness or injury your employees might incur, from a back injury from lifting heavy boxes to a paper cut gone septic to radiation poisoning from close contact with the computer terminal. (People can come up with a lot of strange complaints when money is involved.)

Although your employee may be working in your home, your homeowner's insurance probably won't pay for a problem incurred there, on the grounds that it's actually a workers' compensation case. Rather than making yourself a nervous wreck over all this (creating your own mental health claim), check with your insurance agent and then make an informed decision.

> **Tip...**
>
> ### Smart Tip
> While we're on the subject of insurance, make sure that if you base your office at home you update your homeowner's or renter's insurance policy for all your computer and other equipment, especially if you purchase anything new

Pushing the Envelope, Part 1
Direct-Mail Advertising

In this chapter, we explore what might well be the most fun, exciting, creative—and most demanding—part of mail order: pushing the envelope (or catalog, brochure, or other direct-mail piece). As a mail order maven, a great deal of your resources will go into designing and implementing advertising campaigns to take your sales to the limits and beyond.

Photo© PhotoDisc Inc.

Be prepared. Many mail order entrepreneurs estimate they spend 25 percent of their start-up budget on acquiring mailing lists and developing advertising materials, and 10 to 15 percent of their annual expenses on maintaining these efforts.

The ultimate goal of mail order advertising is not just to inform your customers of the quality or value of your product or service; it's to inspire immediate action—to get the person to pick up the pen or phone or computer mouse and order now. An automaker advertises with the goal of making you, the consumer, believe its cars are the symbol of quality, so that when you're ready to go out and buy, you'll choose its models. In mail order, you want your consumer to call and order that product now, not at a point some months or years down the line.

How are you going to achieve this? Through just about any medium you choose: catalogs, fliers, brochures, sales letters, print ads in magazines and other publications, the Internet, radio, and television. We've divvied all this up into two chapters. This one deals with the direct-mail methods—the catalogs, fliers, and other materials you send winging through the postal system. We'll delve into the mechanics and magic of advertising in magazines, on TV, and in other media in the next chapter: Pushing the Envelope, Part II. As we said, this is the fun part, so let's get creative and get going!

Line Dancing

All direct-marketing ads follow one of two formats: the *one-step* or the *two-step*. Although these sound like Texas line dances for which you have to be light on your

The one-step ad encourages potential customers to order immediately, while the two-step ad introduces the product or catalog.

feet and well-coordinated, they're actually very simple. The one-step ad encourages potential customers to order immediately, while the two-step ad introduces the product or catalog (step 1) and asks the prospect to contact you for more information, like a catalog or brochure (which you then send as step 2).

Why would you want one type of ad instead of the other? Several reasons. You'd choose the one-step when:

- You're advertising one or a few products as opposed to an entire catalog.
- The product(s) can be easily described and understood.
- Potential customers won't need further enticement or encouragement to purchase the product(s).

Take a look at the sample one-step display ad on page 162. Our hypothetical company, Chocoholic Central, isn't trying to cram every product in its catalog into one small ad—instead it's offering one product with simple variations, which are described with a few "brush strokes" of typescript. Part of the ad is an order form that the customer can mail back to us with a check or credit card information. The middle of the order form says "Order Today in Time for the Holidays!" to further encourage that immediate order.

You should note that we've also encouraged telephone orders with a prominent toll-free number and given customers the option of ordering through the Internet with a Web site address.

The Mail Order Two-Step

So when do you use the two-step ad? When you want to:

- Introduce a line of products or your catalog
- Sell products that cannot be easily explained in a small ad
- Develop a list of interested prospects to send that expensive catalog to

Check out the sample two-step display ad on page 163. Instead of advertising one particular product, it generates interest in Chocoholic Central's entire product line and entices the potential customer to order a catalog. And it's not free! We are asking customers to pay for the catalog. (We're also bribing them with a gift, but we'll talk about that in a minute.)

This method is particularly effective because you only send catalogs to people who have already expressed an interest in your products. You know they're interested because they've requested a catalog and they've spent money to get that catalog. What a great way to develop your own mailing list!

Of course, you don't have to entice potential customers with a gift, as the sample ad does. You can give them a discount on their first purchase. Or you can advertise that your catalog is free. The choice is yours. Any way you go, it's still a two-step ad, and it still has the advantage of delivering built-in interest before you send off that expensive catalog or brochure.

The two-step ad is usually used in print media rather than electronic venues like radio, television, and the Internet. And while it's traditionally used for high-ticket items that aren't easily described or won't sell without further encouragement (like swimming pools, sun rooms, furniture, and fine art prints), it's also used for everything from antique roses to books, financial services, and recipes.

Best Product in the Galaxy

Now that you understand the difference between a one-step, a two-step, and a waltz, you'll want to tailor your advertising to your target audience. Yes, we know we've already discussed this, but it bears repeating. Targeting your audience is the most important step in using your advertising budget wisely.

You don't want to target just any old consumers—you want the ones most likely to purchase your product. And to get to these people, you've got to do your homework. Start with the same questions about your target audience that you answered when you did your market research.

Bright Idea

Be creative when considering your audience. For example, baby clothes and children's goods sell well to parents, but grandparents are also big spenders. And Grammy and Grandpa often have more disposable dollars than parents do for non-necessity products like toys and novelty clothing.

Once you've evaluated your potential customers, you've got to be able to reach them. It doesn't matter if you have the most exciting product in the galaxy—if nobody in the galaxy knows about it, it isn't going to sell. So spend some quality time evaluating how to reach your people. If you're selling travel services, you'll want to advertise on The Travel Channel or within the pages of *Travel & Leisure* magazine because that's where travel-oriented people go for information and entertainment. If you opt instead for MTV, *Sports Illustrated,* or *Newsweek,* you're dangerously diluting your advertising dollar because your chance of reaching those dedicated travelers is much slimmer.

If you're selling baby clothes, you'll get more orders for your advertising dollar by placing your ads in magazines aimed at parents rather than in general women's magazines. Why? Because you're focusing your advertising on the specific audience most likely to buy your products: parents. And since parenting magazines have a smaller circulation than their general women's counterparts, your ad costs will be cheaper.

When your ad costs come down, your profits go up. And, as Martha Stewart would say, "That's a good thing."

Reality List

Targeting means more than choosing your audience with care. It also means carefully selecting your mailing list. The absolute best list you could possibly choose would consist of people guaranteed to buy at least one of everything in your line on a weekly basis.

Since that list probably exists only in the realm of fantasy, your absolute best "reality list" is one composed of people who have already purchased similar merchandise at similar prices by mail order. So if you're selling books on rose gardening, you'll want to target people who've already bought mail order books on gardening—and specifically on rose gardening. If you're selling angel figurines, you'll want to target people who have already bought angelic collectibles through the mail. People have specific interests, and once they've decided on what those are, they're generally hooked.

You may not be able to pinpoint all those rose gardeners or angelic types quite that specifically, but the closer you can come—say, by identifying people who like gardening (or, even better, flower gardening)—the better list you'll have.

Mailing Lists Revisited

That said, let's revisit mailing lists. You already know a lot, but there's more. A mailing list can make or break a direct-mail campaign, and a good list can have a greater impact than doubling your ad budget.

You can target your audience more effectively with a mailing list than with any other medium. Say you decide to go with an alternative and advertise on television, perhaps during "I Love Lucy" reruns or "The X-Files" or the "Tonight Show." Although each will have its own demographic profile, you'll get a fairly indiscriminate selection of viewers. You have no way of knowing if they're confirmed mail order buyers or if they routinely refuse all direct mail. You don't know if your audience is made up of teenagers, seniors, young singles, or old marrieds.

Ah, but when you rent a mailing list, you've got your audience targeted to a T. You can choose Midwestern women who've bought bridal gowns through the mail or Northeastern men who like mail order tools and earn more than $50,000 a year.

Common Threads

As we've discussed, in the mailing list world, there are two types of lists: the *compiled* list and the *buyer*, or *response*, list. A compiled list is made up of people who belong to certain groups or organizations—for example, members of alumni organizations or car clubs, members of professional organizations, or even people who have attended certain types of seminars or workshops. A compiled list can also be made up of people

---

Who, What, and Where

Remember the old reporters' adage of always asking who, what, when, where, why, and how? Use the same questions to home in on your target customers and refine your advertising goals:

○ Who are my potential customers?

○ What can I offer that they're not getting now?

○ Where can I find these potential customers?

○ Why should they buy from me instead of from their present source?

○ When (how fast) can I provide my products to them?

○ How (and where) do they now get the products I want to provide?

○ How can I persuade them to do business with me?

with specific demographic characteristics in common—those who live in Manhattan or make more than $30,000 a year or are between 45 and 70 years old. You get the picture. The main point to remember with compiled lists is that the people on them are not necessarily mail order purchasers.

Now, the other type of list—the buyer list—is the one you want to shoot for. Why? Because the people on it are already known mail order buyers. They might be buyers of cookbooks or auto parts or dog toys, but the idea here is that since they've already purchased a product related to yours through the mail, they're more likely to be interested in yours.

People on compiled lists, on the other hand, have not demonstrated that they are mail order buyers. Case in point: A group of would-be mail order mavens put together a mailing aimed at people with CB licenses. They spent about $25,000, designed a nice package and an attractive offer, sent it off to a compiled list of CB licensees—and lost every penny they put into the project. Why? Because the people on the list had not shown any desire to buy. The mail order hopefuls had assumed they were buyers, but all they really knew was that they were CB fans.

Lists Galore

Wondering just how many lists are out there and how selective they can be? Check out these offerings from various list owners and brokers who advertised in just one recent issue of *Catalog Age* magazine:

- ○ Amateur and professional jewelers
- ○ Avid book readers
- ○ Boating enthusiasts
- ○ Career women
- ○ Cat and dog owners
- ○ Gardeners
- ○ Grandparents who buy gifts for their grandchildren
- ○ Health-conscious Hispanics
- ○ High-end travelers (those who spend big bucks)
- ○ Hikers and campers
- ○ Home workshop enthusiasts
- ○ Medical professionals
- ○ Offshore fishermen
- ○ Video producers

This does not mean you should never use compiled lists. It does mean, though, that you should use them carefully. And as a newbie, your best bet is to stay away from them altogether. Stack all the cards you can in your favor: Use buyer lists.

The Formula

Like any good mad scientist, the savvy mail order maven also has a magic formula—for working with lists. That formula is *RFM*: Recency, Frequency, and Money. RFM helps you identify the best lists by asking three questions: How recently have the people on the list ordered something by mail? How frequently do they order? How much money do they spend?

Besides the all-important RFM factor, demographics are crucial in choosing your list. You need to consider income, age, gender, education, type of residence, occupation, and use of credit cards in making purchases. If you're selling romance novels, you would probably choose a girls-only list, because most men wouldn't be interested. Got it? Good.

Another list selection factor is *psychographics*. This is the categorization of people by psychological profile. Political conservatives, for instance, are more likely to be hunters than are liberals. So if you're selling hunting gear, you might try mailing to Republicans. If a list owner or broker says he's got a psychographic profile, ask for it. Check out the profiles listed to see if they match your prospective buyers.

Yet another factor to consider is who else has been renting the same list and how often. This can tell you who your competitors are and how successful they have been with it. If you've got a travel service and you find that another travel service has rented the same list four times in the past year, you can figure they're having good luck with it—which means you probably will, too.

1,2,3, Testing

Mail order mavens do a lot of testing to determine which products are viable and at what prices, which mailing lists are the best, and which ads or other sales materials are most effective. It's extremely difficult to determine the effect of most traditional forms of advertising, but because mail order is a direct-response venue that goes right to the customer, you get—for better or worse—immediate results.

You can find out within a matter of weeks what's working for you and what isn't. And if something isn't working, you can tweak it, or scrap it, or scrape it into another form. Testing requires accurate record-keeping and a certain amount of arithmetic. Indeed, the only way to determine the results of your tests is by number crunching.

You may not like the prospect of analyzing all those figures, but if you don't constantly test and evaluate your ads, you're cutting yourself off from a major avenue to mail order success. Here are the three main elements you'll want to test:

▲

1. *Advertising mediums.* Which sells better for you, display ads in magazines or radio ads on local stations?

2. *Venues within an advertising medium.* By placing the same ad in two magazines with similar readerships, you can determine which one brings in the most orders. You can use this method to test two lists, two television stations, or two of any other venue.

3. *Elements within an ad.* You can test almost any element of an ad, including copy, graphics, and price. Some mail order mavens even test how the color of the envelope in which they mail their sales letter affects their response rate.

Price Testing

Here's how testing actually works. Let's say you're selling a kicky little maternity jumper. You've already decided to use a four-part sales letter (mailing envelope, letter, order card, and business-reply envelope). And you plan on mailing out 35,000 pieces. But first you want to find out which selling price—$45, $49, or $52—will generate the most revenue.

You decide to rent a mailing list from *Impending Motherhood* magazine because impending mothers are the best target customers for maternity wear. You call your list broker and tell him you plan on a final list of 35,000 names but first you want to do a test with 9,000 names—3,000 for each of your "price points," or potential prices. He puts together three lists of moms-to-be with 3,000 *nth* names on each list. As we explained in Chapter 6, *nth name selection* means taking a random sampling by using every seventh name or every tenth name (or whichever number you choose). This eliminates any alphabetical or geographic glitch with the way the list is organized. If you don't use the nth name selection, your first 9,000 names might net you every customer in the Northeast or everyone with a surname from A through D.

Key Code Roundup

Meanwhile, back at your office, you make up three sets of your sales piece, with each set exactly the same—except for two critical differences:

1. Each set has a different price point: $45, $49 or $52.

2. Each set is marked with a different key code (also called a source code, remember?).

These codes—your own secret ones—will tell you which set your customers have responded to. For example, the bottom left-hand corner of the order card for the $45 set bears the code "IMJP45." "IM" stands for *Impending Motherhood*, "JP" means jumper, and "45," of course, indicates the $45 price. The key code for the $49 set is IMJP49, and the code for the $52 set is IMJP52.

Maternity Jumper Key Code Chart

Key Code	Price Point	Phone Orders	Mail Orders	Total Orders	Response (Percent of 3,000)	Gross Sales*
IMJP45	$45	33	30	63	2.1	$2,835
IMPJ49	$49	31	29	60	2.0	$2,940
IMPJ52	$52	24	21	45	1.5	$2,340

*We calculated gross sales by multiplying the total orders by the price point.

You can design your source codes any way that makes sense to you. If you look again at the sample one-step and two-step display ads on pages 162 and 163, you'll see key codes printed beneath the gift boxes. One says V11 and the other reads CL11, which tells us that we placed one in the November issue (11th month) of *Victoria* magazine and the other in the November issue of *Country Living* magazine.

Back to the maternity jumpers. After you design your codes, you record the numbers in your code book, along with a description of your advertising campaign, for future reference.

That done, you send a copy of your sales package to the list broker so that it can be approved by the *Impending Motherhood* people. They give it the go-ahead and send you the three sets of names you rented, printed on pressure sensitive (peel-and-stick) labels. You peel and stick, mail out your materials, and wait for your orders to arrive.

Every morning as you open the orders that have arrived in the mail, you use the key codes printed on the order forms to count how many you've received in each price point. When customers call in with phone orders, you ask them to read the source code off the order form for you. You record all this information in your software program or in a ledger.

At the eight-week point your response will have tapered off and you'll be ready to compare results. Take a look at the "Maternity Jumper Key Code Chart" above. As you can see, the $45 price brought in more orders, but you've made more money by charging $49 per jumper. So when you mail off your 35,000 sales letters, you'll use the $49 price on all of them.

The Big Picture

Testing is extremely important in the mail order business, but like most things in life, it's also important to practice moderation. You can get so carried away with testing that

▲

you lose sight of the big picture—which is, of course, making sales. Don't worry about testing the tiniest things, like the size of your stamp or the color of ink, at least not until you've tweaked all the more important elements.

What are these important elements?

- Your copy (what your ad or sales piece says and how it says it)
- Your offer (free catalog, free gift, money-back guarantee, 30-day trial, etc.)
- Your price
- Your list
- Your format (catalog, sales letter, brochure, television ad, etc.)

Sales Letters

The two main forms of direct mail are sales letters and catalogs. You can design all sorts of variations on these themes, from postcards and "greeting" cards to fliers, brochures, and coupon mailers. Among the most venerable, most popular, and most effective is the sales letter, so let's start off with it.

A sales letter is not just a letter—it's a package comprising several components:

- The letter itself
- The envelope it arrives in
- The order form or reply card
- The reply envelope it comes back to you in

Bells and Whistles

Mail order newbies are often confused about the difference between features and benefits. Your product's features are the bells and whistles it comes with. The benefits are the things it does for you. For instance, the features of a spiffy little sports car would be a convertible top, a five-speed transmission, and a stereo/CD player/coffeemaker. The benefits would be that it gets you where you want to go in the blink of an eye, makes you feel young and sexy, and, of course, attracts attention from the opposite sex.

When you write your sales or ad copy, you want to describe the features, but you also want to be sure to tell your customers about the benefits. These, after all, are the reasons they buy.

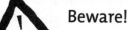

Beware!

If you use testimonials in your sales letters or other materials, they must be from real people who have given you permission to use their comments.

Your sales letter needs to instantly capture your potential customers' attention—preferably as soon as they've got the envelope in their hands—so that they'll open that envelope. (For more on envelopes see "The Envelope, Please" on page 174.) Then, when they do, it must again instantly capture their attention and then keep that attention—so they'll read it through. Besides interest and attention, the main thing to aim for in your sales letter is the sense that you're writing to each potential customer personally.

Roses the Size of Cabbages

Try reading all those sales letters that land in your mailbox. What do they have in common? For one thing, they start off with something that immediately hooks your attention. Maybe it's a description of the offer, enticing you to read on with tidbits of the information you'll get when you buy that book or newsletter. Maybe it's a description of the benefits of using the product, like roses the size of cabbages or more miles to the gallon. Some letters use the flattery approach, assuring you that they have targeted you because you are known for your green thumb or mechanical ability. Others might start off with a question, like "How would you like to…?" or "Wouldn't the world be a better place if everybody…?"

Try the same approaches in your letter. Experiment until you hit on something that sounds good to you and matches your particular product or service.

Then go on to the body of your letter. Again, analyze the ones you have received. What makes them work? Notice that they spend a lot of time describing the product or service. You will want to do the same thing. Emphasize the benefits of your product or service throughout your body copy, repeating those benefits as often as you can using different descriptions so they stick in your potential customer's mind.

If you've got testimonials, use them. They lend credibility to your product and company, and they add another dimension to your copy. It's not just you who thinks your product is great—it's real people, just like your prospect. The sample on page 174 shows you what testimonials typically sound like, how they're formatted, and how you might include them as a separate sheet with your sales letter or other materials. (For more information about using testimonials, see "Sure-Fire Techniques" on page 185 and "Just Ask" on page 186.)

Tip...

Smart Tip

Have a trusted friend or family member proofread your sales letter. Sometimes it's almost impossible to detect minor typos in your own work, and computer spelling and grammar checkers, while helpful, can sometimes interpret things in a strange fashion.

After the main body of your letter, tell your customer what to do to obtain your terrific product. If you're offering a discount or a freebie with a time element, this is the place to mention it. (The advantage of using a time element, like "must be received by June 14th" is that it lights a fire under your customer—who won't want to put off ordering and risk losing out on whatever goodie you're offering.)

The Personal Touch

Check out the sample sales letter on page 173. Then take a look at these sales tips:

- Design the most enticing gift, discount, or free offer you can, and make it prominent in your letter.
- Grab prospects' attention with something they want. Relate it to either the freebie or how your product or service benefits them.
- Use time-proven winning words like "secret" and "free." Everybody wants to know a secret, and everybody wants something for free!
- If you use headlines, try for 10 or more words—longer sells better than shorter.
- Remember that, surprisingly enough, long letters usually yield higher returns than short ones. People like to get letters, and even if they know you're not writing solely to them, in their heart of hearts they like to think you are. So write that way!
- Don't write for thousands of prospective customers—write to just one, as though you're speaking to him or her personally.
- Save the flowery prose for that poetry contest. Instead, use everyday language that appeals to the average person.
- Don't focus only on the features of your product or service; describe the benefits.
- Try letters with indented paragraphs, underlined words, and two colors; they pack more of a punch and outperform plain letters.
- Use gimmicks like boldface type, underlining, and italics sparingly. If you use them too frequently or for no particular reason, they become annoying instead of intriguing.
- Keep your letter clear, clean, free of grammar and style errors, and no more than two pages long. Have someone you trust as a spelling, punctuation, and grammar star check your work before you commit to a print run.
- Relax and enjoy yourself. Have fun!

Beware!
Don't make the common mail order mistake of failing to correspond with your customers on a frequent basis. Tell those repeat customers how much you appreciate them. Let potential and one-time customers know what they're missing—and that you miss their business. The more your customers hear from you, the more often they'll order.

Sales Letter

CHOCOHOLIC CENTRAL

Hi Susan!

I'd like to offer you a very special invitation. *And a free gift.*

I've chosen you to receive this offer because I know you value the little things that make life special for the ones you love—things like shiny red boxes tied with crisp organza ribbons and brimming with gifts you've made or purchased with care.

Imagine how special those gifts would be tucked inside a box handmade of the finest Belgian chocolate and embellished with marzipan flowers and edible gold leaf! Surprise them with that bauble from the jewelry counter in an elegant, edible box that looks like a jewel itself. Tuck that practical handkerchief inside a magical chocolate confection. Or slip a heartfelt message inside that chocolate box.

Your family will swoon in delight. Your friends will wonder how you ever found these special gifts. And your business associates will remember you all year long.

Because I'm so anxious for you to try my chocolate boxes, I'm inviting you to choose any one from my selection of four chocolate boxes and receive it for 10% off! And when you order, I'll send you a rose-and-chocolate scented sachet to tuck into a drawer, in your car, or under your pillow for sweet dreams every night of the year!

I hope you'll take advantage of this special offer. **I can't offer it for long, but I can promise that you'll fall in love with these chocolate gems—and so will those cherished people you give them to.** (If you're not pleased for any reason, just send back the box in its special wrapping, and I'll cheerfully refund your money.)

Just fill out the enclosed reply form and pop it in the mail to me. Don't take too long! Because of the upcoming holidays, my offer must end December 1st.

Very best,

Arianna Arelson

Arianna Arelson

P.S. I've enclosed a page with some letters we've received from other customers like you who have given chocolate boxes in creative and heartwarming ways. Take a look!

123 Cocoa Court, Truffle Bay, FL 30000

(800) 555-4000

www.chocoholic.com

▲

Testimonials

Here's what some of our customers have told us about our elegant, edible chocolate boxes:

"I gave one of your chocolate boxes to my daughter for her 16th birthday with her grandmother's gold locket tucked inside. She says it's the best gift she's ever received. And all her friends want to know where I got the box!"

—Carolee Carter
Memphis, TN

"Every year I try to think up something special for the girls in my bridge club for Christmas. Well, last year I gave them each one of your chocolate boxes. You should have seen their faces—sheer delight!"

—Mrs. Myrtle Dunagin
Lawrence, KS

"I saw your ad in one of my girlfriend's magazines and knew she'd been looking at it. So when it came time to propose, I put the engagement ring inside the heart-shaped chocolate box. She went nuts over that box and said it was the most romantic thing she'd ever seen. P.S. She insisted on saving the box. (It's been in our refrigerator for six months now, along with a piece of wedding cake.)"

—James Amado
Tucson, AZ

We think you'll be just as delighted! And we'd love to hear from you, too!

The Envelope, Please

The envelope is your invitation to your customers, the outer trapping that entices them into your virtual store. What can you do to encourage them to open the envelope and step in? Make it as intriguing as possible. Some mail order mavens suggest using an envelope that looks handwritten. Others go for the official/open immediately look, hoping the customer will think it's from the IRS and rip it open right away (a dangerous tactic; who wants to give their customers a heart attack?) Still others aim for envelopes in bright, can't-miss colors.

But whatever you do, advises Liz L., the children's T-shirt designer, use catchy envelopes. "Unless you're really desperate for mail," she says, "a regular black-and-white envelope from somebody you don't know may be tossed. Use color. Put something in the envelope, an item your customers can touch and feel. That's going to make them want to open the envelope."

People are far more likely to respond to an offer for which they have to actively do something.

Liz did a very successful mailing in which she sent out a simple flier. "There were no pictures," the upstate New Yorker explains. "All it said was [the name of my company], we're here to help your business grow, and we're right here in your own backyard. I included a pack of sunflower seeds. The paper had sunflowers on it, so it all tied in together.

"Of course, there has to be a catch. So on the envelope, there was a sticker that said 'Free gift. Please open immediately.' And they couldn't just let it sit there. It worked. It really worked!

"I found that if you just send a catalog," Liz advises, "people will not respond. They want something. You have to put 'This offer expires on such and such a date,' and there should always be some kind of catch."

What works for one company won't necessarily work for another, because each mail order entrepreneur's target market, merchandise, theme, and ambience are unique (or should be). But whatever your company's style, you should consider the outer envelope a canvas on which to work your mail order magic. Check out these tips and tricks for creating catchy envelopes:

- Go for the personal touch—like a hand-addressed envelope (or one printed with a font that looks handwritten). People are much more likely to open this than one that's obviously been stamped out by a machine.
- Herald a free gift inside. This always gets the envelope opened!
- Print a teaser on the envelope, something like "Look inside for the secret to…" or "Haven't you always wondered…" so that your customer has to open the envelope to find out the rest of the sentence.
- Use oversized envelopes that will stand out from the crowd in a stack of mail.
- Plaster the envelope with colorful stickers.
- Scatter colorful graphics over the envelope.
- Use both sides of the envelope as your canvas—not just the address.
- Design the envelope to look like a fancy invitation.
- Appeal to your customers' five senses.

The Participation Effect

Another quirky thing about direct mail (which is also a quirky thing about human nature in general) is that people are far more likely to respond to an offer for which they have to actively do something. In other words, people like direct-mail offers in which they're asked, for example, to paste a "Yes" or "No" sticker on the reply card.

That's why all those Publishers Clearing House packets are full of stickers and reply cards and tear-offs. They work. Call it the participation effect.

Of course, these gimmicks cost money. But if you can afford them, and they fit your company's style, by all means use them. If not, think about how else you might incorporate the same idea into your order form or reply card. If you're offering a free gift with the order, for instance, you might let them choose the color or style they want by checking a box on your form.

Gimmick or not, the main purpose of the order form or reply card is to encourage orders. So make the form clear, easy to understand, and easy to fill out. Check out the sample order form/reply card on page 177.

Make it Easy

Here's another area where it pays to make things easy: Adding a self-addressed return envelope makes ordering simple for your customer. And, especially when you provide a different-sized envelope (a smaller one to fit your reply card, for instance), having your customer stick the form in the envelope contributes to the participation effect we've already discussed.

Some mail order mavens swear that you get a better response if you use a business-reply envelope (one with postage prepaid by you). Others say this doesn't matter. Do your homework and investigate how your closest competition handles this. Run a few tests and then decide for yourself. But postage prepaid or not, be sure to include that self-addressed reply envelope.

Brochures

Fun Fact

Think it can't be done? *Ballard Designs*, an up-scale home furnishings and décor catalog, started life in 1983 as a two-page, black-and-white brochure. Its featured item? A replica of a table from founder Helen Ballard Weeks' own home, which had been recently featured in *Metropolitan Home* magazine.

A brochure is basically a baby catalog, the perfect vehicle for the mail order newbie who can't afford a big, glossy publication—and possibly doesn't have enough products to fill one. But a brochure should not be cheesy. Like the catalog, it must still convey the impression that your company is an established, high-quality operation.

Your brochure doesn't have to be a full-color photographic masterpiece. With the wondrous array of desktop publishing software available and a generous application of imagination, you can turn line art and paper into a classy brochure. But you should meld

Order Form/Reply Card

Yes! Send My Garden Art Today!

Please mark the Garden Art statues you'd like to receive:

		Quantity	Total Cost
❏ Frog Prince	$20.00	_____	_____
❏ Garden Fairy	$28.00	_____	_____
❏ Daisy Cherub	$40.00	_____	_____
❏ Dancing Cricket	$42.00	_____	_____

Florida residents add 6% sales tax	_____
Shipping & handling	7.00
Total	_____

Name _____

Address _____

City _____ State _____ ZIP _____

Phone ( ) _____

☐ Check   ☐ Visa   ☐ MasterCard   ☐ Discover Card   ☐ American Express

Card # _____ Exp. _____ / __

Signature _____
(as shown on card)

Your order entitles you to a free decorative watering-can planter!

Please check the appropriate box below to indicate your color preference:

❏ Classic Copper
❏ Perfect Periwinkle
❏ Rustic Tin
❏ Wagon Red

The Dancing Daisy Garden

123 Iris St., Clematis, FL 30000, (800) 555-2200

▲

Smart Tip

Tip...

A brochure can be a mini-catalog or it can take the form of a two-, three- or four-fold page printed with your information, sort of a combination sales letter/catalog. Choose the format that works best for you.

your knowledge of your products and your potential customers with your market research and your own judgment before making a final decision on whether to use full-color.

Some products, like horse mane conditioner, don't need a full-color photograph to describe them. Your customers probably know what a bottle of conditioner looks like and won't need to see it up close and personal to purchase. (See the sample brochure page on page 179.) But customers who might buy Chocoholic Central's gift boxes made of chocolate will probably want to see a photo of these glamorous—and highly functional—confections before purchasing. (Or they may not. This is something to test!)

If you design your brochure so that it fits in a No. 10 (business-sized) envelope, you can make it the perfect companion for your sales letter. If you're sending the brochure out on its own without an accompanying letter, try a size that will make it stand out from all the No. 10 envelopes in the mailbox. How about 8 inches by 5 inches? Choose whatever size fits your brochure layout and your budget. But think about how you feel when you see that odd-sized envelope or package in your daily handful of bills and clutter. Don't you automatically think, "Wow! Something special!" and open it first?

Once your potential customers have opened that exciting envelope, you'll need to include some additional features to keep their attention. You might put a personal letter

A Few Formalities

Don't forget that if you plan to sell your ideas, recipes, or formulas in the form of brochures or pamphlets, you'll want to copyright your material. You can copyright cartoon characters, sculptures, paintings, plays, maps, songs, scripts, photographs, and poems as well.

To copyright your material on your own, simply include a copyright notice on it. Three elements make up the copyright notice:

1. The word "copyright," the copyright symbol "©" or the abbreviation "copr."
2. The name of the owner of the copyright (that's you).
3. The year of first publication.

Here's what a copyright notice should look like: *Copyright © 2002 by John Doe*

If you want to get more formal, you can file a copyright with the U.S. government. For information, visit the U.S. Copyright Office, which is part of Library of Congress, at http://lcweb.loc.gov/copyright.

Raisa Magic Mane Conditioner

8-oz bottle makes any mane soft, silky, and easy to braid. Perfect for show days, parades, or just hangin' out in the barn.

RM3353 $8.95

Lucky Shoe

We all know it takes more than luck to win a show. But it doesn't hurt to have this handsome sterling silver horseshoe to hang on the wall at home or in the stable. Measures 12" x 4" and comes gift boxed for giving. (But you can order one for yourself, too!)

RM3358 $21.50

"I've tried mane conditioners before and thought they were all the same. But one bottle of your Raisa Magic Mane Conditioner and I changed my mind! So did my horse, Abbey. We won our first dressage show the first time we used it. Thank you!"

—Vicki Valiant
Burbank, CA

Hay There!

What's More Fun Than Horsin' Around?

Order Toll-Free (800) 555-MANE

Mon.–Fri. 7 A.M. to 6 P.M., Weekends 9 A.M. to 5 P.M., or use the handy order form on page 6.

on the first page of your brochure. Tell your customers exactly why you've designed your product line and what it will do for them. Encourage feedback. People like to feel that the company they're buying from recognizes them as individuals. (Take a look at the brochure-ready personal letter on page 181.)

Another way to keep customers' attention is to sprinkle your brochure with tips, tricks, or tidbits that will be of interest to your target audience. This gives it an added punch without expensive photography or graphics, contributes to that personal touch, and keeps your customers reading on and wanting more.

Consider sending your multifold brochures as self-mailers, folded and tabbed (sealed at each end with those half-moon-shaped stickers), instead of stuffing them into envelopes. Affix your address labels on one side, and you've saved yourself the cost of envelopes!

Catalogs

Now we come to what mail order newbies often think of as the Cadillac of the direct-marketing world, the catalog. It's fun, it's (frequently) glossy, and it can be lucrative—but it can also be incredibly expensive and a wonderful way to lose your proverbial shirt. Before you decide to go with a catalog, do every bit of your homework, think carefully, and plan thoroughly.

Catalogs come in lots of sizes and you don't have to start with a big one. You don't even have to start with a "real" catalog—as we said in the previous section, you can start with a brochure and work your way up to a catalog.

Your catalog must have a central theme. If you've done your homework and developed a target audience, this won't be difficult. You've already come up with your theme: gift chocolates, horse-care products for the equestrian, or auto supplies for the home mechanic. Once you've got that theme, don't deviate. You can't suddenly throw oil filters into your equestrian catalog or horse mane conditioner in with your chocolates. You can develop variations on your theme, offering, say, horse-related gifts with your horse-care products, or gourmet coffees with your chocolates, but you can't stick in something totally out of character. It blows your theme, jars your audience, and plays havoc with your credibility.

> **Tip...**
>
> **Smart Tip**
>
> Half-lives aren't just for radioactive materials. The *half-life* of a catalog is the time span from when you first mail out a particular issue until you receive half the total orders you can expect from it. A catalog's half-life is generally considered to be three to four months, depending on the type of merchandise and the target market.

Brochure Personal Letter

Dear Friend,

I've been in love with horses ever since I can
remember. I think you probably have, too!
After years of wishin' and hopin' and savin', I
was finally able to buy Molly, my beautiful
Swedish Warmblood. Molly and I have been a
team for six years now. We show at dressage
meets about once a month and train at our
local stable (where Molly lives—and I *almost* do)
every other evening.

It's a lifestyle I love, but between working full-time, caring for my
family, and training and hangin' out with Molly, I found that I
had no time to shop for all the horse care products we wanted
and needed. If you're like me, and like all the wonderful friends
I've made at the stables and at shows, I think you've made the
same discovery.

And that's why I started THE HORSEY SET, to bring quality horse
care (and horse fun) products to people who love their carrot-
munching friends but don't have the time to shop for them.

I hope you find the things you and your horse want and need
within these pages. Please let me know. I want to hear from you!

Happy riding,

Darcy

Darcy Daniels

P.S. All THE HORSEY SET products carry a 30-day, risk-free guarantee.
If for any reason you're not pleased with an item, just send it back,
and I'll gladly refund your money.

And that's something you can hang your hat on!

Technicolor Dream

Contrary to what you might think, your catalog doesn't have to be a Technicolor photographer's dream unless you're selling gifts, food, jewelry, or home furnishings. If you're selling auto parts, for instance, your customers aren't likely to be more bowled over by a full-color photo of a spark plug than by a black-and-white one or a line drawing. It's what you do with your copy, your layout, and the theme and mission of your company that counts.

In other words, if your theme is horse-care goods and your mission is to provide quality products at reasonable prices for horse lovers who don't have time to shop, then make those things evident in all your catalog copy. The benefit you're selling is more time with the horse, and you don't need a color photo of that.

If your products call for color photos, you can sometimes get manufacturers to supply color shots of products, which you can pop into your catalog. But take care with these. If you end up with a hodgepodge of different styles, your layout—and your company—will look messy and disorganized.

As in the sales letter and brochure, keep your catalog personal. Use testimonials as often as possible. And consider your product descriptions. Some catalogs go for two or three items per page and describe each item in detail—which makes them read like interesting and instructive little magazine articles. Other catalogs pack up to a half-dozen products on a page with clever, concise copy to describe each. Which format you choose depends on the size of your catalog, the number of products you're offering, and your catalog style.

Think that last one through carefully. You're going to have to keep your catalog style consistent. You can't have one style on one page and another on the next. And you can't switch back and forth from one issue to the next. Remember, your catalog is your store. Once you've established your virtual furnishings and ambience, your customers will expect the same thing on their next visit.

They'll also expect your copy to be factual. They're relying on you to convey how the product looks, sounds, feels, smells, or tastes. If you don't report accurately, they're not going to believe you—or buy from you—a second time. As an added bonus, with accurate reporting you'll get far fewer returns.

Easy Ordering

One of the most important elements of your catalog is the order form. Once you've done all the work of choosing your merchandise, deciding on prices, designing graphics, writing copy, and laying it all out, you want to make it as easy as possible for your customers to place orders.

You'll want to make sure the order form is easy to find. Most mail order mavens print it on heavier paper stock and bind it into the center of the catalog.

It should also be easy for customers to order by phone. Don't make them hunt all

Smart Tip
Remember: Your return policy should be clearly stated on your order form, as well as in all your direct-mail and advertising materials.

Tip...

Creating a Virtual Image

Part of the fun of shopping is the ambience of the stores. And since your customers won't be in an actual store when they peruse your merchandise, you'll need to provide them with a virtual company image. If you're selling trendy clothing or elegant gifts, go all out for a logo that's really trendy or "terribly elegant, dahling." If you're into the warehouse thing, let your customers virtually live the inventory-stacked-to-the-rafters experience.

Like your name and catchphrase or motto, your visual image—the colors, graphics, typefaces, and paper stocks you choose for everything from catalogs to stationery and mailing labels—is a vital factor in your customers' perception of your company.

You can design just about everything with your trusty desktop publishing program. Keep in mind that you're selling not only your own special ambience but also an image of soundness. You want your customers to know your mail order business is reputable.

Have a friend or a family member look over your designs before you commit to a print run. Do they see typos? An amateur quality? Or do they catch the gleam of a business riding the waves of proficiency?

Order Form Checklist

Your order form is one of the most important parts of your catalog. Keep in mind that it must be easy to use. If it looks like an IRS form, your customer may flinch and file it away. Look over the order forms in all the catalogs you've accumulated and borrow the best from each. Then follow this checklist to make sure the one you've designed contains these essential elements:

1. Your company's name and address, phone number, and Web address for ordering, and customer service phone number (if different)

2. A place for your customer's name, address, and daytime and evening phone numbers, so you can easily contact the person if you have a problem

3. Space for your customer to clearly write in the:
   - ❏ Item number
   - ❏ Page number where the item is found
   - ❏ Quantity
   - ❏ Item description (includes size and color)
   - ❏ Price per item
   - ❏ Item price total (if the customer orders more than one of each item)
   - ❏ Monogramming, imprinting, or other personalizing service fee (if applicable)
   - ❏ Gift box or wrapping fee (if applicable)

   Make sure you've got enough lines for an average order, plus a few more. Extra spaces encourage extra orders!

4. Space for an alternate mailing address if item ordered is a gift the customer wants sent directly to the recipient (if this applies to your products)

5. Subtotal (total price of items)

6. Your discount policy (if you have one—for instance, for large orders)

7. Sales tax, clearly described

8. Shipping charges, clearly spelled out

9. Total price of order

10. Payment method. For charge cards, leave clearly identified spaces for your customer to write in the card type, number, expiration date, and the name as shown on the card.

11. Your return policy, clearly spelled out

12. Don't forget the thank you!

   Note: The back of the order form is a good place to add any other information you think your customer should know, like how to order by fax or over the Internet, how to reach customer service, how to purchase a gift certificate, and how to find out more about guarantees or warranties. You can also add a space on the back of the order form for your repeat customers to fill in a change of address. This is also a terrific spot for your customer to fill in the name and address of a friend who might like to receive your catalog. Take advantage of this opportunity to add a free name to your mailing list!

over the catalog for your phone number. Print it in bold numbers that are easy to read, and run it across the bottom of every other page. Make sure you've got your telephone number on your order form, too. And if you've got a Web site that customers can order through, make sure you've got its address printed right along with your phone number. And if you also plan to accept faxed orders, don't forget that fax number!

Sure-Fire Techniques

Buying something by mail order—unless it's a catalog that people look forward to sitting back and perusing at the end of a long day—is generally an impulse affair. If you give your customers a chance to think about it, chances are they won't buy; your direct-mail piece will languish on the kitchen counter or in a desk drawer until it eventually gets thrown away. Your job is to call your customers to action—to get them to order immediately.

We've seen what direct mail looks like and how to design your own pieces for optimum effect. Now let's take a look at some sure-fire techniques for winning customers:

- *Give away freebies.* Remember, everybody likes to get something for free. Everybody appreciates a gift. Depending on your style, budget and target market, you can give away something substantial (but inexpensive) or a mere trinket. If you're selling baby clothes, how about a free bib? For books, you can make your gift a simple bookmark. If you choose something your customers will use often and then imprint it with your company's name, you'll have given away not only a gift but free advertising for yourself.

- *Offer a money-back guarantee.* Your returned merchandise rate will be lower than you might think because most people don't have the time or energy to send something back. This is not, of course, an excuse for sending shoddy products. Instead it's a way to help your customers over the hurdle of sending their money to someone they do not know for something they haven't actually seen. When you offer that guarantee, use strengthening words like "unconditional" or "no questions asked" to show that you're serious about your offer. And don't forget that if you offer a money-back guarantee, you have to honor it—it's the law.

- *Time-date your offers.* Make your offer good only for a limited time. Say something like, "If you respond within the next 30 days, you will receive a free _____" or "This offer is good only through _____." This encourages your customers to order now instead of in the nebulous future. And when you combine a time-dated offer with a money-back guarantee, you will increase your responses.

> **R**emember, everybody likes to get something for free.

▲

Just Ask

By now you're thinking: "I know I should include testimonials in my advertising, but how do I get them?" There are several ways, all beginning with the word "Ask." When customers write to compliment you on your products, services, or company, ask if you can use excerpts from those letters as testimonials. When customers call with compliments, ask if you can write out what they've said and send it to them for a signature so their comments can be used in your sales materials. Some companies actively solicit customer comments by sending out questionnaires and then asking permission from selected customers to use their responses as testimonials.

Don't be shy. Your customers are helping you, but at the same time, you're giving them that little spot in the limelight. You're forging a relationship!

Another way to get fast responses is to offer only a limited quantity of your product. You can also make a special offer, giving a certain discount or freebie to people who respond to one particular ad or mailing, or giving an additional goodie to the first X number of people who respond.

- *Write riveting headlines.* Your direct-mail piece must compete with those scads of advertisements crammed in your customers' mailboxes. Your pitch may be terrific, your product and price may be unbeatable, but if you don't catch their eyes with your opening number—your headline—they're never going to know how special your offer is. Winning headlines generally come in three basic styles: the ego appeal, as in "You have been selected" or "You're invited"; the greed appeal, as in "You have won" or "Free gift inside"; and the news appeal, as in "A new discovery... ." Penning your headline before you write your copy will help you focus on what basic need or desire your product satisfies and what appeal your copy should make.

- *Offer testimonials from satisfied customers.* For your testimonials, always use real first and last names and real hometowns. If you use only initials or first names, your true-life kudos may look invented. (To find out how to get testimonials from your customers, See "Just Ask" above.)

- *Accent with artwork.* Illustrations and photos attract attention. If you use a caption under a picture, make sure it has sales value. People will read captions even when they don't have time to read the rest of the piece.

- *Give them a kick with catchwords.* Certain words trigger emotional responses. Some of the most persuasive in the language, especially when it comes to advertising materials, are: "new," "free," "how to," "love," and "discover." Guess which two are the absolute tops in advertising? "New" and "free"!

- *Help customers respond quickly.* Accept credit cards and toll-free calls. It's much easier for your customer to fill in a credit card number on a form or call and give it to you over the phone than to sit down and write out and send a check.

- *Offer deferred or corporate billing.* With deferred billing, you bill the customer at a later time. Corporate billing means you bill the customer's company (which of course only works with business-to-business products). These techniques are another way to make it easier and faster for your customers to order.

- *Remember the participation effect.* Give your customers plenty to look at, lots to read and, if possible, something to stick, paste, tear off, or insert. If you can't afford these gimmicks, consider something like the seemingly handwritten note that implores the customer to "Read this only if you've decided not to buy."

- *Put a P.S. at the bottom of your letter.* It appears charmingly slapdash, as if you sat down at your kitchen table and scribbled on an afterthought to that valued customer, so it works on the personal level. And it's a terrific place for your call to action. Try something like "P.S. This hand-cast garden gnome will only be available at the rock-bottom price of $19.95 for a limited time, so reserve yours now! Return the enclosed postage-paid reply card today!"

Pushing the Envelope, Part 2
Print, Radio, TV, and Internet Advertising

Mail order is—more than anything else—the fascinating business of advertising. So much so, in fact, that we've devoted another entire chapter to the subject. Here we explore the advertising possibilities beyond those of direct mail, from print ads and radio to television and the Internet.

Display Ads

Print ads are terrific vehicles for getting your message to your target market and come in one of two styles: *classified* and *display*. We're going to talk magazines only because newspapers—while a good read and a good source of bin liners, creative wrapping paper, and packing material—do not make good mail order advertising venues. The reason for this is two-fold: Most newspapers have a very limited geographic range, and their readership is too broad to allow for target marketing.

So with magazines in mind, let's start off with display ads, which usually feature some sort of graphics combined with the printed word and are found throughout a publication (as opposed to classified ads, which consist solely of the printed word and are found only in the classifieds section).

Vampire Today

If you've done your homework and chosen a niche you're familiar with and enjoy, you probably already know which publications will work for you—they're the ones your target audience reads and the ones you probably read, too. These are the best places to start because you already understand at least part of the demographics and psychographics of their readers. If you are a vampire and your target market is vampires, for instance, you probably know *Country Vampire*, *Vampire Today*, and *Fashion Vamp* magazines.

Pick up those issues off your coffee table or nightstand. Study them carefully. Do mail order ads do well here? Compare the number of "traditional" ads with the number

Christmas in July

Most laypersons (which no longer includes you!) don't realize how much time is involved between the production of a magazine and its publication date. Magazines require that ads be submitted at least two months before publication. What this means is that to have your ad come out in the December issue of a magazine, you'll probably need to place the ad in October. This doesn't exactly give you Christmas in July, but it's a good time frame to keep in mind. If you wait until the last minute, it will be too late.

If the closing date has already come and gone but your ad is a small one, you can sometimes get the magazine's production people to squeeze it in somewhere. Call the advertising rep and ask. And the next time, think ahead!

of mail order ads. If a mail order makes up a significant portion, you can figure that other mail order companies are experiencing success with the publication—which means it's a good place to be.

Check for repeated ads featuring products similar to yours. If you're selling a carburetor tune-up kit, see who else is selling the same kind of kit or other auto maintenance merchandise. If all the other ads are for something entirely different, you probably don't want to advertise there. When you hit on a publication with the "right" sorts of ads, head out to the library and skim through six months to a year of back issues. If you see that same ad repeated over and over again, it's because it's making money. And that's good—now you can give it some competition!

But don't imagine you know it all. There may be other vampire publications you have yet to discover. That's why you'll turn to the Standard Rate and Data Service, otherwise known as SRDS. (See the Appendix for contact information.) SRDS publishes directories that list more consumer and trade publications than you might imagine ever existed, along with a short dscription of each one and its editorial content, facts on what sort of people read it, and a breakdown of its circulation figures.

From SRDS' plethora of information, choose a list of possible publications in which to place your ads. Then call the advertising department of each magazine and ask the rep to send you a *media kit*. Media kits contain sample issues, detailed information about editorial content, a breakdown of reader demographics, the publication's ad rates, and an *audited circulation statement*. This is a sworn statement from the publisher, verified by an outside source, that the magazine has the actual circulation claimed in its circulation figures.

> **Smart Tip**
> *Tip...*
>
> While it's important to choose print media (and mailing lists) geared toward your particular audience, it also pays to be creative. Sometimes you can do extremely well with an audience segment that doesn't at first appear to be the best choice. Men's colognes, for instance, sell well in women's magazines. Why? Women like to shop for their men.

> **Smart Tip**
> *Tip...*
>
> Know your media ABCs: There are two primary circulation audit sources, the Audit Bureau of Circulation (ABC) and the Business Publications Audit (BPA).

Lost in Space

Now that you've decided which magazines to advertise in, you'll have to decide what size ad to run. Magazines generally sell *space*, the areas reserved for ads, in standard sizes and formats. The costs for these spaces, especially in widely recognized general-interest publications, can just about take away the breath of an unsuspecting newbie. But don't get alarmed—we'll explore ways to save money on advertising in Chapter 12.

Magazine Ad Space

A standard magazine page is 7 inches by 10 inches, with each page divided into three columns. Each column is 140 lines deep, or 14 lines per inch. While you typically purchase space by the column, in some cases you can buy by the line. If this is your preference, check the magazine's rate card or ask the ad rep.

Type of Ad	Number of Columns	Other
Full page	3	
Two-thirds of page	2	
One-third of page	1	Can also be one-third of page square (instead of running vertically)
One-sixth of page	One-half	
One-twelfth of page	One-quarter	

Naturally, the larger your ad, the more attention it's likely to get. But as they say, size isn't everything, and you can get excellent results with a small ad if your copy, graphics, target market, and choice of magazine all meld in the right mix.

One school of thought is to start with the smallest ad that pulls in money and gradually increase your ad size until it no longer pays for itself. That's where you draw the line. How do you know what small size to start with? Try the smallest one that lets you say what you need to say. A one-step ad, for instance, will take up more space than a two-step because you'll need extra room for the order form. How do you know when the size no longer pays its own way? By testing. You knew that! (If you didn't, go back to the cost per order calculations in Chapter 5 for a quick review.)

The other school of thought dictates that once you've determined what size ad works for you—by studying other ads, by intuition, and by testing—leave it alone. Don't mess with success unless your products, product line, or company theme change enough to warrant a modification. Check out the chart above for a look at typical magazine ad space sizes.

Getting in Position

Ad size is not the only parameter in buying space. There's also the issue of positioning, or where in the magazine your ad gets placed. The chart on page 193 will give you an idea of industry position-think. Most magazines charge extra for the really hot positions. A back cover, for instance, while always a full-page size, costs more than a

full-page ad elsewhere in the book because it's considered a prime position.

Some magazines will let you choose the positioning for your smaller ad; others more or less stick it in wherever it fits on a page. It often depends on how squeezed they are for time when you place your ad, so it pays to place yours as early as possible. Also, the more often you advertise, the better relationship you develop with the sales and production people and the more likely they'll be to work with you on what you want.

> **Smart Tip**
>
> *Tip...*
>
> How many magazines should you advertise in? Let your budget be your guide. Place ads in as many publications as you can afford. The more exposure you have, the more money you'll make. But if you can only afford one at first, that's fine, too.

Fresh Gourmet Coffee

Your next ad decision should by this time have a familiar ring: color or black and white? The answer should also have a familiar ring: Nobody can decide for you. While it's generally true that color pulls more responses than black and white, you may not need color for your particular products. And since color costs more, if you don't need it, don't pay for it—at least not until you can more easily afford it.

Magazine Ad Position	
Ad Position	**Desirability**
Inside front cover	☆
Back cover	☆
Front half of magazine or "book"	☆
Back half of book	
Top half of page	☆
Bottom half of page	
Outside of page	☆
Inside of page	
Closer to editorial content	☆
Before editorial content	☆

Note: ☆ indicates preferred position.

▲

As we've already explored, you'll also have to decide for yourself whether to use photos, line drawings, or no illustrations at all. Some very successful ads use nothing but type. When you think about graphics, think about what you want that illustration to do. Are you just decorating that costly ad space, or are you using the illustration to make a point? If it's just décor, dump it. With all the fun and fancy fonts and borders available through even inexpensive desktop publishing programs, you can do all sorts of decorating tricks without pictures.

If you decide to go with graphics, think about what point you want the illustration to make. If your product makes an impact with a full-monty mug shot—for instance, a fine art print or a piece of furniture—let it stand alone. But in many cases, it's better to illustrate the benefits of the product than to show the product itself. You can show a one-pound bag of gourmet coffee, for instance, or you can show its benefits—an exhausted office worker delightedly inhaling the bracing aroma of fresh coffee. Can you picture how a black-and-white line drawing of the office worker with her cup of java could be more humorous, more individual, and much more effective than a full-color photo of a bag of coffee beans?

Another thing to keep in mind when considering graphics is that if you're advertising technical products that aren't too exciting in photo form in the first place, an illustration can often bring out aspects that aren't readily apparent in a

---

Apples and Oranges

Use the old bean when you test magazine ads. To make sure you're not unfairly skewing your results, follow these guidelines:

○ *Don't compare apples and oranges.* Make sure the magazines in which you're testing ads cater to the same audience. As we've pointed out, you can't compare the results from a maternity dress ad in *Impending Motherhood* with one placed in *Sports Illustrated.*

○ *Don't place test ads in different monthly issues.* If you're selling gifts, for instance, and you place one ad in the December issue of Magazine A and one in the January issue of Magazine B, you can't make a true comparison, because people will naturally buy more gifts before Christmas than after.

○ *Don't ignore holidays and other seasonal factors when analyzing your results.* You may get a phenomenal response when you advertise those patio accessories in June or July issues, but this doesn't mean you'll get the same response in January and February.

---

photograph. A good graphic artist can play up the fancy trackball on a computer mouse, for instance, and even give the mouse a mousier look for a touch of humor that will get your ad noticed.

Start observing the advertising world around you with a professional eye (you are a professional now!) and you'll begin to see that even those expensive television ads are going for the line art look. For your own products, the best advice—again—is to study your competitors' ads, use your best instincts, and test. You'll find out quickly enough what works.

Smart Tip

Tip...

Ad agencies get a 15 percent commission from magazines when they place an ad, so if you pay $1,100 for the space, they get a $165 commission on top of what you're paying them for media placement. You might want to use this as a bargaining chip when negotiating fees.

Rough Guide

The mail order entrepreneurs we interviewed for this book write their own copy and design their own catalogs. Some do their own artwork. Doing it yourself saves money, and after all, nobody knows your products and your market like you do. If you're a newbie, however, you could be shooting yourself in the foot.

Industry experts suggest that you make a draft of your copy and design and then take your work to an advertising pro for polishing. As you learn more, you can eliminate this step, if you like.

How much can you expect to pay an ad agency? Prices vary, depending on which agency you use and what services you outsource. As a rough guide, let's figure you're

From the Drawing Board

You've designed a brilliant display ad and purchased space in a magazine. Now how do you get it from your desktop publishing program to the production department? Most publications like to have the ad copied from your computer onto a Zip disk and then sent to them. Technologically cutting-edge magazines will accept e-mailed ads, so long as they've been designed using a particular format. Other magazines will take a good old-fashioned ad that's been pasted up with film negatives and cardboard.

If you use an ad agency, you won't need to worry about any of this. If you're doing it yourself, ask the magazine for its specifications and guidelines while you're negotiating for ad space.

▲

going to go with a smaller agency. Smaller firms like the business brought to them by start-up entrepreneurs, while big-name firms with offices in three states will usually only work with mega-corporate clients that have million-dollar ad budgets.

When you go with a smaller agency, creative services, such as developing a logo for your company or designing an ad, generally cost $50 to $75 an hour, while production services—anything from entering copy into the computer to market research and media placement—run about $50 an hour. The length of time needed to design or place an ad depends on what you bring to the table—like how much design and research you've already done and the size of the project—and how quick and creative the agency's pros are. The best way to find out how long it will take for your ad to be designed and/or placed is to ask—along with some other important questions:

- Does the agency have mail order experience?
- What other projects have they turned out? Ask to see a few samples.
- What were the success rates of the ads you're reviewing?
- What fees does the agency estimate for your project?
- In what time frame can you expect your ad to be finished?
- Don't forget to check references!

If your advertising budget is tight but you need professional help, try hiring an amateur with a learner's permit. Post a notice for advertising or graphic arts students at a local college. Students are usually hungry for not only money but also professional experience and course credits. And they frequently have brilliant ideas.

Make a trade. You pay the student a modest (but fair) fee to design your ad. The student gets money and a professional job that can be cited on his or her fledgling resume. Who knows—maybe you'll forge the beginning of a terrific business relationship. (The student could develop into the art department you have always wanted!)

Classified Ads

The major appeal of classified ads for the mail order maven is that they're far less expensive than display ads. Add to that the bonus of simplicity—there's no layout to design, no graphics to worry about and no choice of fonts to obsess over. Add another bonus—defined interest. People who peck around in the classifieds are often there because they're looking for something in that particular classification: vacation destinations or collectibles or money-earning opportunities or whatever. So when they see your ad, they already have an expressed interest in what you're selling. By contrast, people who see your display ad have generally just happened onto it; it was on the page they were reading, but they weren't specifically looking for what you're advertising.

People who peck around in the classifieds are often looking for something in particular.

The downsides of classified ads are that you've got an extremely limited space in which to make your pitch, you have nothing with which to catch your prospect's eye except words that graphically look just like everybody else's, and you've got a much smaller audience to work with. Far fewer people read the classified sections than the editorial ones. And some mail order products just can't be sold effectively through the classifieds. High-ticket items, products or services that require lots of explanation, and products that don't lend themselves to two-step ads don't make good classified candidates.

So, aside from cost, why would you want to run a classified ad?

- It's an inexpensive proving ground. You can test new products for relative pennies and, if the response warrants it, step up to a display ad.

- It's a good way to build your mailing list. For each response you get, you also get a name to send a direct-mail kit or catalog to, and to add to those all-important back-end profits.

Weed Out Words

You write the classified ad in basically the same way you write your direct-mail pieces and your display ad: attention-getting headline, riveting copy, the call to action, your address (with the ad's key code discreetly imbedded), or phone number. All in as few words as possible because you are charged by the word. Let's say you're selling a how-to book for crafters and go over each step:

1. *Your attention-getting headline.* "Earn Money With Your Crafts!" People are always interested in making money. It's a proven attention-getter. As an added bonus, you have filled in the target audience for your ad: crafters. And crafters, like most artists, like recognition, so you've got their attention on two counts here. Magazines will usually print your headline in bold at no extra charge, so remember to ask.

2. *Your riveting copy.* Here's where you need to get your idea across as succinctly as possible: "New book tells you how. Results guaranteed." You've got that magic word "new" and that other magic word "guaranteed."

3. *Your call to action.* Remember, this is where you tell your potential customer exactly what to do and when to take advantage of your offer: "Write today for full details!"

4. *Your address and key code.* "Craft Faire, 123 Rose Cottage, Dept. A, Camellia, FL 30000."

Here's your ad in 23 simple words:

Remember to weed out all extraneous words. If you look back at our step-by-step process, you'll see that we originally had a couple of extra words, "Earn money with *your* crafts" and "New book tells *you* how. In the final version, we deleted *your* and *you*. We also deleted *Dept.* and included the *A* (our key code) as part of the street address. The ad still makes sense, and at $20 a word, we've just saved ourselves $60!

The Write Length

Now that we've told you to keep your ad as short as possible, let's gum things up a little by adding that according to industry wisdom, the more words you use to describe your product, the better the ad will pull. Up to a point. Like the display ad, you'll eventually reach a stage where longer isn't any better. How do you find this? By testing. Start off with the shortest possible ad, gradually increase it by 50 percent, and then 100 percent, and see how each size works. You'll soon find out the "write length" to use!

As always, the best way to learn to write classified ads is by studying your competition. Look through the magazines you plan to advertise in. How many ads do you see repeated? Those are the ones to emulate. If they're still there month after month, it's because they're making money.

Summer Reading?

How often should you run your print ads? For classifieds, the answer is: as often as possible. "Consistency is important," says Lisa Tober, an account executive with *Woman's Day* magazine. When readers look at classified ads, they may not want to order at the moment, and they assume they'll find your ad in the next issue, when they'll be ready. If it's not there, you've just lost a customer.

Display ads also rely on consistency, but with the added expense, you may want to schedule yours only for higher-pulling months, which are during the holiday season for most mail order gift items. Traditionally, magazine sales fall off during the summer months (everybody's at the beach reading tacky novels), but your products may do best during these times. It's up to you to do some research and then decide!

Web Sites

A Web site is a fabulous advertising and marketing tool. With you at the helm as a virtual George or Jane Jetson, your site can offer your customers all the magical properties technology has to offer. Cyber shopping carts to load with merchandise, which they can pay for online by credit card. Animation. Sound bytes. Sound tracks. Instant merchandise and stock update capability. Instant gratification!

But when you set aside the fancy gizmos, what are the differences between Internet and paper mail order? One is the type of customer. The person who takes the time to log on to the Net and click on to your site is most likely looking specifically for what you've got to offer and probably qualifies as a potential buyer rather than a mere window shopper. So that's a bonus.

Adventurous Web Shoppers

As another bonus, Web customers, by virtue of the fact that they're shopping online, tend to be more adventurous, more willing to try something new, and more interested in forging a relationship with the site.

What can you do to take advantage of these tendencies? Interact with your customers. Give them something new and exciting. Foster that relationship. Which brings us to the other big difference between Net and paper mail order—the way you interact with your customers.

"Communicate with people," stresses fabric supplier Caryn O. "Let them know about yourself. Let them know what you represent." Caryn spends a lot of time on her site, sharing not only her wares but her business and life philosophies with her member customers. "My members come to my site daily," she says. "They look for new fabrics every day. They can't wait to see what's new. I'm always thinking of new things to do and what I can do differently. I'm constantly changing, and I get lots of compliments on the new additions. People love that.

"If people come to a Web site and see the same things over and over, they're not going to keep coming back. They're going to wait longer and longer, maybe instead of [visiting every] week, now it's [once a] month. You need people to come daily."

Getting customers to visit your site daily is something you can easily accomplish. With a traditional catalog, you cast your merchandise not in stone but on paper, which after all the time and expenses of production, printing, and

> **Bright Idea**
> Hold a contest, suggests Robert Peters of I-1 Internet Group. Put a guest book on your site and advertise that every 100th shopper gets a free catalog. It creates interest and good will and builds your mailing list.

▲

mailing is about as easy to change as stone. With a Web catalog, however, you can make changes daily (or even hourly) if you like, adapting your site to your customers' desires and spending patterns.

Thanks to the magic of the Net, your Web customers can register their preferences for various types of merchandise, and you can use that knowledge to cross- or up-sell them the things you know they want. The Web's stellar bookseller Amazon.com, for example, notes the types of books customers enjoy—mystery, romance, cooking, etc.—and suggests material in those subject areas every time they log on. It's a great way to make those dedicated customers feel remembered and understood.

Amazon.com also offers customers the option of signing up for e-newsletters on their favorite types of books and then sends mini-reviews of new or popular books every few days—with, of course, the option to purchase the book.

No Spamming

Keep in mind that people who shop the e-commerce way don't like hype. They expect to be informed and entertained, but they don't want to be electronically shouted at, patronized, or pandered to. (Which you shouldn't do to your paper customers,

---

Breakthrough!

The Internet offers breakthrough possibilities for computer-oriented entrepreneurs," says the NMOA's John Schulte. And the entrepreneurs we interviewed certainly agree.

Greer T., the children's boutiquer, finds that her Web site brings in new catalog customers. "We get people who see us through our Internet site, request a catalog, and then order," the Ohio retailer reports.

"Our mail order has just exploded because of the Internet," Caryn, the fabric retailer explains. "It's just amazing. A lot of our customers who used to deal with us through the mail now also use the Internet because it's so much easier."

Beth H., the specialty foods marketer, echoes this view. "Our Web page has been very active," she says. "We get a lot of repeat sales from it."

And Mary M., the romantic gifts purveyor, has decided to go all the way with her online store. "We're not even going into production with another paper catalog," the St. Louis resident says. "We're focusing on the Web site. This is the wave of the future. From all the statistics I've researched, it's growing by leaps and bounds."

---

either.) Sending requested e-mail updates is good business and fun interacting, but "spamming," or sending e-junk mail, is definitely poor Netiquette and will not win friends and influence customers. What will? The same elements that win you paper customers—honesty, integrity, fairness, service, and respect. Show your Web customers they're important

Stat Fact
According to the Advertising Mail Marketing Association, more than half of all Web site sales are to new customers.

by how you treat them. Offer discounts, freebies and any other perks you can think up.

Try these tips for winning and keeping Internet mail order customers:

- *Give your customers easy ordering access.* Don't force them to wade through page after page before finding your "order desk." And don't, as so many sites strangely do, make your address and phone number a state secret. Put them out where customers can find them, not just for ordering but for asking questions.

- *Provide alternative ordering methods for customers who are leery about ordering by credit card over the Net.* Offer these folks order forms they can print out and fax or mail to you. And of course, offer your phone number so they can order by phone if they choose.

- *Check and answer your e-mail on a daily basis.* Don't let virtual customers languish any more than you would phone or mail customers.

- *Update your site frequently.* "If something's sold," Caryn says, "get it right off. Don't let it sit there and get people upset because they can't order it."

- *Don't frustrate customers with a site that's slow or difficult to figure out.* You will quickly lose people this way. Keep your site user-friendly and easy to navigate.

- *Feature links to other sites.* This is a terrific public relations move (we'll talk more about PR later in this chapter) because it shows your customers that you're part of your target audience's larger community and that you want to help them by making it easier for them to find others serving their market.

- *Offer customers information and entertainment.* These elements will draw them in, hold their attention, and make them feel you're a part of their world and they're a part of yours. If you're selling travel products, for instance, post an article on the best vacation spots for the season or ten tips for traveling inexpensively. If you're selling coffee, post fun tips on the different blends available.

- *Go easy on the graphics.* Pictures add impact to your site, but if your customers have to wait seemingly endless minutes for your page to become viewable because it's graphics heavy, you're going to lose them. If you use pictures, make sure they're small and load quickly.

- *Check out competitors' sites, just as you check out competitors' other advertising materials.* Borrow the best of what they are doing, then do it better.

▲

Cigars and Golfers

Just having a catalog on the Web doesn't mean having customers. You have to go out and find them, just as you do with a paper catalog. There are all sorts of advertising techniques you can use, says Roy Fletcher of Fletcher Consulting in Pembroke Pines, Florida. Perhaps the simplest is a banner exchange program, in which you make an advertising trade with another Web site. You put your banner on your exchange partner's site and you let that company put its banner on yours. What's a banner? It's a small ad that pops up on a site's home page. When potential customers click on the banner, they're magically transported to your site to shop.

Here again, you need to think of your target market. Choose sites whose customers will be interested in your products or services. While you don't want to mix apples and oranges—trying to put a banner for your horse products on a site that sells tires, for example—you can get creative. You might, for instance, put a banner for your upscale cigars site on a site that caters to upscale golfers, Fletcher says.

A banner exchange program is an advertising freebie because it's a barter. You don't pay for advertising, and neither does your site exchange partner. The more sites you exchange with, the more free advertising you get. Of course, you've got to work the moderation angle here. As we've said, e-shoppers are generally adverse to "junky" advertising, and if you clutter up your site with banners from everybody under the sun, you'll lose your design integrity, not to mention your company's integrity.

The Flow of Traffic

Another good Web advertising tactic is what's known as an affiliate program. This works like a banner exchange, except that there are fees involved. You put your banner on somebody else's site and you pay them per click, say 15 cents for every customer who clicks onto your site. Or you can arrange to pay a percentage of sales, say 8 or 10 percent of each transaction that results from a customer clicking onto your site from that banner.

This is possible through technology that basically acts as a traffic cop, Fletcher says. It tracks banner sales and generates monthly reports for each party, you, and your affiliate program partner, so that you both know exactly how much money you're due.

A good Web site designer can help you explore, design, set up, and maintain both of

> **Fun Fact**
>
> You can blame MAE West for those congested Internet times. Or you can pin the blame on MAE East. MAE stands for Market Area Exchange, and there are two: West in San Jose, California, and East in Washington, DC. They're routing intersections (or roundhouses) for those trillions of bits and bytes of electronic information speeding through the Net, and their daily rush hours are from 3 P.M. to midnight.

these advertising options, as well as a bevy of others, some of which you can do yourself once your designer points you in the right direction. Don't be afraid to ask.

You may not make money with your site the first year, Fletcher admits, but the possibilities for income are definitely there. Besides that, having a Web site is exciting. "It's fun," Fletcher says. "It's where the world is going."

Free Advertising

You can get terrific free advertising by getting your company or products written up in magazines. Most publications have one or more sections devoted to new products in their target market, and they always need something to fill those spaces. Why not your something?

What you need to do first is prepare a press release, a one- or two-page article about your product(s) accompanied by a photo or two. Here's how you do it:

- *Make sure your product is a quality one.* Editors take their duties seriously and won't publish news on merchandise or services that sound shaky or shoddy.

- *Do your homework.* Don't send your release to every magazine in the known world. Choose magazines that cater to your target audience—and don't forget trade publications. If you are selling clothing or jewelry, for instance, include fashion industry magazines on the list of places to send your press release.

- *Call each magazine to find out which editor to send your release to.* Be sure to get correct name spellings and titles. You can request details, such as if the editor has any special press release preferences. Keep your conversation short and professional, but friendly. You may be making a valuable contact!

- *Use the standard press release format.* Start your press release with a catchy lead tailored to your target magazines and follow it up with a concise, fact-driven release. Double-space your material and keep it in an easy-to-read font and type size. Keep it short. Editors are incredibly busy people. If your release is too long, you'll lose their interest.

- *Don't get too carried away with blowing your own horn.* Overblown claims make you sound amateurish.

- *Send reprint-quality slides of your merchandise.* Many smaller magazines have very limited photo budgets, so any artwork they can use is a terrific bonus.

- *Personalize your mailing.* Send a cover letter with your press release, addressed to the editors you've already talked to, reminding them of who you are, and stating that you think their readers will find your products of interest.

- *Follow up.* Wait a few weeks. Then call to make sure the editors have received your release and find out if they have any questions.

- *Be persistent.* If your first release doesn't garner coverage, send another one and then another in a regular publicity program. But don't send the same release over and over. You don't want to bore the editors to death. Vary your lead, your story, and your products.

Radio

In the beginning, it's probably best to stick to direct-mail and print advertising. But as your company grows, you might want to expand to other advertising venues—radio, for instance. Local stations, not just in your town but all over the country, make excellent vehicles, and time (which is the radio equivalent of magazine space) is more affordable than you might think—as low as $6.50 per spot.

Get hold of the SRDS radio directories and do your homework. Choose stations whose listeners are demographically and psychographically matched to your target audience. If you're selling nose and navel rings, for instance, you're not going to do all that well with golden oldies stations whose listeners are more into Perry Como than psychedelic T-shirts.

Radio time is divided into five periods, of which the most expensive are morning drive time, 6 A.M. to 10 A.M., and evening drive time, 3 P.M. to 7 P.M., when you've got all those captive audiences trapped in their cars on the freeway. The other periods are 10 A.M. to 3 P.M., 7 P.M. to midnight, and the night owl zone of midnight to 6 A.M. Surprisingly enough, the dead zones are often much better advertising times for mail order products. Nobody knows for certain why this is so—maybe insomniacs have more time to write down your company's name and address and mail away for things, or they might be desperate for something to think about besides the sleep they're losing, or perhaps they just like to order by mail. The point is, it works.

Radio, P.I.

Radio has a couple of advantages over other advertising mediums. One is that the station will produce the ad for you at no extra cost. (Make sure you're on-site when production is in progress so you can fix whatever doesn't come out the way you want it to.)

The other advantage is that some stations will accept *P.I.* deals for payment. This has nothing to do with private investigators; it means *per inquiry*. In a P.I. deal, you pay nothing up front

> **Bright Idea**
>
> Once you've got that magazine coverage, take advantage of it. Include "as seen in *Vampire Today* (or whichever) magazine" in your sales materials. This is another type of testimonial and gives you loads of credibility.

Beware!
Unlike print ads, radio, and TV spots are difficult to monitor. Unless you glue yourself to your set, you can't be entirely sure that your ad is being aired as per your contract. If you go for this type of advertising, be sure to plan some sort of "random check" monitoring strategy.

for the cost of advertising. Instead, you pay the station a percentage of the profits you make on each inquiry you receive from your on-air ad.

You'll have to convince the station that your advertising can pull in enough money to make this worth its while, but smaller stations, especially ones with open time in the dead hours, are good candidates.

Television

Well, we've all seen the one-shot television commercials for "Greatest Polkas of All Time CD Collection—just $19.95 plus shipping and handling!" Those commercials air over and over again, one product after another, because they work. As with radio, television is probably not the best venue for the newbie. Why not? For one thing, television works best for one-shots, which we do not recommend, and for another, it's an expensive venue. But as with radio, when your company grows, you might want to give it a try.

The Fringe Zone

The television day is divided into four parts:
- *Daytime:* from dawn until 4 P.M.
- *Early fringe:* from 4 P.M. to 8 P.M. and all day on weekends
- *Prime time (the most expensive):* from 8 P.M. to 11 P.M. (take off one hour for central time zone stations)
- *Late fringe:* from 11 P.M. to dawn.

Like radio, the most expensive time is not necessarily the best for mail order advertising. In fact, the late fringe can be an ideal source of advertising revenue for mail order entrepreneurs.

As with any other advertising medium, target your market. Check out SRDS and *TV Guide*. Television doesn't give you as much demographic and psychographic range for local programming as radio does, but with the ever-expanding reach of cable stations, you should be able to find a vehicle that complements your audience and products.

Local TV stations will often produce your ad for you. Let them! Give them your guidelines or copy, which should run along the same lines as a print ad. Remember that you can show the benefits of your product better with television than with just about any other medium, so take advantage of it.

▲

If you choose to advertise on TV, you should be aware that television has a built-in mail order price threshold. Most products sell best at a top range of $24.95. But check out your competition. Most products sold on TV go for $19.95. Why? Because that's what sells!

Public Relations

Even though you may never come face to face with the customers who view your advertisements, public relations is an important consideration. Good public relations can get your company's name out to people who may not otherwise hear of you and can also keep your current customers thinking fondly of you so they'll continue ordering.

There are all sorts of low-cost public relations techniques you can use. Try some of the following:

- *Volunteer as a guest speaker at the meetings of local associations or clubs that serve your target audience.* If you're selling chocolates, talk to women's groups, cooking classes, and even kids' clubs about the history of chocolate. If you bring samples, you will probably make customers for life. If you've got a business-to-business company, talk to local business groups. Remember that word-of-mouth is a powerful advertising tool and get creative!
- *Join organizations that match your target audience and volunteer for things that will get your company recognized—and thought well of.* Most people respect volunteers

---

Helping Others

Helping others while you help yourself is good for the soul and also a great public relations strategy. Caryn, the fabric merchandiser, has made advocating her customers' businesses a fundamental part of her Web site. Members' wares, along with contact information, are displayed on the site free of charge. "We try to encourage our members to support each other," Caryn says. "We try to get them business as well. We're very big [on the concept that] we'll do better if you do better, and we'll do anything to help you do better."

Caryn receives frequent calls from grateful members thanking her for directing business their way. "We're just happy to help," the Roswell, Georgia, entrepreneur says. "The thing people forget is that when you help somebody else, it truly comes back to you. If you continue to help other companies, when they need products, who do they come back to?"

within an organization and consider them experts in the organization's area of interest. So volunteering can heighten your company's credibility.

- *How about going live on the air? Volunteer yourself for a local radio station's chat show.* You can discuss your niche—health products or horses or chocolates. Listeners can call in with questions. When they talk to you on the air, they'll be interested in ordering your products. And remember word-of-mouth. They'll tell their friends and relatives.

- *Go green.* Use recycled materials as often as possible and stress this fact in your catalog or other printed materials and when you talk to people. Explain that your company helps the environment by conserving fossil fuels, too: When people shop by mail, they're not out running all over town burning smog-producing gasoline.

- *Offer your products as prizes for charity events.*

Use your imagination! If your niche is horse products, can you supply ribbons for show winners? If it's gardening, can you sponsor a yard beautification program? Whatever you can do to get your name in front of the public in favorable ways will add to your company's image—and your income.

> **Bright Idea**
> Have everyone in your audience sign a guest register when you give talks at local club or association meetings. They'll be flattered, and you'll have more names for your in-house mailing list.

The Check's in the Mail
Money Management

Whether you're a chronic number cruncher or one of the finance-phobic, you'll want to give your company periodic financial checkups. "Why?" you ask. "I already did all that math stuff in the start-up chapter." Yup. That was the prenatal exam for the precious baby that's your business. Once you've gone through the birthing process and that precocious tot is toddling around, you'll want periodic checks to make sure your enfant terrible is as healthy as you imagine. If there's a problem, you'll find out before it becomes critical. For instance, if you discover that your income barely covers your printing and operating expenses, you can change the size of your ads or the number of catalogs you mail out.

"With this type of business," Kate W., the team logo merchandiser says, "you have to keep a close eye on your cash flow because it's a very expensive venture. You have to know what's making you money and what's not. If a certain type of advertising isn't making any money, you need to know that before you continue to do it for another two months."

Financial checkups don't have to be negative. After all, they can indicate how well you're doing—which may be even better than you expected. If you've been saving for a new printer or a software upgrade, or if you're hoping to take on an employee, you can judge how close you are to achieving your goal.

Making a Statement

An income statement, also called a profit-and-loss statement, charts the revenues and operating costs of your business over a specific period of time, usually a month. Check out the income statements on pages 211 and 212 for our two hypothetical mail order companies, Chocoholic Central and OnCall Designer. Chocoholic Central, our homebased newbie, has no employees except its owner and so far has a net profit of $31,860. OnCall Designer, with three years of business under its belt, makes its base in an industrial park near the airport, has one full-time employee in addition to the owner, and brings in annual net profits of $62,436. Neither owner draws a salary; they both rely on a percentage of the net profit for their income.

You'll want to tailor your income statement to your particular business. To make the statement really accurate, you'll need to prorate items that are paid annually, such as business licenses and tax-time accounting fees, and pop those figures into your monthly statement. For example, if you pay $600 annually for insurance, divide this figure by 12 and list the resulting $50 as your monthly insurance expense.

Use the worksheet on page 213 to create your own income statement. You'll be surprised at how much fun finances can be!

Coming Up with a Response

You know how to figure your cost per order on a print or classified ad. (If you don't, go back to Chapter 5). You know how to conduct a test mailing of a catalog or other direct-mail piece, sending to, say, 3,000 or 5,000 names before committing yourself to a huge run of 20,000 or more. (Chapter 10, remember?) But how do you determine how much of a response—and how much money—a mail order product is likely to bring in? And more specifically, at what point will you break even and begin making a profit?

Sample Income Statement 1

CHOCOHOLIC CENTRAL

INCOME STATEMENT
For the Month of July 1999

Monthly Income	
Gross sales	$4,900
Cost of sales*	1,209
Gross Monthly Income	**$3,691**
Monthly Expenses	
Rent	$N/A
Box rental	20
Phone/utilities	640
Call center	N/A
Electronic card processing	31
Employees	N/A
Miscellaneous postage	20
Licenses	8
Legal services	30
Accounting services	25
Office supplies	10
Shipping supplies	50
Insurance	90
Subscriptions/dues	37
Web hosting	30
Internet service provider	20
Loan repayment	N/A
Miscellaneous	25
Total Monthly Expenses	**$1,036**
Net Monthly Profit	**$2,655**

Cost of sales is the company's advertising and mailing costs.

Sample Income Statement 2

OnCall Designer

INCOME STATEMENT
For the Month of July 1999

Monthly Income	
Gross sales	$19,600
Cost of sales*	7,500
Gross Monthly Income	**$12,100**
Monthly Expenses	
Rent	$1,200
Box rental	N/A
Phone/utilities	1,175
Call center	1,350
Electronic card processing	45
Employees	2,000
Miscellaneous postage	40
Licenses	20
Legal services	100
Accounting services	100
Office supplies	50
Shipping supplies	100
Insurance	90
Subscriptions/dues	57
Web hosting	300
Internet service provider	20
Loan repayment	200
Miscellaneous	50
Total Monthly Expenses	**$6,897**
Net Monthly Profit	**$5,203**

*Cost of sales is the company's advertising and mailing costs.

Monthly Income Statement Worksheet

For the Month of _____

Monthly Income	
Gross sales	$
Cost of sales*	
Gross Monthly Income	$
Monthly Expenses	
Rent	$
Box rental	
Phone/utilities	
Call center	
Electronic card processing	
Employees	
Miscellaneous postage	
Licenses	
Legal services	
Accounting services	
Office supplies	
Shipping supplies	
Insurance	
Subscriptions/dues	
Web hosting	
Internet service provider	
Loan repayment	
Miscellaneous	
Total Monthly Expenses	$
Net Monthly Profit	$

Smart Tip

The National Mail Order Association (NMOA) is a valuable asset to any mail order newbie, as attested by many of the people we interviewed for this book. Don't hesitate to call on the organization for help. You can visit the NMOA at www.nmoa.org.

We took the question to John Schulte of the National Mail Order Association, who kindly provided us with an "Advanced Break-Even Worksheet" (starting on page 220) and a detailed explanation of how to use it. It may bear a resemblance to those annual forms from the IRS, but it's a lot more fun—and a lot easier to work with. Make lots of copies of the worksheet to use with different product pricing variables. Use your first one to work out the break-even point for the hypothetical mail order proposition Schulte uses to explain the step-by-step calculations on the worksheet. (See the "Advanced Break-Even Worksheet Instructions," starting on page 222.)

What's an average response? There is no easy answer to that one, Schulte says. Response rates depend on a number of factors, including the type and quality of your mailing list, the kind of product or service you're offering, the time of year, and the type of customer you have targeted. If you're selling big-ticket items like $100,000 tractors, for instance, you might be delighted with a one-tenth of 1 percent response. If you're selling the mega-toy of the year during the holiday season, you could expect as high as a 90 percent response.

Hey, Big Spender

As a mail order entrepreneur, you need to keep your costs pared to the bone to make a profit. So whether you're inquiring about print advertising space, printing or lettershop services, copywriting, graphics, or vendors' products, the key is to negotiate. Don't accept the first price someone quotes you. Ask for a better deal and, surprisingly enough, you'll often get it.

Besides bargaining, shop around. Get quotes from several printers or list brokers or call centers. Evaluate not only price but also factors like the estimated amount of time needed to complete a project and company qualifications. Don't be afraid to ask questions. Nobody expects you to be an expert on everything, especially not immediately. If you don't ask, you won't learn.

You may be able to get a head start on finding the best prices for different services from an unlikely source. "When you purchase a bulk mail permit," Kate W. says, "the postal service provides a whole packet of information. Based on [our] ZIP code, they gave us a directory of companies that do a number of services. Through that directory, we interviewed several companies and found [a print shop] that was conveniently located and had the best price."

There are many things you can do to wisely manage your money in the print ad arena. Magazines will often give you special deals because a) they need to make money, and you may turn out to be a big advertising spender, and b) they realize that as a mail order entrepreneur most of your revenue comes from advertising and that you just might need a little help. Most magazine ad reps are not going to give you the deals we're about to discuss without being asked—and even then, you'll have negotiate. But you can frequently get them to agree to your requests. Try these ideas:

- *Mail order special.* As we've just explored, magazines know that your customers aren't going to walk into your store and be swept off their feet by a cardboard cutout display ad at the cash register. You don't have a store in which to place a cardboard cutout; your ad is your only means of generating income. So they'll often give you a sizable discount, up to 40 percent, just because you have a mail order business.

- *Off-season rates.* Like tropical islands or ski resorts, some magazines have off-seasons, when their advertising volume takes a downturn. And like those vacation destinations, these publications will often give you a better-than-normal rate for advertising during the lull. Of course, you have to make sure your own seasonal curve will bear the cost. If you're selling suntan oil in January, this might not be worth the proposed savings.

Rating Ad Rates

One way to determine the cost-effectiveness of advertising in a particular publication is by calculating an efficiency ratio between the circulation and ad rates. This ratio is your cost per thousand, or CPM. If you think this sounds like something only math majors can figure out, you're wrong. A CPM is simply the cost of advertising divided by the magazine's circulation in thousands. If the circulation is 30,000 and the rate for a full-page ad is $600, you'd divide $600 by 30 and arrive at a CPM of $20.

Then you'd compare this with another potential advertising candidate, say, one with a circulation of 50,000 and a full-page ad rate of $700. Dividing $700 by 50, you'd have a CPM of $14.

If one magazine's CPM is considerably lower than the other's, and you can only afford to advertise in one of them, you've got a good place to start your decision-making process. But you'll still need to take all those demographics into consideration. If the cheaper magazine doesn't address your target market as closely, think twice!

- *Flying standby.* Sometimes magazines, like airlines, find at the eleventh hour before going to press that they don't have all their space sold. Since blank space looks bad, the usual solution is to fill it with public service ads like the ones you see for the Red Cross or the Humane Society. This is good karma but bad for the books. You can save the day by offering to purchase space at a standby rate, for which you may get as much as 50 percent off the usual rate. You'll have to inform the magazine ahead of time that you'd like this arrangement so its salespeople will know to call you, and you'll need to be able to have an ad ready at a moment's notice. (Sometimes you can have one on standby already at the magazine.) You also usually have to already have a good relationship with the magazine. But what a savings!

> **Smart Tip** Tip...
>
> Looking for ways to increase your income? Set a goal for your average sale amount per order. When you reach that average, set new goals. This strategy helps you determine what you need to do to increase sales. If your average order is $50, for instance, and you're selling chocolates, you might come up with special promotions to boost the average to, say, $75 per order.

- *Mail order, P.I.* You remember the PI (per inquiry) from our review of radio advertising in Chapter 11, right? Well, it can work for print ads, too. In a PI arrangement, the magazine runs your ad "for free." In exchange, you give it a percentage of whatever money you make off inquiries from that ad. Sometimes the inquiries come to you, and you do all the book work and send the magazine its share every month (or whenever you've agreed). Sometimes the inquiries go to the magazine, which takes its portion off the top and sends the balance to you.

- *Frequent flier.* Magazines will usually give you a discount for advertising frequently. The size of the discount depends on whether you advertise every month, or three, four, or six times a year. This can be a terrific deal, but do not commit to it until you've done your testing and ascertained that the ad is working.

- *Regional remnants.* Remnants aren't just for fabric! National magazines often have regional issues, which allow advertisers to run ads only in the areas they want to target or to test ads by running them in different regions. Because of this, however, one regional issue or another may end up with blank, or *remnant*, space. You can negotiate to purchase last-minute remnant space the same way as in the standby arrangement, again with up to a 50 percent discount.

- *Help if necessary.* Not all magazines are going to go for this one, but it doesn't hurt to ask. A "help if necessary" ad means that, if you've paid for your ad in advance and you don't get any results from it, the magazine will help you out by running the ad again (and even again after that) if necessary until you at best make a profit or at worst break even.

- *Trading places.* Occasionally a magazine will make a trade—free advertising in exchange for your product(s). You can see that this won't always work, but depending on your merchandise, the type of magazine, and the type of mind behind the magazine, it can be a good and fair trade.

- *Spread discount.* In the magazine industry, a "spread" isn't a low-fat butter substitute; it's an ad (or an article) with two or more pages. While this is probably not an option for you as a newbie, you may get to the point where you can afford to purchase a spread. The good news here is that while spreads are terribly expensive, magazines will often give you a discount of up to—you guessed it—50 percent.

- *Cash it in.* Most magazines will give you a 2 percent discount if you pay within 10 days of placing your ad. To find out if this is offered, you'll have to examine the magazine's rate card or SRDS listing. If you see an early-payment discount, take it. Just deduct the discount amount when you send in your paid-within-10-days check.

- *In-house agency.* Form your own advertising agency! Magazines give agencies a 15 percent discount on every ad they place, so when you form your own agency,

The Trick Shot

Clever mail order entrepreneurs come up with all sorts of tricks to keep costs down. "We cut our photography expenses in half," Kate W. says, "yet we doubled the number of photographs."

In Kate's first catalog, she featured group photos of her products on nearly every page, which required long, complicated photo shoots of her inanimate models. "There was a lot of artistic stuff," the team logo merchandiser says. "You had to put things so they all looked good together. Rather than setting down a coffee mug—one piece—and photographing it, we had to completely design and lay out everything."

The result was that her labor costs were astronomical. The following year, the tenor—and the expense—of the photo shoot changed. "We used about half the group-shot pictures from last year," Kate explains, "and then we did a lot of single product inserts. When you're only shooting one product, you can get 10 or 12 done in an hour vs. one every three hours. You learn that if you're going to bring costs down, you have to change your original ideas."

you qualify for the same discount. The trick here is to keep your identity as low-key as possible. You don't want to lie about being in-house, but you don't want to trumpet the fact either; some magazines will try to avoid giving you the agency discount if they know your agency is in-house. Give your agency a different name than your company and then print up special agency stationery with which to send your ad and instructions.

When you go wheeling and dealing, remember that magazines usually don't like to admit that they give any of these special deals. You may not find most of them on the rate card, so you'll have to ask. When you do, be firm but friendly—not pushy. Keep in mind that you're establishing relationships here, ones that ideally will take you far into the future, earning tidy sums for your company and for the magazine. Let the ad reps know that you're a serious businessperson and that, as one, you're looking for a deal. They'll respect your position. Make sure you respect theirs. And don't forget to say "Thank you."

The Tax Man Cometh

Once you earn all that money with your cleverly negotiated ads, someone else will be queuing up for a piece of the action: Uncle Sam. If your budget allows, you should engage an accountant. You probably won't need one for your daily or monthly concerns, but it's well worth the expense to have someone in the know at the reins when April 15 rolls around and for those rare but Panicsville questions that come up now and then.

Your tax deductions should be about the same as those for any other small or home-based business. These deductions include all normal office expenses plus interest, taxes, insurance, and depreciation (this is where the accountant comes in handy). You can deduct the percentage of your home that's used as an office, so long as you're using it solely as an office. The total amount of the deduction is limited by the gross income you derive from business activity minus all your other business expenses, apart from those related to the home office. And you thought that new board game you got for your birthday had complicated rules!

Tip...

Smart Tip

You can call the IRS with questions from just about anywhere in the country using the convenient toll-free number listed in your local White Pages. You may have to go through voice-mail menu hell and hold for what seems an eternity, but once you get a live being on the line, they're well-informed and surprisingly friendly. You can also ask Uncle Sam questions via e-mail through the IRS's Web site at www.irs.gov.

Basically, the IRS doesn't want you to come up with so many home office deductions that you end up paying no taxes at all. If, after reading all the lowdown, you're still confused, consult your accountant.

On the Road Again

What else can you deduct? Business-related phone calls, the cost of business equipment and supplies (again, so long as you're truly using them solely for your business), subscriptions to professional and trade journals, and auto expenses. Deductible auto expenses accrue when you drive your trusty vehicle in the course of doing business or seeking business. In other words, you're chalking up deductible mileage when you motor out to vendors' or manufacturers' offices to pick up samples and when you take a spin upstate to attend a trade show.

It's wise to keep a log of your business miles. You can buy one of several varieties at your local office supply or stationers, or you can make one yourself. Keep track as you go. It's no fun to have to backtrack at tax time and guesstimate how many miles you drove to how many clients' locations how many times during the year.

Let Me Entertain You

You can deduct entertainment expenses, such as wining and dining a vendor during the course of a meeting or hosting potential customers at a coffee hour. Keep a log of all these expenses as well, especially if they come to less than $75 a pop. And if you're entertaining at home, have your vendors or customers sign a guest book.

You must have a business-related purpose for entertaining, such as a sales presentation. General goodwill toward your potential customers or vendors does not make it, so be sure your log contains the reason for the partying.

Planes, Trains, and Automobiles

When you travel for business purposes, you can deduct air fares, train tickets, rental car mileage, and the like. You can also deduct hotel and meal expenses. And you can even—under certain circumstances—deduct recreational side trips you take with your family while you are traveling on business. Since the IRS allows deductions for any trip you take to expand your awareness and expertise in your field of business, it makes sense to also take advantage of any conferences or seminars you can attend.

Tip...

Smart Tip

The IRS loves documentation. The more receipts and logs you accumulate and carefully organize, the happier you'll be if an audit rears its ugly head.

Advanced Break-Even Worksheet

Date:_____

Key Code:_____

Product or Service: _____

1. Selling price of product or service $_____

2. Variable costs of filling an order:

     a. Wholesale cost of product or service $_____

     b. Royalty $_____

     c. Handling expense $_____

     d. Postage and shipping expense $_____

     e. Premium, include handling and shipping $_____

     f. Use tax, if any (#1 x _____%) $_____

     g. Credit card processing charge
        (#1 x _____% transaction fee) $_____

     Total Cost of Filling the Order   **$**_____

3. Administrative overhead

     a. Rent, utilities, maintenance, credit checks,
        collections, etc. (_____% of #1) $_____

     Total Administrative Cost   **$**_____

4. Estimated percentage of returns, refunds, or cancellations   _____ %

5. Expense in handling returns:

     a. Return postage and handling (#2c + #2d) $_____

     b. Refurbishing returned merchandise (_____% of #2a) $_____

     Total Cost of Handling Returns   **$**_____

Advanced Break-Even Worksheet, continued

6. Chargeable cost of returns (_____% of #5 total) $_____

7. Estimated bad debt percentage   _____ %

8. Chargeable cost of bad debts (#1 x #7) $_____

9. Total Variable Costs (#2 + #3 + #6 + #8) $_____

10. Unit profit after deducting variable costs (#1 - #9) $_____

11. Return factor (100% - #4)   _____ %

12. Unit profit per order (#10 x #11) $_____

13. Credit for returned merchandise (_____% of #2a) $_____

14. Net profit per order (#12 + #13) $_____

15. Cost of mailing per 1,000 $_____

16. Number of orders per 1,000 mailings needed to break even:

   Mailing cost (#15) divided by net profit (#14) $_____

Source: The National Mail Order Association.

▲

Advanced Break-Even Worksheet
Instructions

Let's take a look at a hypothetical mail order proposition and go through the various steps to see what costs must be included to determine how many orders per thousand you must get to break even.* First, the worksheet should carry the date, the name of the proposition, and the key code for that particular mailing. You'll need this information for future reference.

1. We start with the retail selling price of the merchandise or service. In this case, let's say we're selling the *Green Thumb Gardening Book* for $25 with ten days' free examination and a premium, a "seed planting gauge," included as an extra incentive to examine the book. The customer gets to keep the planting gauge whether he buys or returns the book. Fill in $25 under item #1.

2. Here we enter #2a, the wholesale cost of the book (including shipping carton) which is $6. This gives us a good markup of more than 400 percent. For one-shot mailings, a larger selling margin is necessary, especially on lower-cost items.

   The next consideration is royalty, item #2b. If you're selling a book or an item on which a royalty or commission needs to be paid to the author, manufacturer or inventor, this expense should be included as a part of the total cost of the merchandise or service. In this hypothetical case, there is no royalty because the book is purchased from another publisher.

   The handling expense, item #2c, includes the opening of the mail, data entry, and processing the order for fulfillment. This amounts to 95 cents. Postage and shipping expense (#2d) is 60 cents. As we included a premium in this offer (the planting gauge), we must add its cost (30 cents) as part of the expense of filling the order (item #2e). If your state has a use tax this must also be added (#2f). For this example, we will not be adding a use tax. In most cases, you will also have to add a credit card processing expense, as most people use their credit cards for orders. Let's take 3 percent (including transaction fee) as an example. Multiply item #1 by 3 percent and you get 75 cents for #2g. Adding all the expenses under #2, it costs $8.60 to fill an order.

3. But there are other costs that must be included. How about administrative costs, which include rent, light, heat, use of equipment, maintenance, credit checks, collection follow-up, office supplies, and the like? Many firms make a flat charge of 10 to 20 percent of the retail price (#1) to cover these expenses. Let's use 10 percent of $25.00, or $2.50, and enter this under #3a as the total administrative cost.

4. The next question is what percentage of your customers will return the merchandise if sold on a free examination offer? Suppose we take 10 percent as an average and post this under item #4.

*All numbers used in this worksheet are hypothetical and do not relate to any actual known numbers.

Advanced Break-Even Worksheet
Instructions, continued

5. How much does it cost to handle returns? It certainly costs as much as it did to ship the books. So let's charge $1.55 (#2c plus #2d) for item #5a. (Of course, some customers will pay the shipping for returning the merchandise but let's not count on it.) Also consider that some of the books may be damaged in shipping, so let's allow 10 percent of the cost of the book (10 percent of #2a), 60 cents in this example, for refurbishing (#5b). This brings the total cost of handling returns (item #5) to $2.15 per order.

6. As we are figuring that 10 percent of the orders will be returned, refunded, or canceled (item #4), the total cost of handling returns will be 10 percent of $2.15 (item #5), or 21.5 cents per order. Let's just say 21 cents.

7. Bad debts (money owed from customers who never pay up) are another expense that must be considered. This percentage will vary from about 5 to 25 percent, depending on the proposition, the way the offer is presented, and the list used. Let's take 10 percent as an average figure and enter it here.

8. So our bad debt cost is 10 percent (item #7) times $25.00 (item #1). This amounts to $2.50 that must be allowed for the cost of bad debts. Enter $2.50 for item #8.

9. The total variable costs are item #2 ($8.60) plus item #3 ($2.50), item #6 ($ .21) and item #8 ($2.50), amounting to $13.81.

10. After deducting the total variable costs of $13.81 (item #9) from the selling price of $25 (item #1), we're left with a unit profit of $11.19.

11. But there is a return factor of 10 percent (item #4) that must be accounted for. Deducting item #4, or 10 percent, from 100 percent leaves 90 percent of the unit profit. Post 90 percent for item #11.

12. Taking 90 percent (item #11) of $11.19 (item #10) leaves a unit profit of $10.07 per order. Post this amount for item #12.

13. Any merchandise that is returned after examination will be put back into your inventory to liquidate or perhaps be sent back to the manufacturer. This represents a credit against the original cost of the merchandise. Since we estimate the returns to be 10 percent (item #4), we would have a credit of 10 percent of our cost (item #2a, $6), or 60 cents.

14. Adding the unit profit per order (item #12) to the credit for returned merchandise (item #13), we have a net profit per order of $10.67.

15. Suppose the cost of your mailing package—carrier envelope, letter, circular, order form, reply envelope, mailing list, lettershop labor, postage, etc.— amounts to $100 per thousand. What about creative and production charges such as editorial preparation, artwork, advertising, consultation, copy, engravings, and typesetting that must be paid for?

▲

Advanced Break-Even Worksheet
Instructions, continued

You have the choice of charging these expenses against the test mailing or amortizing them over your projected mailing possibilities. If you charge it all in one lump sum against the test, it will show a distorted picture. This could kill the test before you give it a chance. It's better to spread this part of the cost over the total quantity of a projected mailing. If the creative and production charges amount to $1,000 and you figure you can mail to 2 million names if the test is successful, you could charge 50 cents per thousand names against the cost of the mailing. If the test is a flop, you'll have to absorb the expense anyway, so why not give it a reasonable chance to come through? Enter $100.50 ($100 plus 50 cents) under item #15.

16. Dividing the cost of mailing 1,000 letters (item #15), $100.50, by the net profit per order (item #14), $10.67, tells us that you need 9.4 orders, or .94 percent per thousand, to break even.

Suppose your break-even point on a test mailing is 9.4 orders or .94 percent, less than a 1 percent response. How many orders more than 9.4 per thousand should you get to justify going ahead with a larger mailing? That depends on whether there's the potential to win long-term customers or if this is a one-shot deal. If you are selling merchandise that provides some kind of residual income, such as vitamins or another product that people reorder regularly, you may be happy with just breaking even to bring in new customers and having future sales make up your profit. But with one-shot propositions, you should look for some kind of return on investment, since you're taking a bigger risk with your money—and that means getting enough orders to take you past your break-even point.

To give you an idea of how the money grows when you get just a few orders more than what's needed to break even, we've laid out an illustrative scenario. For this example, we will get one-third more orders than our break-even point of 9.4. This would give us a total of 12.5 orders per thousand, or 3.1 orders more than the break-even point. (This is a 1.25 percent response.)

With 3.1 orders more than the break-even point and a unit profit of $10.67 per order, the net profit would be $33.08 per thousand (3.1 x $10.67). On a 100,000 mailing, the net profit would be $3,308. On 500,000 it would be $16,540. And on 1,000,000 it would $33,080.

A word of caution! The time that elapses between the date of a test mailing and the date of the final mailing may affect your results. For example, a test made in January that pulls 12.5 orders per thousand might pull only 9.4 or less if mailed in June. So test in the slow months, if possible, and mail in the good months to eliminate unprofitable mailings.

Source: The National Mail Order Association.

Happy Mailings
or Empty
Envelopes?

Most people succeed in the mail order
business by following the tried-and-true business methods of
persistence and plain old-fashioned hard work, with a healthy
dose of optimism sprinkled throughout. If we have illustrated
anything in this book, we hope it's that becoming a successful

mail order entrepreneur involves a lot of work—rewarding and sometimes exhilarating work, but darn hard work nonetheless.

We also hope we've managed to convey that becoming a mail order maven is not the same as becoming an overnight success. It takes lots of market research, loads of planning, tons of testing and analysis, and an abundance of creativity to gain those repeat customers.

Don't Look Back

When the mail order entrepreneurs interviewed for this book were asked for some words of advice for beginners, they gave—not surprisingly—some very thoughtful responses.

"I think in any type of mail order business you want to identify a need and target your mailing," says Beth H., the gluten-free foods purveyor in Connecticut. "If you try to saturate a market that is very broad, you are just dooming yourself to failure. You really need to start small and remain focused. You need to know who your competition is. I think you have to have an excellent product and top-notch service. And you have to be consistent. If you can do all of those things, then I think you have a good shot at a good business."

In Missouri, Mary M., the provider of romantic gifts and romance-themed home décor, says, "You probably need to do most of the work yourself. Keep your investment as low as possible. Research your competitors. Take some business courses. Put yourself out there. You can't find out a lot if you're just sitting at home. You've got to get out there and network."

"Ask everybody questions," adds Liz L., the children's T-shirt designer in New York. "Find someone you know and like at your local post office. If you have any questions, they will help you. And I am sure every community has an office you can call with questions if your local post office can't handle something. Attend seminars at your local college. Join groups. Get involved and really get into your field. Read trade magazines."

In Kansas, Kate W., the university team logo merchandiser, also suggests reading. "Read, read, read," she says. "Read everything you can get your hands on before you start." In addition, she recommends having an interest in your target market. "If you're going to do it solo," Kate advises, "make sure it's something you have a genuine interest in. If I wasn't so loyal to [my niche] and excited about it every day, it would be really hard to put in the long hours consistently."

"Go very slowly," cautions Caryn O., the fabric supplier in Georgia. "Going too fast can put you out of business quickly. If you can't fill your customers' needs, you'll be shocked how quickly you can go out of business. It's just as detrimental as having no business. So go slow. It'll work out. Get it right. Get it down to a science. It gets easier and easier."

Yin and Yang

If you're the type of person who can handle the ups and downs of entrepreneurship in general and the yin and yang of creativity and number crunching that makes up the mail order maven's world, you'll probably thrive. If not, you may discover during your company's first year of life, or a little beyond, that the business isn't for you. You may feel that instead of happy mailings, you are experiencing empty envelopes.

Whether or not you're earning money, the success of your business is contingent on a happiness factor. Because of the amount of work and responsibility involved in running your own business, you may discover that you'd be just as happy—or more so—working for someone else. And that's OK. With everything you will have learned, you'll be a great job candidate.

None of the people interviewed for this book, from a brand-new newbie to a veteran with 15 years of experience, seem to have any intention of packing it in. Rather, they appear to delight in doing what they enjoy and helping others with the same interests.

"We share a lot," Caryn says. "We know so many of our members that you wouldn't believe it. We have customers all over the world. We've met some of the most wonderful people. It's really a fun thing."

Although the mail order entrepreneurs who so generously helped with this book serve different markets and have different levels of experience, they all have one important thing in common—a winning attitude. If you go into this business with the right stuff—a willingness to work hard and learn everything you can, the confidence to promote yourself and your business, and the drive to succeed—chances are, you will.

Appendix

Mail Order Resources

They say you can never be rich enough or young enough. While these could be argued, we say you can never have enough resources. Therefore, we present for your consideration a wealth of resources for you to check into, check out, and harness as part of your own personal information blitz.

These resources are intended to get you started on your research. They are by no means the only ones out there. We have done our research, but businesses—like those expired mailing list nixies—do tend to move, change, fold, and expand. As we have repeatedly stressed, *do your homework*. Get out there and do some investigating.

The best place to start? If you haven't yet joined the Internet age, do it! Surfing the Net is like waltzing through the fabled Library at Alexandria, with a breathtaking array of resources literally at your fingertips.

Advertising Rate Information

Standard Rate and Data Service (SRDS), 1700 Higgins Rd., Des Plaines, IL 60018-5605, (800) 851-7737, (847) 375-5000, www.srds.com (*Note:* Most local public libraries carry copies of SRDS directories—an option if you don't want to invest in your own right away.)

Associations

Advertising Mail Marketing Association, 1901 N. Fort Meyer Dr., #401, Arlington, VA 22209-1609, (703) 524-0096, www.amma.org

The Direct Marketing Association, 1120 Ave. of the Americas, New York, NY 10036-6700, (212) 768-7277, www.the-dma.org

Mail Advertising Service Association International, 1421 Prince St., Alexandria, VA 22314-2806, (888) 333-6272, (703) 836-9200, www.masa.org

National Mail Order Association, 2807 Polk St. N.E., Minneapolis, MN 55418-2954, (888) 496-7337 (for ordering books and reports only), (612) 788-1673, www.nmoa.org

Books

Building a Mail Order Business: A Complete Manual for Success, William A. Cohen, Ph.D., John Wiley & Sons

Home-Based Mail Order: A Success Guide for Entrepreneurs, William J. Bond, McGraw-Hill

How to Start a Mail Order Business, Mike Powers, Avon Books

How to Start and Operate a Mail-Order Business, Julian L. Simon, McGraw-Hill

Call Centers

All USA Communications, 10526 Cermak, #300, Westchester, IL 60154, (888) 413-0210, (708) 236-1200, www.allusa.net

Call Center Plus, 2519 N. 330 E., North Logan, UT 84341, (888) 753-2030, (435) 753-2030, www.callcenterplus.com

Viking Fulfillment Services Inc., 7145 Boone Ave. N., #200, Minneapolis, MN 55428, (612) 533-2526

Credit Card Services

CreditCards.com, 9200 Sunset Blvd., 6th Fl., Los Angeles, CA 90069, (888) 327-4748, (310) 724-6400, www.creditcards.com

Merchant Express, 20A Northwest Blvd., PMB 102, Nashua, NH 03063, (888) 845-9457, www.merchantexpress.com

Delivery Services

FedEx, (800) GO-FEDEX, www.fedex.com

UPS, (800) PICK-UPS, www.ups.com

USPS, (800) THE-USPS, www.usps.gov

Helpful Government Web Sites

Bureau of the Census, www.census.gov

Federal Trade Commission, www.ftc.gov

U.S. Postal Service, www.usps.gov; for mail rate calculators: www.usps.gov/business/calcs.htm

(*Note:* Ask your local bulk-mail processing center—which you can locate by calling your nearest post office—for copies of *Publication 95, Quick Service Guide* and the *Mailers Companion*)

Magazines and Publications

Catalog Age, Cowles Business Media, 11 River Bend Dr. S., Box 4949, Stamford, CT 06907-0949, (800) 775-3777 (subscriptions), (203) 358-9900 (editorial), www.catalogagemag.com.

The Catalog & Web Marketer, Maxwell Sroge Publishing, 522 Forest Ave., Evanston, IL 60202-3005, (847) 866-1890, www.catalog-news.com

Direct Marketing, 224 Seventh St., Garden City, NY 11530, (800) 229-6700, (516) 746-6700

Target Marketing, 401 N. Broad St., Philadelphia, PA 19108, (800) 627-2689, (215) 238-5300, www.targetonline.com

(*Note:* Most magazines will send a sample issue free of charge if you call and ask. So do it!)

Mailing Lists

Allmedia, 17060 Dallas Pkwy., #105, Dallas, TX 75248-1905, (800) 466-4061, (972) 818-4060

▲

American List Counsel, 88 Orchard Rd. CN-5219, Princeton, NJ 08543, (800) ALC-LIST, (908) 874-4300, www.amlist.com

Database America, 100 Paragon Dr., Montvale, NJ 07645-0416, (800) 223-7777, (201) 476-2000, www.databaseamerica.com

(*Note:* Check into any issue of magazines like Catalog Age or Target Marketing—advertisements for list brokers, managers and owners abound.)

Mail Order Consultants

John Schulte & Associates, 2807 Polk St. N.E., Minneapolis, MN 55418-2954, (612) 788-1673, e-mail: schulte@nmoa.org

Maxwell Sroge Co., 522 Forest Ave., Evanston, IL 60202-3005, (847) 866-1890, www.catalog-news.com

Richard Siedlecki, 4767 Lake Forest Dr. N.E., Atlanta, GA 30342, (404) 303-9900, e-mail: sied@mindspring.com

Mail Order Software

MAILER'S Software, 22382 Empressa, Rancho Santa Margarita, CA 92688-2112, (800) 800-MAIL, (949) 589-5200, www.800mail.com

Mail Order Wizard, Haven Corp., 1227 Dodge Ave., Evanston, IL 60202-1008, (800) 676-0098, (847) 869-3434, www.havencorp.com

Mailware, Core Technologies, 900 Cesery Blvd., #107, Jacksonville, FL 32211, (904) 221-1227, www.core-tech.com

(*Note:* Most software vendors will send you a free or nominally priced demo if you ask.)

Mail Order Web Sites

ALC List Connection, www.amlist.com. (Terrific how-to articles and checklists!)

Catalog-News.com, www.catalog-news.com

Media Central, www.mediacentral.com

NetMarketing, www.netb2b.com

Smart Business Supersite Catalog Page, www.smartbiz.com/sbs/cats/catalogs.htm

Seminars and Conferences

The Direct Marketing Association, 1120 Ave. of the Americas, New York, NY 10036-6700, (212) 768-7277, www.the-dma.org

National Mail Order Association, 2807 Polk St. N.E., Minneapolis, MN 55418-2954, (888) 496-7337 (for ordering books and reports only), (612) 788-1673, www.nmoa.org

(*Note:* Your local community college or university may also sponsor seminars and workshops.)

Shipping and Packaging Supplies

Anchor Box Co., 5889 S. Gessner Rd., Houston, TX 77036, (800) 522-8820, (713) 778-1500, www.anchorbox.com

Associated Bag Co., 400 Boden Rd., Milwaukee, WI 53207, (800) 926-6100, (414) 769-1000, www.associatedbag.com

Geopac, P.O. Box 3660, 521 Main Ave. S.W., Hickory, NC 28601, (828) 322-5258, www.geopac.com

Successful Mail Order Businesses

Bella Famiglia, Greer Thottam, 4800 Higbee Ave., Canton, OH 44718, (888) 423-5523, (330) 479-1464, www.beautiful family.com

The Fabric Club, Caryn O'Keefe, P.O. Box 767670, Roswell, GA 30076, (800) FAB-CLUB, (404) 344-9432, www.fabricclub.com

The Gluten-Free Pantry, Beth Hillson, P.O. Box 840, Glastonbury, CT 06033, (800) 291-8386, (860) 633-3826, e-mail: pantry@glutenfree.com, www.glutenfree.com

Just for Fans, Kate Wolford, 11936 W. 119th St., #105, Overland Park, KS 66213, (800) 934-FANS, (913) 681-3634, e-mail: sales@just4fans.com, www.just4fans.com

Little Lizzie, Liz Landa, P.O. Box 593, Rhinebeck, NY 12572, (914) 876-8130, e-mail: littlelizzie1@yahoo.com

Love & Lace, Mary Martin and Michelle Harrison, 3953 Hartford St., Dept. Z, St. Louis, MO 63116-3909, (800) 246-3583, e-mail: sales@loveandlacegifts.com, www.loveandlacegifts.com

Rubber Vodka Logs (McMahon Inc.), Mike McMahon, P.O. Box 39, Byron, CA 94514, (925) 516-0985, www.rubbervodka.com

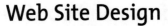
Web Site Design

Fletcher Consulting, Roy Fletcher, 11214 Pines Blvd., #240, Pembroke Pines, FL 33026, (888) 438-8311, (954) 438-8311, www.fcon.com

Pulsity, 53 W. Jackson Blvd., #550, Chicago, IL 60604, (800) 617-8263, (312) 341-1977, www.pulsity.com

Glossary

Additional profit center: a method of earning money other than through sales to mail order customers, such as renting mailing lists to other direct marketers.

Audited circulation statement: a sworn statement from a magazine publisher, verified by an outside source, that discloses the magazine's circulation.

Back end: a mail order company's list of repeat customers.

Bulk mail: mail sent at discounted prices and according to special postal guidelines; also called *standard mail*.

Call center: a company that answers phones and takes orders from customers for a mail order business.

Catalog house: a company that supplies preprinted catalogs and drop-shipped merchandise to mail order entrepreneurs.

Charge-back: the refunding of money for returned or disputed merchandise that was paid for by credit card.

Classified ad: a print advertisement without graphics found only in the classified section of a publication.

Compiled list: a mailing list composed of people in specific categories, e.g., doctors, lawyers, Manhattan residents.

Cost per order: the cost of an advertisement divided by the number of orders received.

Cost per thousand (CPM): the cost of an advertisement divided by a magazine's circulation in thousands.

CPM: see *cost per thousand*.

Cross-sell: to attempt to raise the total amount of a customer's order by suggesting the purchase of related products.

Dba (doing business as): also called a *fictitious business name*, a dba is the name a business legally registers for itself.

Direct mail: see *direct marketing*.

Direct marketing: the use of printed materials such as sales letters, brochures, and catalogs to advertise products and services available for order via mail, telephone, fax, or e-mail; another term for mail order; also called *direct mail* and *direct response*.

Direct response: see *direct marketing*.

Display ad: a print advertisement that has graphics and can be placed almost anywhere in a publication.

Drop-ship: an arrangement in which a third party such as a manufacturer or a wholesaler sends products directly from its warehouse to the mail order retailer's customers

Early fringe: the television time slot from 4 P.M. to 8 P.M.

Evening drive time: the radio time slot from 3 P.M. to 7 P.M.

FDA: Food and Drug Administration.

Fictitious business name: see *dba*.

Focus group: a group of people gathered for the purpose of conducting market research.

Front end: a list of prospects to whom material has been mailed but who have not purchased products or services.

FTC: Federal Trade Commission.

Fulfillment: the process of filling and shipping mail orders; fulfillment often also includes taking the orders.

Fulfillment house: a company that fills and ships orders; fulfillment houses frequently also take orders by phone or mail.

General catalog: a catalog that sells a wide variety of merchandise.

Half-life: the time span between when an issue of a catalog is mailed out and when half the total number of orders expected from it are received; generally considered to be three or four months, depending on the type of merchandise and the target market.

Help if necessary: a stipulation in which a magazine reruns an ad at no additional charge until the advertiser garners a response.

In-house agency: an advertising agency formed and run by a company to address its own advertising needs.

Jobber: a wholesale-product distributor.

Key code: an identifying code made up of numbers and letters, or an address addition, such as "Dept. A," that is placed on all sales materials to indicate which advertisement or mail campaign a response originated from; also called a *source code*.

Late fringe: the television time slot from 11 P.M. to dawn.

Lettershop: a company that processes direct-mail pieces, performing services such as placing inserts, folding, stapling, sorting, and stamping.

List broker: a company or individual specializing in mailing-list rentals.

Mailing list: a roster of names and addresses used by direct marketers.

Mail or Telephone Order Merchandise Rule: an FTC ruling that regulates direct-marketing practices.

Media kit: the package magazines send to potential advertisers that contains sample issues, an *audited circulation statement* and information about editorial content, reader demographics, and ad rates.

Merge/purge: to combine duplicate mailing list entries and remove invalid ones, such as those for people who have moved and provided no forwarding address.

Morning drive time: the radio time slot from 6 A.M. to 10 A.M.

Nixie: a mailing list address that has changed and for which no forwarding information has been provided.

Nth name selection: a random-sampling method of mailing list name selection in which every seventh or 10th name, for example, is used to compile a broad cross-section of names.

One-shot: a single mail order product marketed and sold by itself rather than as part of a line of products.

One-step: a print ad that incorporates an order form.

Overwrap: a second catalog cover made with cheaper paper than the rest of the book; used to test new products, advertise specials, or promote other materials.

Per inquiry (P.I.): a method of paying for advertising by giving the media source a percentage of the profits made on each inquiry the ad generates.

P.I.: see *per inquiry*.

Pick and pack: a company that handles packing and shipping.

Piggyback products: sales materials from one mail order advertiser tucked in with the sales package of another advertiser.

Postal inspector: a direct-marketing regulator employed by the U.S. Postal Service and empowered to arrest those who engage in illegal mail order activities.

▲

Proprietary rights: a company's right to manufacture a product.

Psychographics: a method of targeting mail order customers by psychological profile.

Qualified buyer: a customer who has already purchased products or services by mail order.

Rate card: a card or sheet that lists a magazine's advertising prices.

Recency, Frequency, Money (RFM): a mailing list selection formula in which a list is evaluated according to how recently the people on it have ordered something by mail, how frequently they order and how much money they spend.

Remnant: magazine ad space that remains unsold immediately prior to publication and is offered to advertisers at a discounted rate.

Response list: a mailing list composed of people who have previously responded to specific mail order campaigns; for instance, people who buy gardening books or people who buy horse-care products.

Roll out: to mail out materials in a direct-marketing campaign.

Salting: the practice of inserting fictitious names and addresses into a mailing list so that the company renting the list to others can tell if it has been used illegally; also called *seeding*.

Seeding: see *salting*.

Select: a specific category, such as age, geographic region, or income bracket, by which names on a mailing list can be sorted and selected for mailings.

Source code: see *key code*.

Space: areas set aside by magazines or other publications for advertising.

Specialty catalog: a catalog that sells a specialized selection of goods.

Spread: an ad that covers two or more pages in a publication.

Standard mail: see *bulk mail*.

Standard Rate and Data Service (SRDS): a service that provides media information and rates on print, radio, television, and Internet advertising sources.

Two-step: a print advertisement that encourages customers to call or write for more information rather than allowing them to order directly from the ad.

Up-sell: to attempt to raise the total amount of a customer's order by suggesting the purchase of more than one of the same product.

Index

Star ___ ____ __des

Software

To order our catalog call 800-421-2300.
Or visit us online at smallbizbooks.com

AUG 1 3 2005	DATE DUE	
JAN _ _ 2008		
AUG 0 1 2006		
DEC 2 2 2007		

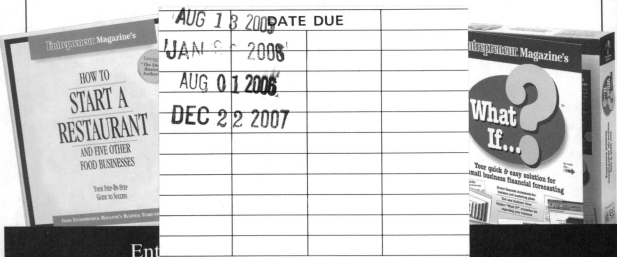

Entrepreneur Magazine's
HOW TO START A RESTAURANT
AND FIVE OTHER FOOD BUSINESSES

YOUR STEP-BY-STEP GUIDE TO SUCCESS

FROM ENTREPRENEUR MAGAZINE'S BUSINESS START-UP

Entrepreneur Magazine's
What If...?
Your quick & easy solution for small business financial forecasting

Create financial statements for business and marketing plans

Ent___

SmallBizBooks.com